AF711811

PRINCIPLES OF TRANSNATIONAL CIVIL PROCEDURE

The ALI (American Law Institute) and UNIDROIT (the International Institute for the Unification of Private Law) are preeminent organizations working together toward the clarification and advancement of the procedural rules of law. Recognizing the need for a "universal" set of procedures that would transcend national jurisdictional rules and facilitate the resolution of disputes arising from transnational commercial transactions, *Principles of Transnational Civil Procedure* was launched to create a set of procedural rules and principles that would be adopted globally. This work strives to reduce uncertainty for parties that must litigate in unfamiliar surroundings and to promote fairness in judicial proceedings. As recognized standards of civil justice, the *Principles of Transnational Civil Procedure* can be used in judicial proceedings as well as in arbitration. The result is a work that significantly contributes to the promotion of a universal rule of procedural law.

The American Law Institute was organized in 1923 following a study conducted by a group of prominent American judges, lawyers, and law professors. Their recommendation that a lawyers' organization be formed to improve the law and its administration led to the creation of The American Law Institute.

UNIDROIT was founded in 1926 as a specialized agency of the League of Nations. It exists as an independent intergovernmental organization on the basis of a multilateral agreement, the UNIDROIT Statute. Its purpose is to study needs and methods for modernizing, harmonizing, and coordinating private law between states and groups of states and to prepare legislative texts for consideration by governments.

ALI/UNIDROIT Principles of Transnational Civil Procedure

As Adopted and Promulgated

By

The American Law Institute

At Washington, D.C., U.S.A.

May 2004

and By

UNIDROIT

At Rome, Italy

April 2004

CAMBRIDGE UNIVERSITY PRESS

A·L·I·

UNIDROIT

CAMBRIDGE UNIVERSITY PRESS
Cambridge, New York, Melbourne, Madrid, Cape Town, Singapore, São Paulo

Cambridge University Press
32 Avenue of the Americas, New York, NY 10013-2473, USA

www.cambridge.org
Information on this title: www.cambridge.org/9780521855013

© 2006 The American Law Institute (entire work)
© 2006 UNIDROIT ("Principles" only)

This publication is in copyright. Subject to statutory exception
and to the provisions of relevant collective licensing agreements,
no reproduction of any part may take place without
the written permission of Cambridge University Press or The American Law Institute.

First published 2006
First paperback edition 2007

Printed in the United States of America

A catalog record for this publication is available from the British Library.

Library of Congress Cataloging in Publication Data

Principles of transnational civil procedure / American Law
Institute, UNIDROIT.
p. cm.
Includes bibliographical references and index.
ISBN-13: 978-0-521-85501-3 (hardback)
ISBN-10: 0-521-85501-2 (hardback)
1. Civil procedure. 2. Judicial assistance. 3. Conflict of laws – Civil procedure.
I. American Law Institute. II. International Institute for the Unification of
Private Law. III. Title.
K2205.P75 2005
347′.05 – dc22 2005018255

ISBN 978-0-521-85501-3 hardback
ISBN 978-0-521-70614-8 paperback

Cambridge University Press has no responsibility for
the persistence or accuracy of URLs for external or
third-party Internet Web sites referred to in this publication
and does not guarantee that any content on such
Web sites is, or will remain, accurate or appropriate.

THE AMERICAN LAW INSTITUTE

OFFICERS[†]

Roswell B. Perkins, *Chair of the Council*
Michael Traynor, *President*
Roberta C. Ramo, *1st Vice President*
Allen D. Black, *2nd Vice President*
Bennett Boskey, *Treasurer*
Susan Frelich Appleton, *Secretary*
Lance Liebman, *Director*
Elena A. Cappella, *Deputy Director*
Michael Greenwald, *Deputy Director*

COUNCIL[†]

Kenneth S. Abraham	Charlottesville	Virginia
Shirley S. Abrahamson	Madison	Wisconsin
Philip S. Anderson	Little Rock	Arkansas
Susan Frelich Appleton	St. Louis	Missouri
José I. Astigarraga	Miami	Florida
Sheila L. Birnbaum	New York	New York
Allen D. Black	Philadelphia	Pennsylvania
Bennett Boskey	Washington	District of Columbia
Amelia H. Boss	Philadelphia	Pennsylvania
Michael Boudin	Boston	Massachusetts
William M. Burke	Costa Mesa	California
Elizabeth J. Cabraser	San Francisco	California
Hugh Calkins	Cleveland	Ohio
Gerhard Casper	Stanford	California
William T. Coleman, Jr.	Washington	District of Columbia
Edward H. Cooper	Ann Arbor	Michigan
N. Lee Cooper	Birmingham	Alabama
Lloyd N. Cutler	Washington	District of Columbia
George H. T. Dudley	St. Thomas	U.S. Virgin Islands
Christine M. Durham	Salt Lake City	Utah
Kenneth C. Frazier	Whitehouse Station	New Jersey
George Clemon Freeman, Jr.	Richmond	Virginia
Paul L. Friedman	Washington	District of Columbia
Conrad K. Harper	New York	New York
Geoffrey C. Hazard, Jr.*	Philadelphia	Pennsylvania
D. Brock Hornby	Portland	Maine
William C. Hubbard	Columbia	South Carolina

† As of December 20, 2004
* *Director Emeritus*

Vester T. Hughes, Jr.	Dallas	Texas
Mary Kay Kane	San Francisco	California
Herma Hill Kay	Berkeley	California
Carolyn Dineen King	Houston	Texas
Carolyn B. Lamm	Washington	District of Columbia
Douglas Laycock	Austin	Texas
Pierre N. Leval	New York	New York
David F. Levi	Sacramento	California
Betsy Levin	Washington	District of Columbia
Hans A. Linde	Salem	Oregon
Martin Lipton	New York	New York
Myles V. Lynk	Tempe	Arizona
Robert MacCrate	New York	New York
Margaret H. Marshall	Boston	Massachusetts
John J. McKetta, III	Austin	Texas
Vincent L. McKusick	Portland	Maine
Daniel J. Meltzer	Cambridge	Massachusetts
Robert H. Mundheim	New York	New York
Kathryn A. Oberly	New York	New York
Roswell B. Perkins	New York	New York
Harvey S. Perlman	Lincoln	Nebraska
Ellen Ash Peters	Hartford	Connecticut
Louis H. Pollak	Philadelphia	Pennsylvania
Roberta C. Ramo	Albuquerque	New Mexico
Mary M. Schroeder	Phoenix	Arizona
Sherwin P. Simmons	Miami	Florida
Wm. Reece Smith, Jr.	Tampa	Florida
Jane Stapleton	Canberra	Australia
Robert A. Stein	Chicago	Illinois
Larry S. Stewart	Miami	Florida
John T. Subak	Boca Grande	Florida
Michael Traynor	San Francisco	California
Bill Wagner	Tampa	Florida
Patricia M. Wald	Washington	District of Columbia
Elizabeth Warren	Cambridge	Massachusetts
William H. Webster	Washington	District of Columbia
George Whittenburg	Amarillo	Texas
Herbert P. Wilkins	Boston	Massachusetts
James H. Wilson, Jr.	Atlanta	Georgia
Diane P. Wood	Chicago	Illinois

Emeritus Council Members

Roger C. Cramton	Ithaca	New York
William H. Erickson	Denver	Colorado
Thomas E. Fairchild	Madison	Wisconsin
Nicholas deB. Katzenbach	Princeton	New Jersey
Hale McCown	Yellow Springs	Ohio
Ernest J. Sargeant	Boston	Massachusetts
Lawrence E. Walsh	Oklahoma City	Oklahoma

UNIDROIT

INTERNATIONAL INSTITUTE FOR THE UNIFICATION OF PRIVATE LAW

LIST OF MEMBER STATES

Argentina
Australia
Austria
Belgium
Bolivia
Brazil
Bulgaria
Canada
Chile
China
Colombia
Croatia
Cuba
Cyprus
Czech Republic
Denmark
Egypt
Estonia
Finland
France
Germany
Greece
Holy See
Hungary
India
Iran
Iraq
Ireland
Israel
Italy
Japan
Luxembourg
Malta
Mexico
Netherlands
Nicaragua
Nigeria
Norway
Pakistan
Paraguay
Poland
Portugal
Republic of Korea
Romania
Russian Federation
San Marino
Serbia and Montenegro
Slovakia
Slovenia
South Africa
Spain
Sweden
Switzerland
Tunisia
Turkey
United Kingdom
United States of America
Uruguay
Venezuela

March 2004

THE UNIDROIT GOVERNING COUNCIL (2004–2008)

Berardino Libonati	President of UNIDROIT
Martin Adensamer	Austria
Tuğrul Arat	Turkey
Antonio Boggiano	Argentina
Hans-Georg Bollweg	Germany
Sergio Carbone	Italy
Michael Bendik Elmer	Denmark
Henry Deeb Gabriel	United States of America
Ian Govey	Australia
Attila Harmathy	Hungary
Arthur S. Hartkamp	Netherlands
Gerard William Hogan	Ireland
Kiyoshi Hosokawa	Japan
Anthony Inglese	United Kingdom
Alexander S. Komarov	Russian Federation
Lyou Byung-Hwa	Republic of Korea
Didier Opertti Badán	Uruguay
Jorge A. Sánchez-Cordero Dávila	Mexico
Biswanath B. Sen	India
Stanislaw J. Soltysinski	Poland
Bruno Sturlese	France
Anne-Marie Trahan	Canada
Evelio Verdera y Tuells	Spain
Ioannis Voulgaris	Greece
Pierre Widmer	Switzerland
Zhang Yuqing	People's Republic of China

EXECUTIVE OFFICERS UNIDROIT

BERARDINO LIBONATI, President
HERBERT KRONKE, Secretary-General
WALTER RODINO, Deputy Secretary-General

PRINCIPLES OF TRANSNATIONAL CIVIL PROCEDURE

REPORTERS

*GEOFFREY C. HAZARD, JR., University of Pennsylvania Law School, Philadelphia, Pennsylvania
MICHELE TARUFFO, University of Pavia, Pavia, Italy

ASSOCIATE REPORTER

** ANTONIO GIDI, Salvador, Brazil; University of Houston Law Center, Houston, Texas

U.S. ADVISERS***

JOHN J. BARCELO, III, Cornell Law School, Ithaca, New York
JAMES J. BROSNAHAN, San Francisco, California [from 2000]
STEPHEN B. BURBANK, University of Pennsylvania Law School, Philadelphia, Pennsylvania
JEROME A. COHEN, New York, New York
GEORGE W. COOMBE, JR., San Francisco, California
EDWARD H. COOPER, The University of Michigan Law School, Ann Arbor, Michigan
SHELDON H. ELSEN, New York, New York [from 1999]
JAMIE S. GORELICK, Washington, District of Columbia
PHILIP L. GRAHAM, JR., New York, New York
CONRAD K. HARPER, New York, New York
FRIEDRICH K. JUENGER, University of California at Davis School of Law, Davis, California [deceased 2001]
MARY KAY KANE, University of California, Hastings College of the Law, San Francisco, California
BENJAMIN KAPLAN, Harvard University Law School, Cambridge, Massachusetts [from 1999]
HAROLD HONGJU KOH, Yale Law School, New Haven, Connecticut
STEVEN J. LABENSKY, Phoenix, Arizona [to 2000]
ANDREAS F. LOWENFELD, New York University School of Law, New York, New York
JOSEPH T. MCLAUGHLIN, New York, New York
DAVID W. RIVKIN, New York, New York
LEE H. ROSENTHAL, United States District Court for the Southern District of Texas, Houston, Texas
VANESSA RUIZ, District of Columbia Court of Appeals, Washington, District of Columbia
ANTHONY J. SCIRICA, United States Court of Appeals for the Third Circuit, Philadelphia, Pennsylvania [from 2002]
PETER D. TROOBOFF, Washington, District of Columbia
DETLEV F. VAGTS, Harvard University Law School, Cambridge, Massachusetts
DIANE P. WOOD, United States Court of Appeals for the Seventh Circuit, Chicago, Illinois

* Also served as UNIDROIT Co-Reporter. The other UNIDROIT Co-Reporter was Rolf Stürner.
** Also served as Secretary to the UNIDROIT Working Group.
*** Status as of May 17, 2004.

INTERNATIONAL ADVISERS*

BRYAN BEAUMONT, Federal Court of Australia, Sydney, Australia
ANDREW S. BELL, Sydney, Australia
FEDERICO CARPI, International Association of Procedural Law, Bologna, Italy
FEI ZHONGYI, Supreme Court of China, Beijing, China [from 2001]
RICHARD FENTIMAN, Queens' College, University of Cambridge, Cambridge, England
PETER GILLES, Johann Wolfgang Goethe-Universität Frankfurt, Frankfurt, Germany
DAVID GODDARD, Wellington, New Zealand
LORD GOLDSMITH, Q.C., Attorney General for England and Wales, London, England
STEPHEN R. GOLDSTEIN, Hebrew University of Jerusalem, Jerusalem, Israel
LORD ANDREW HARDIE, Edinburgh, Scotland
J. A. JOLOWICZ, Trinity College, Cambridge, England
DIANNA P. KEMPE, Paget, Bermuda
KONSTANTINOS D. KERAMEUS, Athens University School of Law (Director, Hellenic Institute of International and Foreign Law), Athens, Greece [from 2002]
CATHERINE KESSEDJIAN, University of Panthéon-Assas (Paris II), Paris, France
TAKESHI KOJIMA, Chuo University Law Department, Tokyo, Japan
SERGEI LEBEDEV, International Law School of the Moscow State University for International Relations, Moscow, Russia [from 2002]
WANG LIMING, People's University, Beijing, China [from 2001]
KOICHI MIKI, Keio University, Tokyo, Japan
RAMÓN MULLERAT-BALMAÑA, Barcelona, Spain
L. J. PRIESTLEY, Q.C., Sydney, Australia; Retired Justice, Court of Appeal, Supreme Court of New South Wales [from 2001]
JORGE A. SÁNCHEZ-CORDERO DÁVILA, Mexico City, Mexico [from 2002]
CARLOS SÁNCHEZ-MEJORADA Y VELASCO, Mexico City, Mexico [from 2002]
SANG HYUN SONG, Law School, Seoul National University, Seoul, Korea
**ROLF STÜRNER, University of Freiburg, Freiburg, Germany
TANG WEIJIAN, People's University, Beijing, China [from 2001]
YASUHEI TANIGUCHI, Tokyo, Japan
JANET WALKER, Osgoode Hall Law School of York University, North York, Ontario, Canada
GERHARD WALTER, University of Bern Institute for Swiss and International Civil Procedure, Bern, Switzerland
GARRY D. WATSON, Osgoode Hall Law School of York University, North York, Ontario, Canada
LINA ZHENG, Hong Kong, Hong Kong

LIAISON

HOUSTON PUTNAM LOWRY, Meriden, Connecticut, for the American Bar Association Section of International Law and Practice

EX OFFICIO

ROSWELL B. PERKINS, New York, New York
Chair of the Council, The American Law Institute
MICHAEL TRAYNOR, San Francisco, California
President, The American Law Institute
LANCE LIEBMAN, New York, New York
Director, The American Law Institute

* Status as of May 17, 2004.

** Also served as UNIDROIT Co-Reporter.

ALI/UNIDROIT WORKING GROUP

PRINCIPLES OF TRANSNATIONAL CIVIL PROCEDURE

REPORTERS

*GEOFFREY C. HAZARD, JR., University of Pennsylvania Law School, Philadelphia, United States

ROLF STÜRNER, University of Freiburg, Freiburg, Germany

CHAIR

**RONALD T. NHLAPO, South African Law Commission, Pretoria, South Africa

MEMBERS

NEIL H. ANDREWS, Clare College, University of Cambridge, Cambridge, England

AÍDA R. KEMELMAJER DE CARLUCCI, Supreme Court of Mendoza, Mendoza, Argentina

FRÉDÉRIQUE FERRAND, Université Jean Moulin, Lyon, France

MASANORI KAWANO, Nagoya University School of Law, Nagoya, Japan

PIERRE LALIVE, University of Geneva, Geneva, Switzerland

CONSULTANT

MICHAEL JOACHIM BONELL, University of Rome, Rome, Italy

SECRETARY

***ANTONIO GIDI, Salvador, Brazil; University of Houston Law Center, Houston, Texas

EX OFFICIO

BERARDINO LIBONATI, Rome, Italy
President, UNIDROIT

HERBERT KRONKE, Rome, Italy
Secretary-General, UNIDROIT

* Also served as ALI Co-Reporter. The other ALI Co-Reporter was Michele Taruffo.

** Member of the Governing Council of UNIDROIT.

*** Also served as ALI Associate Reporter.

MEMBERS CONSULTATIVE GROUP

PRINCIPLES OF TRANSNATIONAL CIVIL PROCEDURE (AS OF FEBRUARY 13, 2004)

MARC T. AMY, Louisiana Court of Appeal, Third Circuit, Abbeville, Louisiana
NEIL H. ANDREWS, Cambridge, England
JOSEPH R. BANKOFF, Atlanta, Georgia
ROBERT S. BARKER, Pittsburgh, Pennsylvania
PETER V. BAUGHER, Chicago, Illinois
JOHN STEPHEN BECKERMAN, Camden, New Jersey
PASCALE BLOCH, Paris, France
SANFORD L. BOHRER, Miami, Florida
ROBERT G. BONE, Boston, Massachusetts
GARY BRIAN BORN, London, England
KAREN KENNEDY BROWN, United States Bankruptcy Court for the Southern District of Texas, Houston, Texas
STEPHEN McG. BUNDY, Berkeley, California
JOHN P. BURTON, Santa Fe, New Mexico
ROBERT L. BYER, Pittsburgh, Pennsylvania
ROBERT C. CASAD, Lawrence, Kansas
OSCAR G. CHASE, New York, New York
STEPHEN YEE CHOW, Boston, Massachusetts
JACK J. COE, Westlake Village, California
DAVID K. COHEN, London, England
MICHAEL MARKS COHEN, New York, New York
DENISE D. COLLIERS, Philadelphia, Pennsylvania
THOMAS FIELD COPE, Denver, Colorado
MARINA CORODEMUS, New Jersey Superior Court, New Brunswick, New Jersey
AVELINO V. CRUZ, Makati City, Philippines
CHRISTOPHER SCOTT D'ANGELO, Philadelphia, Pennsylvania
LOUIS F. DEL DUCA, Carlisle, Pennsylvania
A. MECHELE DICKERSON, Williamsburg, Virginia
JAMES SHOLTO DOUGLAS, Supreme Court of Queensland, Brisbane, Australia
PETER D. EHRENHAFT, Washington, District of Columbia
DAVID N. ELLENHORN, New York, New York
C. RONALD ELLINGTON, Athens, Georgia
JOHN N. FELLAS, New York, New York
ROBERT G. FLANDERS, JR., Rhode Island Supreme Court, Providence, Rhode Island
JOSEPH Z. FLEMING, Miami, Florida
ERIC M. FREEDMAN, Hempstead, New York
MARK ERIC GEBAUER, Harrisburg, Pennsylvania
JOHN L. GEDID, Harrisburg, Pennsylvania
JAMES PAUL GEORGE, Fort Worth, Texas
MARGARET GILHOOLEY, Newark, New Jersey
GERALD GILLERMAN, Cambridge, Massachusetts
CARL F. GOODMAN, Bethesda, Maryland
GEORGE J. GRUMBACH, JR., New York, New York
DAVID W. GRUNING, New Orleans, Louisiana
JOHN O. HALEY, St. Louis, Missouri
WILLIAM M. HANNAY, Chicago, Illinois
RICHARD E. V. HARRIS, Piedmont, California
TREVOR CLAYTON HARTLEY, Surrey, England
KATHERINE J. HENRY, Washington, District of Columbia
MIGUEL ÁNGEL HERNÁNDEZ ROMO, Mexico City, Mexico
MARIA TANKENSON HODGE, St. Thomas, U.S. Virgin Islands
RANDY J. HOLLAND, Delaware Supreme Court, Georgetown, Delaware
EDWIN E. HUDDLESON, III, Washington, District of Columbia

Richard W. Hulbert, New York, New York
Michael Hwang, Singapore, Singapore
Samuel Issacharoff, New York, New York
Makoto Ito, Tokyo, Japan
Michele C. Kane, Burbank, California
Robert B. Kent, Lexington, Massachusetts
Mark R. Killenbeck, Fayetteville, Arkansas
Donald Barnett King, St. Louis, Missouri
Jeffrey D. Kovar, Washington, District of Columbia
Steven C. Krane, New York, New York
Peter B Kutner, Norman, Oklahoma
Earle F. Kyle, IV, Brooklyn Park, Minnesota
Michele Langer, Philadelphia, Pennsylvania
E. Bruce Leonard, Toronto, Ontario
David I. Levine, Berkeley, California
Victor B. Levit, San Francisco, California
William H. Levit, Jr., Milwaukee, Wisconsin
Eric L. Lewis, Washington, District of Columbia
Houston Putnam Lowry, Meriden, Connecticut
Robert E. Lutz, II, Los Angeles, California
Myles V. Lynk, Tempe, Arizona
Champ Lyons, Jr., Alabama Supreme Court, Montgomery, Alabama
Morton M. Maneker, New York, New York
Raymond B. Marcin, Washington, District of Columbia
Richard L. Marcus, San Francisco, California
Judy Perry Martinez, New Orleans, Louisiana
Pedro Julio Martinez-Fraga, Miami, Florida
David Charles Mason, Missouri Circuit Court, 22nd Judicial Circuit, St. Louis, Missouri
Toni M. Massaro, Tucson, Arizona
James R. Maxeiner, Bronxville, New York
Daniel J. McAuliffe, Phoenix, Arizona
Judith D. McConnell, California Court of Appeal, San Diego, California
Stephen J. McEwen, Jr., The Superior Court of Pennsylvania, Media, Pennsylvania
H. Brent McKnight, United States District Court for the Western District of North Carolina, Charlotte, North Carolina
Daniel John Meador, Charlottesville, Virginia
Patrick E. Mears, Grand Rapids, Michigan
Rona Robbins Mears, Dallas, Texas
Richard A. Michael, Chicago, Illinois
Linda S. Mullenix, Austin, Texas
Fred F. Murray, Washington, District of Columbia
Peter L. Murray, Portland, Maine
Lawrence W. Newman, New York, New York
John B. Oakley, Davis, California
James M. O'Fallon, Eugene, Oregon
Dario U. Oscós Coria, Mexico City, Mexico
James E. Pfander, Champaign, Illinois
Steven R. Plotkin, Louisiana Court of Appeal, Fourth Circuit, New Orleans, Louisiana
Sheldon Raab, New York, New York
Myrna Sharon Raeder, Los Angeles, California
Bernard D. Reams, Jr., San Antonio, Texas
Judith Resnik, New Haven, Connecticut
William L. Reynolds, Baltimore, Maryland
James K. Robinson, Washington, District of Columbia
Eduardo C. Robreno, United States District Court for the Eastern District of Pennsylvania, Philadelphia, Pennsylvania
Thomas D. Rowe, Jr., Durham, North Carolina
Sol Schreiber, New York, New York
Karl E. Seib, Jr., New York, New York
Amos Shapira, Tel Aviv, Israel
Edward F. Sherman, New Orleans, Louisiana
Gene R. Shreve, Bloomington, Indiana
Gerald K. Smith, Phoenix, Arizona
Brian F. Spector, Miami, Florida
E. Blythe Stason, Jr., DeKalb, Illinois
Joan E. Steinman, Chicago, Illinois

IAN A. L. STROGATZ, Philadelphia, Pennsylvania
STEPHEN N. SUBRIN, Boston, Massachusetts
SYMEON C. SYMEONIDES, Salem, Oregon
COLIN C. TAIT, Norfolk, Connecticut
H. SIMMONS TATE, JR., Columbia, South Carolina
LOUISE E. TEITZ, Bristol, Rhode Island
ELIZABETH G. THORNBURG, Dallas, Texas
JAY TIDMARSH, Notre Dame, Indiana
R. PATRICK VANCE, New Orleans, Louisiana
VINCENZO VIGORITI, Florence, Italy
JAY M. VOGELSON, Dallas, Texas
STEVEN T. WALTHER, Reno, Nevada
MICHAEL P. WAXMAN, Milwaukee, Wisconsin
RALPH U. WHITTEN, Omaha, Nebraska
PETER WINSHIP, Dallas, Texas
ANDREW J. WISTRICH, United States District Court for the Central District of California, Los Angeles, California
NICHOLAS J. WITTNER, Irvine, California
ERIC K. YAMAMOTO, Honolulu, Hawaii
ROBERT J. ZAPF, Los Angeles, California
JOACHIM ZEKOLL, New Orleans, Louisiana

INTERNATIONAL CONSULTANTS

PRINCIPLES OF TRANSNATIONAL CIVIL PROCEDURE (AS OF FEBRUARY 13, 2004)

Mohammed Aboul-Enein, Egypt
Ivo Alehno, Latvia
Arruda Alvim, Brazil
Thereza Alvim, Brazil
Torbjörn Andersson, Sweden
Roland Arazi, Argentina
Sergio Artavia B., Costa Rica
Kichimoto Asaka, Japan
Lorena Bachmaier Winter, Spain
Wallace R. Baker, France
Samuel P. Baumgartner, Switzerland
Jean-Paul Béraudo, France
Roberto Berizonce, Argentina
Bi Yuqian, China
Paolo Biavati, Italy
Henrik Bielenstein, Sweden
Martín Böhmer, Argentina
Alegria Borrás, Spain
Brunella Brunelli, Italy
John J. A. Burke, Latvia
Lucio Cabrera Acevedo, Mexico
Cai Yanmin, China
Petrônio Calmon, Brazil
Carlos Camps, Argentina
Nedo Carlucci, Argentina
Carlos Alberto Carmona, Brazil
Paulius Čerka, Lithuania
Chen Gang, China
Chen Guiming, China
Valdis Cielava, Latvia
Vinodh Coomaraswamy, Singapore
Victor Rolando Días Ortiz, Mexico
Ignacio Díez-Picazo Gimenez, Spain
Angelo Dondi, Italy
Voravuthi Dvavasin, Thailand
Nikolai Eliseev, Russia
Enrique Falcón, Argentina
Eduardo Ferrer Mac-Gregor, Mexico
Joaquim-J. Forner Delaygua, Spain
Gian Franco Ricci, Italy
José Lebre de Freitas, Portugal
Elisabet Fura-Sandström, Sweden
Alejandro M. Garro, Argentina
Chiara Giovannucci Orlandi, Italy
Andrea Giussani, Italy
H. Patrick Glenn, Canada
Cipriano Gómez Lara, Mexico
Peter Gottwald, Germany
Andrea Graziosi, Italy
Jurgita Grigienė, Lithuania
Pablo Grillo Ciocchini, Argentina
Ada Pellegrini Grinover, Brazil
Indra Gudrone, Latvia
Leandro Guzmán, Argentina
Lars Heuman, Sweden
Juan Carlos Hitters, Argentina
Foo Chee Hock, Singapore
Hu Yaqiu, China
Huang Songyou, China
Stefan Huber, Germany
Daniel John, Singapore
Elena Vitalyevna Kabatova, Russia
Inga Kačevska, Latvia
Gen Kajitani, Japan
Lee Seiu Kin, Singapore
Jan Kleineman, Sweden
A. Kostin, Russia
Phaedon J. Kozyris, Greece
Egidijus Krivka, Lithuania
Mārcis Krūmiņš, Latvia
Eduard Kunštek, Croatia
Anibal Quiroga Leon, Peru
Magdangal de Leon, Philippines
Li Hao, China
Lauris Liepa, Latvia
Charles Lim, Singapore
Per-Henrik Lindblom, Sweden
Hartmut Linke, Germany
Liu Rongjun, China
Gualberto Lucas Sosa, Argentina

Stefan Luginbuehl, Switzerland
Claes Lundblad, Sweden
Michele Lupoi, Italy
Luigia Maggioni, Luxembourg
Francisco Málaga, Spain
Juan Carlos Marín G., Mexico
Luiz Guilherme Marinoni, Brazil
Roberto Martínez Guerrero, Mexico
Junichi Matsushita, Japan
Gabriele Mecarelli, France
Wagner Menezes, Brazil
Valentinas Mikelénas, Lithuania
Toshihumi Minami, Japan
Toru Motobayashi, Japan
Bo Nilsson, Sweden
Roberth Nordh, Sweden
E. Nozyreva, Russia
Olakunle Olatawura, Nigeria
Daina Ose, Latvia
Eduardo Oteiza, Argentina
Pan Jianfeng, China
Ernesto Pedraz Penalva, Spain
Ricardo Perlingeiro, Brazil
Jorge W. Peyrano, Argentina
Thomas Pfeiffer, Germany
Reynato S. Puno, Philippines
Qi Shujie, China
Lea Querzola, Italy
Hilmar Raeschke-Kessler, Germany
Ricardo Ramalho Almeida, Brazil
Walter Rechberger, Austria
Jorge Rojas, Argentina
Fabio Rota, Italy
Jānis Rozenbergs, Latvia
Carlos Alberto Salles, Brazil
Bruno Sassani, Italy
Cássio Scarpinella Bueno, Brazil
Haimo Schack, Germany
GP Selvam, Singapore
Patricia Shaughnessy, Sweden
Elisabetta Silvestri, Italy
Joaquim Simões Barbosa, Brazil
José Luís Siqueiros, Mexico
Marcel Storme, Belgium
Thomas Sutter-Somm, Switzerland
Petri Taivalkoski, Finland
Morio Takeshita, Japan
Makoto Tanabe, Japan
Tian Pingan, China
Flora Triantaphyllou, Greece
Nicolò Trocker, Italy
Vincenzo Varano, Italy
Alejandro Verdaguer, Argentina
Elena Vershinina, Russia
Hernany Veytia Palomino, Mexico
Ramón Viñas, Spain
Gunta Višņakova, Latvia
Spyros Vrellis, Greece
Luiz Rodrigues Wambier, Brazil
Teresa Arruda Alvim Wambier, Brazil
Kazuo Watanabe, Brazil
Thomas Willging, United States
Xu Hui, China
Yukio Yangida, Japan
Alvin Yeo, Singapore
Pelayia Yessiou-Faltsi, Greece
Gvido Zemribo, Latvia
Zhang Weiping, China
Zhang Wusheng, China
Zhao Gang, China
Elena Zucconi Galli Fonseca, Italy

FOREWORD

The proposals for law reform published in this volume result from a happy collaboration between the International Institute for the Unification of Private Law (UNIDROIT) and The American Law Institute (ALI).

UNIDROIT, based in Rome (Italy), was founded in 1926 as a specialized agency of the League of Nations. After World War II it continued as an independent intergovernmental organization on the basis of a multilateral agreement, the UNIDROIT Statute. Its purpose is to study needs and methods for modernizing, harmonizing, and coordinating private law between states and groups of states and to prepare legislative texts for consideration by governments. Membership is restricted to states. The currently 59 member states are drawn from the five continents and represent all varieties of different legal, economic, and political systems as well as different cultural backgrounds. The organization has over the years prepared over 70 studies and drafts. In recent years, nine Conventions plus various "soft-law" instruments such as Model Laws, Guides, and the UNIDROIT Principles of International Commercial Contracts (1994 and 2004), www.unidroit.org/english/principles/contracts/main.htm, were adopted. At present, the focus is on secured-transactions law (Convention on International Interests in Mobile Equipment (Cape Town, 2001), www.unidroit.org/english/conventions/mobile-equipment/main.htm), and capital-market law. It is envisaged to further develop the Principles of International Commercial Contracts.

ALI, based in Philadelphia, was founded in 1923 by American judges, professors, and practicing lawyers with the goal of recommending simplification of American law and the law's improved adaptation to social conditions. The ALI is a private organization with nearly 4,000 members, selected on the basis of professional achievement and demonstrated interest in the improvement of the law. For 82 years it has been devoted to law reform, drafting and publishing Restatements of the common law, Principles of law, proposed Statutes, and various studies. For the past decade, ALI's agenda has included transnational work, recommending rules for coordinating insolvency disputes among the three North American Free Trade Agreement (NAFTA) nations and currently considering recommendations concerning U.S. enforcement of foreign judgments, transnational coordination of intellectual-property disputes, and the law of the World Trade Organization (WTO).

This work on *Principles of Transnational Civil Procedure* was begun in 1997 as an ALI project on Transnational Rules of Civil Procedure (later titled Principles and Rules of Transnational Civil Procedure), with Professor Geoffrey Hazard, then ALI Director, and Professor Michele Taruffo as Reporters; Professor Antonio Gidi joined the project soon thereafter, first as Assistant Reporter, then as Associate Reporter. When it became clear that cooperation with a distinguished international institution was desirable, ALI began its collaboration with UNIDROIT in 1999, and the focus of the project began to shift from Rules to Principles. For the UNIDROIT process, Professors Hazard and Rolf Stürner were the Reporters and Professor Gidi was Secretary. In the ALI process, the Reporters benefited from the constructive criticism of Advisers from many countries, a Consultative Group consisting of ALI members, and a group of International Consultants, as well as from annual discussion and consideration by the ALI's Council and membership. In the UNIDROIT process, a distinguished Working Group devoted four week-long meetings at the UNIDROIT headquarters in Rome to vigorous analysis of the Reporters' drafts.

In addition to the formal procedures of the two sponsoring organizations, the drafts were subjected to close critical review at numerous professional meetings and conferences held around the world. The great number of countries visited and of national systems taken into account and compared was crucial not only in demonstrating that the project and its goals were feasible on a broader scale than originally envisioned, but also in providing access to practitioners and scholars from many different jurisdictions, whose comments and criticisms enabled the Reporters both to refine their work and to make it more practicable.

UNIDROIT and ALI are proud that the work has been completed, confident that it will have influence as the growth of global commerce increases the need for dispute-resolution systems that deserve public confidence, and hopeful that this project will lead to further efforts to help national legal systems adapt to an interconnected world. In the process we have learned again what an early ALI leader once said, that "law reform is not for the short-winded."

HERBERT KRONKE
Secretary-General
The International Institute for the Unification of Private Law

LANCE LIEBMAN
Director
The American Law Institute

December 23, 2004

REPORTERS' PREFACE

Presented herewith are the Principles of Transnational Civil Procedure. Appended to the Principles are the Rules of Transnational Civil Procedure, which are the Reporters' model implementation of the Principles, which may be considered for adoption in various legal systems.

There are, understandably, skeptics who think the idea premature at best that there can be "universal" procedural rules, and others who, though sympathetic to the idea, have reservations about the present execution of the concept. These reservations are at two levels. First, there is doubt that it is feasible to overcome fundamental differences between common-law and civil-law systems and, among common-law systems, to cope with the peculiarities of the U.S. system. We think, however, that the reservations based on the civil-law/common-law distinction reflect undue anxiety. The U.S. system is unique among common-law systems in having both broad discovery and jury trial. Thus, a second-level reservation is that, if such a project is feasible, it is not feasible if it corresponded in any substantial way to characteristic U.S. procedure.

We conclude that a system of procedure acceptable generally throughout the world could not require jury trial and would require much more limited discovery than is typical in the United States. This in turn has led us to conclude that the scope of the proposed Principles of Transnational Civil Procedure is limited to commercial disputes and excludes categories of litigation such as personal-injury and wrongful-death actions, because barring jury trial in such cases would be unacceptable in the United States. The definition of "commercial disputes" will require some further specification, but we believe that it is adequate to frame the project.

In this era of globalization, the world is marching in two directions. One path is of separation and isolationism, with war and turmoil: In such a world, this project is useless and unwelcome. The other path is increasing exchange of products and ideas among the peoples of the world; this path underscores the need for a transnational civil procedure.

Geoffrey C. Hazard, Jr. (Reporter, ALI/UNIDROIT)
Rolf Stürner (Reporter, UNIDROIT)
Michele Taruffo (Reporter, ALI)
Antonio Gidi (Associate Reporter, ALI)

November 22, 2004

PREFACE

The explosion in transnational commerce has changed the world forever. International commerce and investment are increasing at an enormous rate and the rate of change is continuing to accelerate. The legal procedures applicable to the global community, however, have not kept pace and are still largely confined to and limited by individual national jurisdictions.

The *Principles of Transnational Civil Procedure* comprise an unprecedented international analysis and a unique statement of an internationally acceptable basis for dealing with the legal aspects of international disputes and controversies.

The Principles seek nothing less than to provide a system of legal procedures applicable to a wide-ranging variety of disputes throughout the world. It is an undertaking of enormous magnitude and its potential to improve cross-border and multinational commerce, trade, and investment is inestimable.

Too often, local legal and commercial procedures in practice operate, whether intentionally or otherwise, in a manner that favors local parties in transnational disputes. International investment and credit decisions must take into account local proclivities of this kind and, consequently, prospective commerce and investment are inevitably and invariably curtailed in order to allow for them.

International trade and investment is thereby diminished to the direct disadvantage of the parties involved and, indirectly, to the disadvantage of their communities and their public. On a macroeconomic scale, the sum of these diminished opportunities in aggregate is extraordinarily large. International commerce and the communities affected by it are impoverished as a result.

The Principles provide an exceptionally valuable pattern for "Best Practices" dispute-resolution procedures but they are, as well, international benchmarks that can be used in connection with efforts to improve standards and systems in countries around the world. For the participants in international commerce, they are ideally suited to improve and enhance the climate for international commerce and investment. Parties to international transactions will be able to adopt the Principles, with or without modifications, in their transactions or to incorporate them by reference in their arrangements.

The Principles are a welcome and highly constructive contribution to the advancement of international cooperation in the legal and commercial area, where contributions of this magnitude and significance are still regrettably rare. The Principles should achieve general recognition as have the ALI's *Guidelines Applicable to Court-to-Court Communications in Cross-Border Cases* that, as in the case of the Principles, have been translated into many of the world's leading languages and distributed to leading judges and lawyers around the world. The *Guidelines* are already making a positive contribution to international insolvency systems and procedures in the same way that the Principles can and will contribute to the advancement of international legal systems and procedures.

The Principles carry the potential to provide for an unequaled advance in international commerce that will bring with it consequent benefits to all of the world's economies. The drafters of the Principles have given the international community the tools to improve significantly the world's legal systems. The Principles, therefore, reflect not only an advance in international legal systems and procedures, but also the means to advance and improve international commerce generally for the benefit of everyone affected by it. It is a challenge and an opportunity that the legal and commercial communities should not fail to grasp.

E. Bruce Leonard
Chairman
International Insolvency Institute
and ALI member

Toronto, Ontario
December 21, 2004

PREFACE

It is a pleasure and an honor to write a preface to this transcendental work for the evolution of law at the universal level. Its inspiration is found in the spirit of two extraordinary attorneys: Geoffrey Hazard, from the University of Pennsylvania Law School, and Michele Taruffo, from the University of Pavia. They developed the blueprint for this ambitious project on transnational-civil-procedure rules, and The American Law Institute (ALI) decided to take it up in 1997. The ALI project began with Rules, the International Institute for the Unification of Private Law (UNIDROIT) suggested the need for Principles, and final approval by both organizations was of the Principles only, with the Rules conceived as the Reporters' model of how the Principles might be implemented in a particular jurisdiction.

The challenge was Herculean, especially considering the difficulty comparative law has faced in transferring legal devices and concepts from one legal system to another.[1] It has been asserted that the more an institution is integrated into the political and legal environment in a specific country, the more difficult it is to assimilate it into another one.[2] In addition, it has been stated that the majority of these legal concepts are intimately linked to the political structures of a country and, therefore, to the distribution of power among the three state branches: the Executive, the Legislative, and the Judicial. Such is the nature of Civil Procedural Law. If this is true, it would seem natural that drafting universal uniform civil-procedure rules would have been impossible. Only two determined legal spirits like those of Professors Hazard and Taruffo, practicing in two legal systems supposedly quite different in their legal underpinnings, could have imagined and so strongly influenced the creation of the *Principles of Transnational Civil Procedure*.

[1] Hein Kötz, "La protection en justice des intérêts collectifs. Tableau de Droit Comparé." Accès à la Justice et État-Providence, under the direction of Mauro Capelletti, with a preface by René David (Paris: Económica, 1984), 105.

[2] Kötz, "La protection en justice des intérêts collectifs," 107.

On May 22, 2000, at the head offices of UNIDROIT in Rome, as a result of the study[3] conducted by the esteemed German Professor Rolf Stürner, a Working Group was summoned[4] in order to analyze and propose the foundation for the Principles and Rules of Transnational Civil Procedure. When UNIDROIT President Berardino Libonati welcomed the group's members,[5] he praised the proposed effort to unify such a technical and sensitive area as procedural law. "The globalization process," he underlined, "set the conditions in order to enhance it." His comment was prescient and his perspective has provided invaluable support to the effort.

Yet those present felt that something more incredible was taking place. It was the outset of one of the most important and exciting legal projects of recent times. The task involved several challenges for the prestigious members of the Working Group, as well as the institutions concerned: UNIDROIT and the ALI. These two prominent organizations chose to join forces to accomplish a common purpose. After having agreed to travel down such an unpredictable path, they should now feel proud of the results and their significant contribution to legal evolution at a universal level.

The international legal community should also take pride in the success of a project of this magnitude, especially given the challenges it faced and the unfortunate fate that other international legal projects of this scope have suffered.

The initial context of the project can perhaps best be described as transitional. During most of the 20th century, a concept espoused by Professor

[3] The study of Professor Rolf Stürner of Freiburg University was requested by UNIDROIT to determine whether the project was feasible and to decide about the convenience of implementing it both by UNIDROIT and ALI. In Frédérique Ferrand, "La procédure civile internationale et la procédure civil transnationale: Incidence de l'integration économique régional." *Uniform Law Review* [*Revue de Droit Uniforme*], NS – vol. 8, nos. 1/2 (2003), 422.

[4] In 1999, the UNIDROIT's Chair Council agreed to join with the ALI in the publication of the *Principles of Transnational Civil Procedure*, using as a support the feasibility study by Professor Rolf Stürner. The Working Group consisted of the Chair, Ronald Thandabantu Nhlapo from South Africa, and Co-Reporters, Professors Geoffrey C. Hazard, Jr. (USA) and Rolf Stürner (Germany). Other members were Neil H. Andrews (UK), Aída R. Kemelmajer de Carlucci (Argentina), Frédérique Ferrand (France), Masanori Kawano (Japan), and Pierre Lalive (Switzerland). Antonio Gidi was the Secretary and the Assistant Reporter (later Associate Reporter) for the ALI. Michele Taruffo (Italy) was Co-Reporter for the ALI. Michael Joachim Bonell was Project Coordinator for UNIDROIT. In Herbert Kronke, "Efficiency, Fairness, Macro-Economic Functions: Challenges for the Harmonisation of Transnational Civil Procedure." *Uniform Law Review* [*Revue de Droit Uniforme*], NS – vol. 6, no. 4 (2001), 740.

[5] Report on the First Session, Rome, 22 to 26 May 2000, UNIDROIT 2001 Study LXXVI-Doc. 3 (Prepared by Antonio Gidi, Secretary to the Working Group), www.unidroit.org/english/publications/proceedings/2001/study/76/76-03-e.pdf.

Konstantinos D. Kerameus[6] prevailed. He supported the view that, despite the functional connection with substantive law, procedure ruled the judicial power system and that, therefore, the nature of its norms should be considered as of *ordre public*. Administration of justice was an expression of political authority and its institutions developed a state function. For this reason, the basic principles of procedure often have constitutional significance. Professor Stephen Goldstein's arguments in this respect are particularly useful:

> First, there are norms which are peculiar to a given system, which reflect the peculiar history of that system, but which do not, at all, represent a general norm of due process or natural justice. Second, there are constitutional norms that do reflect general norms of natural justice, but are not the only possible manifestations of such general norm. Third, at least in theory, one could posit a given constitutional norm which is the only possible manifestation of a general norm of natural justice.... In general, however, there are very few examples of constitutional norms that do not at all reflect a universal norm of due process or natural justice. Most of the constitutional norms in most systems do reflect such universal norms.[7]

Within this concept, some asserted that procedural law was a "State sovereignty prerogative"[8] since judicial power is one of the three main state branches and, as such, it was a structural expression of national sovereignty. The Mexican expression of the concept is quite eloquent in this respect.

However, in the last part of the 20th century, this new concept set the stage for drastic changes based on a fundamental difference. Judicial organization and procedural law *strictu sensu* follow different functions: procedural law rules the relationships between the parties and between the parties and the court.[9] It is what Professor Herbert Kronke,[10] the Secretary-General of UNIDROIT, appropriately calls "substantive procedural law" or "substance of the proceedings." In its strict meaning procedural law can be qualified as procedural "software" and can be subject to harmonization processes. On the other hand, the rules regarding judicial organization are considered "procedural hardware" and they belong to the sovereignty of each national state.

[6] Konstantinos D. Kerameus, "Some Reflections on Procedural Harmonisation: Reasons and Scope." *Uniform Law Review* [*Revue de Droit Uniforme*], NS – vol. 8, nos. 1/2 (2003), 448.

[7] Stephen Goldstein, "The Proposed ALI/UNIDROIT Principles and Rules of Transnational Civil Procedure: The Utility of Such a Harmonization Project." *Uniform Law Review* [*Revue de Droit Uniforme*], NS – vol. 6, no. 4 (2001), 793–794.

[8] Marcel Storme, "Procedural Law and the Reform of Justice: from Regional to Universal Harmonisation." *Uniform Law Review* [*Revue de Droit Uniforme*]. NS – vol. 6, no. 4 (2001), 765.

[9] Kerameus, "Some Reflections," n.6, 448.

[10] See Herbert Kronke, "Efficiency, Fairness, Macro-Economic Functions: Challenges for the Harmonisation of Transnational Civil Procedure. *Uniform Law Review* [*Revue de Droit Uniforme*]. NS – vol. 6, no. 4 (2001), 744, 746.

This new tendency is evident in several new European Civil Procedure Codes. Examples include the Spanish *Ley de Enjuiciamiento Civil* from April 30, 1992, the Italian *Provvedimenti urgenti per il processo civile,* from November 26, 1990, and the French *Nouveau Code de procédure civile.*[11]

Emerging multinational arbitration proceedings also accurately reflect this new concept, a notable example being the United Nations Commission on International Trade Law's (UNCITRAL's) 1985 model law of commercial arbitration.

This model law represents one of the many instances of "contractualization" in the private-law movement.[12] We find similar movements supporting the standardization of civil-procedure law, where again inclusion of the emergence of international commercial regions has not been unfamiliar.[13]

Against this backdrop, we can more fully appreciate the importance of various proposals within the American continent seeking to harmonize civil procedure. Recent examples include a Civil Procedure Model Law for Latin America (1988),[14] and the Mercosur region protocols of *Las Leñas*[15] and *Ouro Preto*[16] (the most recent civil-procedure instruments).[17] The driving forces behind the standardization movement are quite varied and have been extensively discussed.[18] One such force is the growing need for legal certainty in a world where people and corporations have seemingly unfettered mobility. Ensuring legal certainty places enormous responsibility on those in charge of managing justice, but it also creates confidence when people believe that

[11] Storme, "Procedural Law," n.8, 771.

[12] H. Patrick Glenn, "Prospects for Transnational Civil Procedure in the Americas." *Uniform Law Review* [*Revue de Droit Uniforme*], NS – vol. 8, nos. 1/2 (2003), 490. About the "contractualization" in civil-procedure law, see Antonio Gidi, "'Vers un procès civil transnational': Une première réponse aux critiques," in *Vers un procès civil universel? Les règles transnacionales de procédure civile de* l'American Law Institute, ed. Philippe Fouchard (Paris: Panthéon-Assas, 2001), 140.

[13] In the American continent, there are many free-trade agreements and treaties; one of the most significant is the North American Free Trade Agreement (NAFTA). In Mercosur, there are the Protocols of Leñas 1992 and Ouro Preto, from 1994. In Claudia Lima Marques, "Procédure civile internationale et Mercosur: Pour un dialogue des sigles universelles et régionales." *Uniform Law Review* [*Revue de Droit Uniforme*], NS – vol. 8, nos. 1/2 (2003), 472.

[14] *Anteproyecto del Codigo Procesal Civil Modelo para Iberoamerica*, Revista de Processo, Vols. 52 y 53.

[15] The Protocol of Leñas (1992) deals with judicial cooperation in the civil, commercial, labor, and administrative ambits. In Lima, "Procédure civile internationale et Mercosur," n.12, 472.

[16] The Protocol of Ouro Preto (1994) deals with provisional measures. In Lima, "Procédure civile internationale et Mercosur," n.13, 471.

[17] In Lima, "Procédure civile internationale et Mercosur," n.13, 472.

[18] Storme, "Procedural Law," n.8, 768.

equivalent systems of civil procedure will assure them access to justice in a system renowned for its efficiency, transparency, predictability, and procedural economy.[19]

As the emerging views of the international legal community matured, this type of legal enterprise became feasible. This time, the Working Group was able to tackle it with a uniquely creative perspective.

The *Principles of Transnational Civil Procedure* are intended to help reduce the impact of differences between legal systems in lawsuits involving transnational commercial transactions. Their purpose is to propose a model of universal procedure that follows the essential elements of due process of law. The Rules and Principles involve "a universal equitable process in the commercial area"[20] and are distinguishable for their contribution to the attainment of a truly equal access to justice.

The Project was developed with a dualistic structure: a system of basic Principles of civil procedure accompanied by specific Rules. This structure reconciles important needs of both major legal systems: the Anglo-Saxon preference for concrete rules, and the continental European, Latin American, and Asian emphasis on the formulation of abstract principles rather than detailed rules.[21] By taking into consideration this cultural diversity, the dualistic structure allows its incorporation into the different legal systems in a more harmonious way.[22] The formulation of the Principles has been quite novel in comparison to the regional[23] or universal human-rights conventions,[24] as well as their jurisdictional interpretation.[25]

[19] Storme, "Procedural Law," n.8, 768.

[20] Frédérique Ferrand, "Les 'Principes' relatifs à la procédure civile transnationale sont-ils autosuffisants? – De la nécessité ou non de les assortir de 'Règles' dans le projet ALI/UNIDROIT." *Uniform Law Review* [*Revue de Droit Uniforme*], NS – vol. 6, no. 4 (2001), 995.

[21] Ferrand, "Les 'Principes' relatifs," 1013.

[22] Ferrand, "Les 'Principes' relatifs," 1013.

[23] Art. 6 paragraph 1 of the European Convention for the Protection of Human Rights and Fundamental Freedoms of November 4, 1950, whose text was taken up again verbatim by the European Union Charter of Fundamental Rights adopted by the European Council of Nice December 7, 2000; the Interamerican Convention of Human Rights of November 22, 1969, adopted by the Member States of the Organization of American States in San Jose, Costa Rica, coming into force on July 18, 1978; the African Charter of Human and Peoples' Rights, which came into force on October 21, 1986; and the Protocol Ouagadougou, from June 9, 1998.

[24] Arts. 14 and 16 of the International Covenant on Civil and Political Rights of New York, known as the New York Pact of December 19, 1966.

[25] See the jurisprudence of the European Charter of Human Rights, especially the one regarding the interpretation of article 6, paragraph 1 of the European Convention for the Protection of Human Rights and Fundamental Freedoms.

On the other hand, the Rules do more than merely illustrate the development of the Principles. They intentionally avoid interpreting several Principles that differ across legal cultures and thereby assure the recognition of the main principle of standardization that underlies the project's objectives.[26]

Thus, there are several reasons why I am writing this Preface: One of them is my dual role as a member of UNIDROIT's Governing Council since 1990 and of the ALI since 2001. This dual role allowed me to understand and synchronize the perspective of both institutions and to appreciate the effort needed to accomplish this seemingly impossible project. The skeptics, vastly outnumbering us, the aficionados, had several reservations: Some considered writing "universal" process rules premature;[27] others sympathized with the cause but held a number of reservations regarding its implementation.

These reservations varied: The fundamental differences between the common-law system and the civil-law system were considered insurmountable. Even more, within the common-law system itself, the peculiarities inherent in the U.S. procedural system added more complexity. The ALI/UNIDROIT Working Group estimated and demonstrated, however, that the differences between the systems of common law and continental law had been exaggerated. The differences were not irreconcilable as had been dogmatically claimed. There are fundamental principles of civil procedure that transcend the differences between the system of continental law and that of common law.[28] The examples of the "Woolf reforms" in the United Kingdom are, in this sense, quite eloquent.[29] The Principles and Rules show an extended scope of convergence between these two legal systems.[30] The Working Group skillfully managed to orient its goal toward, and fit into, the sphere of commercial controversies.

There are other reasons for writing this Preface. I am a Mexican attorney. This is my origin and the context I use to explain myself. Mexico is part of the continental system, particularly the Latin American legal subsystem that has

[26] Thomas Pfeiffer, "The ALI/UNIDROIT Project: Are Principles Sufficient, Without the Rules?" *Uniform Law Review [Revue* de Droit Uniforme], NS – vol. 6, no. 4 (2001), 1033.

[27] Draft Principles and Rules, UNIDROIT 2001 Study LXXVI – Doc. 4 (Prepared by Geoffrey C. Hazard, Jr., Rolf Stürner, Michele Taruffo, and Antonio Gidi), www.unidroit.org/english/publications/proceedings/2001/study/76/76-04-e.pdf.

[28] See Antonio Gidi, "Notes on Criticizing the Proposed ALI/UNIDROIT Principles and Rules of Transnational Civil Procedure." *Uniform Law Review* [*Revue de Droit Uniforme*], NS – vol. 6, no. 4 (2001), 821.

[29] Geoffrey C. Hazard, Jr., "International Civil Procedure: The Impact of Regional Economic Integration." *Uniform Law Review* [*Revue de Droit Uniforme*], NS – vol. 8, nos. 1/2 (2003), 439.

[30] Vladimir V. Prokhorenko, "Some Aspects of Unification of Civil Procedure Law." *Uniform Law Review* [*Revue de Droit Uniforme*], NS – vol. 8, nos. 1/2 (2003), 493.

been stigmatized by a misplaced reputation for excessive formalism. In the last decade, my country adopted dynamic participation in free-trade zones. It has entered into multiple free-trade agreements, three of which were signed with the most important universal economies: the United States of America and Canada (NAFTA), the European Union, and recently Japan. This has helped my country better understand the consequences of globalization, including how to manage the accompanying increase in social friction, legal controversy, and litigation. The Mexican system shares the conviction that the greater costs and degree of social turbulence might be mitigated if the procedural differences between competing legal systems[31] were to diminish. In this regard, the Principles and Rules have a special importance.

The opportunity to convene a seminar in Mexico to discuss the ALI/UNIDROIT Transnational Civil Procedure Project finally occurred in February 2002. The Mexican forum exceeded all expectations. Attorneys from across the Mexican legal landscape came together: from government officials, including the Legal Counselor of the President himself, to federal and local judges, arbitrators, and practitioners.

Two events occurred that were unforeseeable in the Mexican academy, and to me they symbolize the importance of this seminar: The first was the attendance of two Justices of the Mexican Supreme Court[32] who dedicated a full session to discuss the project. Their presence was emblematic of the high level of interest in the project. The second was the presence of the editor of the Model Code of Civil Procedure Project of the Conference of Chief Justices of Mexico.[33]

Since the seminar, the Principles and Rules have continued to be discussed in Mexico, and they have become a necessary point of reference. The ALI/UNIDROIT document has begun to have a significant impact on the development of legal systems, as can be discerned in the legal structure of Mexico.

It would be disingenuous to assert that the Mexican system provides a model for harmonizing its civil-procedure rules with those of its main commercial partners. Nothing could be further from the truth. Nonetheless, the notion of "approximation" of legal systems would be more accurate if approximation is understood as an arduous reformation process making

[31] Ferrand, "La procédure civile internationale," n.3, 422.

[32] Justices Olga Sánchez Cordero and Juan Silva Meza attended this working meeting.

[33] Judge Díaz Ortiz is the editor charged by the Conference of Chief Justices of Mexico to create the Mexican Model Code of Civil Procedure. This Model Code would be established subject to the consideration and approval of the federal states that comprise the Mexican Union.

legal systems more compatible.[34] This notion of approximation shifts the debate from the dogmatic fundamentals of civil-procedure law to a more pragmatic approach focusing on the final resolution of the controversy. This is what Professor Storme has referred to as "il principio del finalismo."

With this evolutionary view in mind it is worthwhile to evoke recent changes in the Mexican legal system. The Mexican Code of Commerce (Co. Com.) was reformed in 1993[35] and incorporated UNCITRAL's model law of International Commercial Arbitration. Article 1435 of the Co. Com. states that, following the arbitral statements, the parties are free to elect the procedure they would like to use and the arbitral tribunal will adjust its actions accordingly. When agreement is lacking, the tribunal may, within this regulatory framework, conduct the arbitration in any manner it deems appropriate. The discretion given to the arbitral tribunal includes determining the admissibility and relevance of evidence, as well as the value of the proofs.

The constitutionality of this article was challenged in the Supreme Court of Justice of Mexico (SC). The core argument was that it breached the constitutional guarantees of hearing and of due process of law.[36] Yet, despite this significant concern, the Supreme Court of Justice of Mexico affirmed the constitutionality of the Co. Com reform.[37]

This decision represents a radical shift in the interpretative principles of our legal system. The ALI/UNIDROIT Principles and Rules were present both in the Mexican Justices' spirit and in their deliberations. It may not be a coincidence that Justice Silva Meza, author of the decision, was the Chair of the ALI/UNIDROIT Mexican Seminar.

[34] Professor Kerameus in this respect states: "The third, and final, issue of definition pertains to the frequent and growing use of the terms 'unification,' 'harmonization,' and 'approximation.'... *Unification* implies the adoption of common rules on a given matter, where it is irrelevant whether such adoption is dictated by a treaty, by some other official act (for instance, a directive of the European Union), or by sheer imitation. By contrast, *harmonization* gives expression to a certain rapprochement among various legal systems and the elimination of most, but not all disparities, while at the same time some other disparities persist and coexist with otherwise identical norms. We may say that harmonization is a form of mini-unification. Within the European Union, harmonization is usually called *approximation*." See Kerameus, "Some Reflections," n.6, 444.

[35] *Diario Oficial de la Federación*. Mexico, July 22, 1993.

[36] See art. 14 of the Mexican Constitution, which has been the object of several polemic interpretations. This article states that no one can be deprived of life, freedom or properties, possessions, or rights, but by a judgment before tribunals previously established in which the essential formalities are followed, and according to laws of due process previously adopted. The observance of these guarantees of hearing and due process are binding upon every Mexican authority, even the legislative.

[37] Supreme Court of Mexico's Decision. June 30, 2004. 759/2003.

The Supreme Court's decision has had several repercussions that can now be recognized. It supports the new concept of universal procedural law and therefore validates the basis upon which others might choose to adopt general universal procedures like that found in the ALI/UNIDROIT Principles and Rules.

As a result of this new decision by the Supreme Court of Mexico, the potential to achieve an approximation with the different legal systems multiplies. The Principles and Rules offer an extraordinary framework of reference for Mexican jurisdictions, including arbitration, and can help assure transparency, predictability, and effective procedural equality among the parties of different nationalities, residences, and addresses.[38] Mexican arbitrators may now seek guidance from the Principles and Rules in order for determining appropriate procedures. In addition the movement toward procedural harmonization would also positively influence the Mexican Model Code of Civil Procedure.

The American continent has been historically open to concepts of legal approximation, and procedural law is no exception. I agree with Professor Glenn's statement[39] suggesting that the Americas are more open to universal movements of harmonization because there is no regional harmonization that hinders the Americas from adhering to such movements. Implementation can materialize through legislative or judicial authorities under the present national or subnational structures. The Mexican legal system confirms it. It is natural to expect reticence from those who adhere to traditional notions of sovereignty, constitutional law, and local culture, but every social process demonstrates this. From this broader perspective, the Supreme Court's decision turned out to be more than a mere premonition. The Mexican experience shows that the Principles and Rules have already started proving their utility and importance, and that over time they will make it possible for justice to begin abolishing national borders.

Jorge A. Sánchez-Cordero Dávila
Member of the Governing Council
of UNIDROIT and ALI member

Mexico City, Mexico
November 22, 2004

[38] Ferrand, "La procédure civile internationale, n.3, 429.
[39] Glenn, "Prospects for Transnational Civil Procedure," n.12, 488.

A DRAFTER'S REFLECTIONS ON THE PRINCIPLES OF TRANSNATIONAL CIVIL PROCEDURE

The Idea

The publication in 2005 of this work by The American Law Institute and the International Institute for the Unification of Private Law (UNIDROIT) completes an undertaking that originated about 10 years earlier.

Professor Michele Taruffo and I conceived the idea in conversation during a coffee break at an international conference on comparative civil procedure, in which we were sharing reflections on our prior collaborations in that subject. Professor Taruffo, of the University of Pavia, is a leading expert in the comparison of procedure, particularly in various civil-law systems, including those of Germany, France, Spain, and, of course, Italy. I have long been a student of common-law procedures, particularly their history and the variations in the federal legal systems in the United States. In our previous work, Professor Taruffo and I had addressed such problems as discovery, the burden of proof, and *res judicata*. We had also completed a book about the American system addressed to lawyers from other countries and to curious minds in the United States.[1]

The basic idea for the Transnational Civil Procedure project was simple: If a "civilian" and a "common lawyer" could so comfortably come to understand each other, the subjects of their professional knowledge must be fundamentally similar. And if the subjects were similar, it must be possible to formulate a single system in mutually coherent terms. Fortunately, Professor Taruffo was fluent in English as well as several Romance languages, for – being an American – I was not multilingual (although I had a grounding in Latin and Spanish). I believe it was equally important that Professor Taruffo

[1] Geoffrey Hazard and Michele Taruffo, American Civil Procedure (New Haven, CT: Yale Univ. Press, 1993).

and I had been continually engaged as practicing lawyers in our respective systems as well as being academic scholars.

The Proposal

We proposed a project to draft a code of civil procedure that would be intelligible and operable in regimes of both the civil law and the common law. We hoped that the project would be approved for sponsorship by The American Law Institute. At that point I was about to retire as Director (executive director) of the Institute; my relationship as Director had been a happy one, so we considered the prospects for approval to be favorable. In fact, before submitting our proposal to the ALI Council, Professor Taruffo and I had already spent more than a year in preliminary drafting of the final product, thereby satisfying ourselves that the enterprise was indeed feasible.[2] Having regard for possible conflict of interest on the Director's part, the ALI appointed a special committee to consider the proposal. The review was supportive and the project approved, although (as we learned subsequently) with some trepidation.

However, in deliberations about the project, it was recognized that, if possible, there should be co-sponsorship with another organization with international standing. The ALI is an American not-for-profit, nongovernmental organization of professionals in the law, including judges, lawyers, and professors of law. It had a long and widely recognized record of serious engagement in projects promoting the "clarification and simplification" of the law, to use a phrase in its charter. The Institute was the sole sponsor of most of its projects, including the Restatements of the Law (for example, in Contracts and Torts) and legislative projects such as the Model Penal Code and the Model Code of Evidence. However, the Institute had also undertaken projects in cooperation with other organizations. For several years we had been pursuing a challenging but very promising project in comparative insolvency law ("bankruptcy" law) with counterparts from Canada and Mexico.[3] For many years the Institute had cooperated with another American organization in developing and then revising the U.S. Uniform Commercial Code.

[2] We remembered a poignant scenario in Western intellectual history: Many of the academics who fled from the Nazis in the 1930s had thereafter obtained American research grants on the basis of projected work that they had in fact already completed before leaving Europe. Thus, we knew that a proposed experiment is very likely to succeed when it is based on a previously tested prototype.

[3] American Law Institute, Transnational Insolvency: Cooperation Among the NAFTA Countries (Huntington, NY: Juris Publishing, Inc., 4 volumes, 2003).

Membership in the Institute included a number of legal scholars, judges, and lawyers from other countries, particularly England, Germany, and Canada.

UNIDROIT was a "natural" for cooperative participation. That organization and the ALI had a cordial relationship arising from UNIDROIT's work on and publication of the UNIDROIT Principles of International Commercial Contracts. That work was modeled in part on the ALI Restatements. Also, the late Professor E. Allan Farnsworth of Columbia University was both a member of UNIDROIT's Council and a member of the ALI and the Reporter for the ALI's Restatement Second of Contracts. UNIDROIT expressed interest in exploring the possibility of a joint venture.

The UNIDROIT Evaluation

UNIDROIT engaged Professor Rolf Stürner of the Faculty of Law of the University of Freiburg to conduct an evaluation of the proposal. Professor Stürner was ideally qualified. He is both a leading scholar in comparative civil procedure and a judge and he has extensive experience in dealing with common-law procedures. With Peter L. Murray of the Harvard Law School faculty he had also undertaken a major project that has now resulted in a book, *German Civil Justice*,[4] involving comparison of the German legal system with that of the United States.

Professor Stürner submitted a report to UNIDROIT giving qualified approval of a project involving a joint venture. That approval was of the concept and of its probable feasibility. The primary qualification was that the project should aim at a statement of principles of civil procedure rather than a code of rules. On this basis, and after some further discussion, the joint venture was approved.

The ALI and UNIDROIT set up a joint Working Group, in accordance with their usual project procedures. The Working Group consisted of Professor Stürner and myself as Co-Reporters, a Chair, and the following members:

Professor Neil H. Andrews, Clare College, University of Cambridge, Cambridge, England
Justice Aída R. Kemelmajer de Carlucci, Supreme Court of Mendoza, Mendoza, Argentina
Professor Frédérique Ferrand, Université Jean Moulin, Lyon, France

[4] Peter Murray and Rolf Stürner, *German Civil Justice* (Durham, NC: Carolina Academic Press, 2004).

Professor Masanori Kawano, Nagoya University School of Law, Nagoya, Japan
Professor Pierre Lalive, University of Geneva, Geneva, Switzerland

The Chair of the Working Group was Mr. Ronald T. Nhlapo of the South African Law Commission. The other members of the Working Group were all specialists in civil procedure, with much comparative-law knowledge and experience. Mr. Nhlapo was an exceptionally effective presiding officer, despite – or perhaps by reason of – the fact that he was not a specialist in the field. Dr. Antonio Gidi from ALI and Professor M. J. Bonell from UNIDROIT served as Co-Coordinators, with Dr. Gidi also serving as Secretary.

The ALI/UNIDROIT Working Group

The ALI/UNIDROIT Working Group convened for week-long annual sessions over a four-year period. At each meeting, a full text of the work was submitted for detailed discussion. The text thus submitted each year had been developed by the team of Reporters by modifying the previous draft. The Co-Reporters of the Working Group received valuable advice and assistance from Dr. Antonio Gidi. Dr. Gidi had his foundational legal training in Brazil; he subsequently received a master's degree in Italy and a doctorate in comparative civil procedure in both Brazil and the United States. Throughout, he carried the burden of maintaining the text and securing the accuracy of the revisions. He was also continuously sensitive to subtle differences between common-law and civil-law approaches.

The mandate of the Working Group was that it review text, question provisions controversial or difficult to understand, and suggest alternatives or alternative approaches. Thanks to the competence and courtesy of its members, all discussions were conducted in English, although French has an equivalent status in UNIDROIT's work. Interim French versions were made to assist in clarifying the meaning, and a complete French version has been made of the final text. Fortunately, the competence in English of all participants facilitated a free and informal method of discussion.

This method of discussion is worth emphasizing. After some awkwardness at the beginning, discussion proceeded without the elaborate introductions and expressions of respect and deference often typical in international deliberations. On the contrary, discussion was simple, direct, professional, and sympathetic. The common aim was to "get it right." One can say that a draft text is a series of questions in the form of an answer. The common objective was to make "the answer" as good as possible.

The ALI Proceedings

Meanwhile, The American Law Institute proceeded according to its usual methods. These involve designation of the Reporters (Professor Taruffo and I were designated as Co-Reporters, and Dr. Gidi was designated first as Assistant Reporter, then as Associate Reporter), selection of Advisers, and recruitment of a Members Consultative Group. In the ALI project procedure, the Advisers are selected by the Director upon consultation with the Institute's Council, its officers, and the Reporter. The Director is Professor Lance Liebman of Columbia Law School, who succeeded me in 1999. The principal officer at the beginning of the project was Professor Charles Alan Wright, the President. Upon Professor Wright's untimely death in 2000, Michael Traynor became President. Professor Wright, Mr. Traynor, and Professor Liebman were all very interested in and supportive of the enterprise.

The ALI Advisers included leading judges, lawyers, and scholars from the United States and a number of other countries as well. The American Advisers notably included Professor Edward H. Cooper and Dean Mary Kay Kane, co-authors of a leading treatise on procedure under the U.S. Federal Rules of Civil Procedure. They provided detailed comments on every draft. Other ALI Advisers included judges, lawyers, and scholars from Australia, Canada, China, England, France, Greece, Hong Kong, Italy, Japan, Korea, Mexico, Russia, Spain, and Switzerland. The ALI Members Consultative Group included many other Americans and also ALI members from Australia, Canada, Italy, Mexico, the Philippines, and Singapore. In addition, many other colleagues from countries throughout the world participated in one or more conferences addressing the project. Their names are listed as International Consultants.

The procedure followed for the ALI deliberations is essentially similar to that utilized in the ALI/UNIDROIT Working Group. However, in the ALI procedure the text at each stage goes through three reviews, first by the Advisers and Members Consultative Group, then by the ALI Council, and finally by the membership at its Annual Meeting held each May.

Principles and Rules

The ALI accepted the proposal by UNIDROIT that the project formulate principles of civil procedure rather than a code. At the first meeting of the Working Group, Professor Stürner presented a preliminary draft of principles and Professor Andrews presented another. Those drafts were adopted as the basis of discussion and further work instead of the code form originally created. As the work progressed, most attention was focused on the Principles, with only incidental attention being given to the previously drafted Rules. Along the way it was firmly decided that the final product would be the Principles. However, the Rules were to be revised to conform to the Principles, to be designated as the work of the Reporters rather than the project sponsors, and to be considered an example of how the Principles might be implemented in practice. Such is the finished product.

The decision to frame the project as Principles left open a central issue, however: What is an appropriate level of detail in expression of legal "principles," as distinct from legal "rules" or a "code"? This question posed three kinds of problem. First, as a technical matter, what level of detail is appropriate to fulfill the project's purposes at the stage of implementation? At that stage, generalities are of limited use, for as the saying goes, the devil is in the details. For example, the principle of fair notice can be stated very simply as "fair notice." But specification of the content of notice and the procedure for its delivery are important details; the Principles require a copy of the complaint to be included. And, as an aspect of giving notice, the Principles require a court to inquire whether there has been compliance with the notice procedure before entering a judgment by default of the defendant's appearance, which is also an important detail. Cumulatively, specification at this level of detail conveys a much more concrete conception of the procedure contemplated in the finished product.

Second, as a practical matter, procedure based on the Principles, if adopted, would have to be accommodated in existing legal systems. No legal text, even a code in the classic Justinian tradition, is entirely self-contained. From the drafting perspective, as a practical matter not all matters of detail can be addressed within the limitations of time and intellectual capacity in a given project. Hence, it was necessary to presuppose an existing local procedural system and to refer to the rules of that system for myriad particulars. The force of that consideration obviously goes in the opposite direction from the requirement, stated earlier, of providing technical detail. A balance always had to be considered.

Third, as a diplomatic matter, a reform proposal should not demand more change than necessary of a system's existing rules. In my experience of the American scene at any rate, successful reform is essentially conservative; the more substantial the purpose the more conservative the implementation.

In general, the Working Group, the Advisers, and the Reporters considered that a fairly fine level of detail was necessary to express our conception of the procedures being recommended. Nevertheless, on a number of issues we decided to abandon some draft provisions that seemed too specific.

Many of these decisions are reflected in the succession of drafts as the work proceeded.

Scope: "Transnational Commercial Disputes"

The Principles and Rules are designed for administration in a relatively small sector of civil litigation. The first delimitation of scope is to international transactions. Concerning this limitation, relatively few disputes addressed in the legal system of any regime arise from transactions or occurrences having an international dimension, as distinct from wholly domestic ones. A second limitation is to "commercial" disputes. Relatively few legal disputes arise from business transactions, as distinct from motor-vehicle accidents, divorce and other domestic-relations matters, employment disputes, and so on. An issue at the outset and throughout the project, therefore, was whether a project of such limited scope was worthwhile.

The rationale for limiting the scope was twofold, both positive and negative. The positive consideration was that parties to transactions in international commerce, and their legal representatives, generally have a very well-informed understanding of legal disputes. Hence, they could accept the idea of a cosmopolitan approach to procedural justice, and hence be receptive to the idea of a "neutral" set of procedures, rather than ones rooted in various national legal cultures. Second, the negative or exclusionary consideration was that most modern legal systems have several different procedural codes for various categories of legal dispute, involving modifications of the system's basic civil-procedure regime. No modern legal system has one procedural system for all civil litigation. Familiar variations include procedures in employment disputes, in divorce and other domestic-relations matters, and in insolvency proceedings. These are all excluded from the *Principles of Transnational Civil Procedure*, thus bypassing many complications. Another excluded category is personal-injury litigation (notably automobile accidents and claims of defective products causing human injury). This category is prominent in the United States, where the background structures of medical care and disability insurance are so different from those in most other modern economies. Trying to deal with that category in this project, although no doubt welcome to many Europeans, would have been extremely controversial in the United States.

This is not to say that the procedural system delineated in the Principles could not be adopted for adjudication of other types of disputes in addition to those arising from international commerce. Indeed, systems essentially similar to that in the Principles function today in general litigation in domestic courts throughout the world. We were so informed regarding the basic systems in Australia, Canada, and the Philippines, for example. Moreover, the definition of "commercial" is somewhat different from one legal system to another. It is contemplated that a more precise definition of scope would be required in any system of procedural rules based on the Principles.

Pleading, Disclosure of Evidence, and Decisional Hearing

A civil legal dispute requires consideration of legal rules and of facts and evidence. The legal rules include those governing procedural matters, such as the form in which issues are to be identified and resolved; substantive legal rules, such as the law of contract; rules governing remedies, such as those for calculating damages; and sometimes rules of private international law or choice of law. "Facts and evidence," a term commonly employed by lawyers in the civil systems, includes concepts of relevance and probative inference (i.e., factual matters to be proved) and documentary, testimonial, and expert evidence (i.e., means of establishing relevant factual matters). A court must be suitably informed of both law and fact and the parties or their advocates should have reasonable opportunity to contribute information accordingly.

It is universally recognized that the initial vehicle for contentions of fact and law is pleading, first in the plaintiff's complaint and then in the defendant's response. It is almost universally recognized that the plaintiff should spell out the factual basis of its claim, whether based on a written contract or a course of dealing, or on some kind of tort (in the common-law term) or civil wrong (the civil-law term). That is the rule in all modern procedural systems except in the U.S. Federal Rules of Civil Procedure. Under the U.S. Federal Rule (which has also been adopted by many state-court systems), the plaintiff is allowed to engage in "notice pleading," which requires only a general reference to the transaction on which the suit is based. However, in actual practice the claims of plaintiffs in U.S. litigation typically are stated at the same level of detail as in other regimes. Lawyers for plaintiffs in American litigation do this chiefly because they want the judge, to whom the pleadings will be presented in the course of administering the case, to understand the facts of the case, according to the plaintiff's version, and to appreciate that the plaintiff's case has real merit. Also, contrary to popular calumny, plaintiffs' lawyers in the United States ordinarily scrutinize carefully the prospects of a claim before filing it.[5] Careful scrutiny of the case's prospects usually yields

[5] This pattern is a matter of self-interest on the part of plaintiffs' lawyers as well as professional responsibility. If a case is prosecuted on the basis of a contingent fee (as is often

sufficiently detailed information that a requirement of "fact pleading" can, in fact, be fulfilled.

In any event, in commercial disputes the claimant usually has fairly specific knowledge of the factual basis of a claim. Moreover, since the dispute is international, there is the possibility of some "cultural dissonance" even among countries in the Western community. Specificity in statement of the claim and similar specificity in the defendant's response reduce the possible effects of such dissonance. Hence, the Principles require that statement of the factual basis of a claim and defense be reasonably specific.

In civil-law systems, the plaintiff is also required to state the legal basis of its claim. In traditional common-law systems, the legal basis can be left implicit, to be inferred from the factual allegations. Explication of the legal basis of a claim is nevertheless at least customary in some common-law systems. Such an explication is required in some cases in the federal courts in the United States, for example, in order to comply with jurisdictional requirements. The Principles require such explication in all cases, partly for the same reason, that is, so the court can determine whether the case is governed by this procedure rather than the general procedural law. Also, in international disputes there is less reason to be confident that the judges will be immediately familiar with the substantive law that ought to be applied.

A plaintiff can make specific factual allegations only on the basis of having, "in hand" so to speak, evidence on which eventually to prove the case. However, a plaintiff may lack sufficient proof of some legally required element of a claim, or lack corroborating evidence to support proof of such an element, while knowing or believing that such evidence is in possession of the defendant or some third party. (A significant third party in commercial transactions could be a bank involved in handling a money transfer, for example.) The potentially available evidence may be positive in that it would tend to prove the contention in issue, or negative in that it would contradict or disparage the contention. A similar situation can confront a defendant regarding evidence for a defense, such as payment or waiver.

The procedural problem is definition of the circumstances, if any, under which a party seeking such evidence can require its production by an opposing party or a third party. In international and some common-law parlance, this is the problem of "discovery." The problem is very sensitive, largely

the situation), the lawyer invested time and effort and typically also litigation expenses such as expert-witness fees. Lawyers do not like to make bad investments. Where a case is prosecuted on the basis of a firm fee, the lawyer ordinarily must be concerned not to waste the client's money on a weak case.

because of experience with sweeping demands for documents emanating from litigation in the United States.

On one hand, it seems profoundly unfair that a party could withhold or prevent disclosure of evidence that would resolve or be strongly indicative in resolving a critical issue in a legal dispute. This consideration holds, even allowing for recognition of generally recognized rights of privacy or confidentiality, including protection of client–attorney communications as recognized in the Principles. This consideration becomes more compelling in modern conditions, where relevant evidence typically takes the form, not simply of testimony by percipient witnesses, but of documents (and now e-mail) in some private or public repository. On the other hand, there are rights or at least interests of privacy, even for parties invoking the coercive authority of the state through litigation. And the idea that one disputant can ransack another's files, through a "fishing expedition," is abhorrent to some mentalities and at least troublesome to all.

The civil law has generally tried to deal with this problem along two lines. One is that a disputing party may have a substantively protected right to a document in another's possession. A ready example is a depositor's right to bank information about his or her account. Another approach is exercise of the court's authority to require production of such evidence once its existence and relevance have become apparent through preliminary hearing. The common law has dealt with the problem by definition of the documents subject to disclosure. Such definition easily includes specifically identified documents whose relevance is apparent. Not so easy is a definition of documents by category, when a demanding party must articulate a category whose material content is unknown. The classic common-law definition is found in the English *Peruvian Guano* case,[6] in language that is clear in concept but inevitably ambiguous in application. The U.S. Federal Rules largely avoided ambiguity through a very broad definition of discoverability: any material that "appears reasonably calculated to lead to the discovery of admissible evidence."[7] That definition has been very controversial, not alone outside of the United States. The Principles seek a ground close to that in *Peruvian Guano*, but with recognition that application of the concept may be modified as a case progresses beyond the pleading stage.

[6] The court's language is as follows: *Compagnie Financiere v. Peruvian Guano Co.*, Ct. Appeal, 11 QBD 55, 20 Dec. 1882, per Brett, L.J.: "documents . . . which, it is not unreasonable to suppose, . . . contain information which may, either directly or indirectly, enable the party . . . either to advance his own case or to damage the case of his adversary."

[7] Federal Rules of Civil Procedure, Rule 26(b)(1).

The final stage of a civil dispute is decisional hearing. Traditionally, the civil-law systems have a series of hearings, first to identify the issues, then to receive evidence essentially issue by issue until the point of decision is reached. Traditionally, the common law contemplated a single "trial" at which all issues, factual and legal, would be resolved. However, many civil-law systems now aim for concentrated hearings, in which all or most evidentiary matters are determined. And common-law systems have long since had pretrial hearings for identifying crucial issues, scheduling and organizing further proceedings, and considering dispositive motions, such as the motion for dismissal and the motion for summary judgment.

Viewed functionally, these two approaches increasingly resemble each other. The civil-law systems have tended to consolidate the interchanges between court and parties into fewer and more encompassing hearings, while the common-law systems have recognized that more than one stage of such interchanges is typically necessary. In any event, in substantial commercial litigation, particularly of an international character, fair procedure requires planning, coordinating, and scheduling court proceedings into as few hearings as practicable.

It is common ground that in a case tried without a jury, the judge (or judges in a multijudge panel) decides the issues of fact as well as the issues of law. It is also common ground that the court should provide written explanation for its important rulings, particularly those determining the merits. The Principles also recognize that there should be a right of appeal from a court of first instance, but that reference should be made to local law for appellate procedures.

Finally, concerning resolution of issues of fact and application of legal rules to disputed evidence, there is the question of jury trial. No legal system outside the United States uses juries in civil litigation, except for very limited categories of cases that do not generally include commercial litigation. In the United States, however, jury trial is generally a matter of constitutional right in both federal and state courts, even in complex business litigation. The Principles simply defer to the law of the forum on this issue, as they must where domestic constitutional rights are involved. The Principles are compatible with the right of jury trial, if proper local adjustment is made concerning the rules of evidence and the technique of judicial instruction to the jury about governing legal rules. Comprehensive discovery, especially depositions in the fashion of the U.S. Federal Rules, is now familiar in the United States in disputes tried to a jury but is not essential in a jury-trial system. Procedures essentially similar to those in the Principles prevailed in most civil litigation in the United States under the constitutional jury-trial guarantees as they functioned prior to adoption of the Federal Rules, which occurred only in 1938.

Conclusion

At the beginning of the project for Principles of Transnational Civil Procedure, many observers thought that the enterprise would be too "American." At various stages in the project, many American observers thought the project had taken on a European or even a Continental cast. The Reporters have thought that the system worked out in the Principles was very similar to at least one of the various civil-procedure systems prevailing in their respective home countries. However, as remarked by Justice Kemelmajer de Carlucci of the ALI/UNIDROIT Working Group concerning one of the many details being addressed, "This idea seems fair and I support it, even though it is not a part of my country's system." That was the prevailing attitude during the course of the project. Perhaps the Principles are about right.

Geoffrey C. Hazard, Jr.

November 22, 2004

SUMMARY OF CONTENTS

Foreword *page* xxiii

Reporters' Preface xxvii

Preface, by E. Bruce Leonard xxix

Preface, by Jorge A. Sánchez-Cordero Dávila xxxi

A Drafter's Reflections on the Principles of Transnational Civil Procedure, by Geoffrey C. Hazard, Jr. xli

Introduction 1

PRINCIPLES OF TRANSNATIONAL CIVIL PROCEDURE (with commentary) 16

PRINCIPLES OF TRANSNATIONAL CIVIL PROCEDURE (with commentary), French Version 51

APPENDIX: REPORTERS' STUDY 99

RULES OF TRANSNATIONAL CIVIL PROCEDURE (with commentary) 100

A Bibliography of Writings about the ALI/UNIDROIT Project 157

Index 163

CONTENTS

Foreword *page* xxiii
Reporters' Preface xxvii
Preface, by E. Bruce Leonard xxix
Preface, by Jorge A. Sánchez-Cordero Dávila xxxi
A Drafter's Reflections on the Principles of Transnational Civil Procedure, by Geoffrey C. Hazard, Jr. xli

Introduction 1

PRINCIPLES OF TRANSNATIONAL CIVIL PROCEDURE (with commentary)

Principle

Scope and Implementation 16
Comment 16
1. Independence, Impartiality, and Qualifications of the Court and Its Judges 17
Comment 18
2. Jurisdiction Over Parties 18
Comment 19
3. Procedural Equality of the Parties 20
Comment 21
4. Right to Engage a Lawyer 22
Comment 22
5. Due Notice and Right to Be Heard 22
Comment 23
6. Languages 24
Comment 24
7. Prompt Rendition of Justice 25
Comment 25

Principle

8. Provisional and Protective Measures 25
Comment 26

9. Structure of the Proceedings 28
Comment 28

10. Party Initiative and Scope of the Proceeding 29
Comment 29

11. Obligations of the Parties and Lawyers 30
Comment 31

12. Multiple Claims and Parties; Intervention 31
Comment 32

13. *Amicus Curiae* Submission 32
Comment 33

14. Court Responsibility for Direction of the Proceeding 33
Comment 34

15. Dismissal and Default Judgment 34
Comment 35

16. Access to Information and Evidence 36
Comment 37

17. Sanctions 38
Comment 38

18. Evidentiary Privileges and Immunities 39
Comment 39

19. Oral and Written Presentations 40
Comment 40

20. Public Proceedings 41
Comment 41

21. Burden and Standard of Proof 42
Comment 42

22. Responsibility for Determinations of Fact and Law 42
Comment 43

23. Decision and Reasoned Explanation 44
Comment 44

24. Settlement 44
Comment 45

25. Costs 45
Comment 46

Principle

26.	Immediate Enforceability of Judgments	46
	Comment	46
27.	Appeal	47
	Comment	47
28.	*Lis Pendens* and *Res Judicata*	47
	Comment	48
29.	Effective Enforcement	48
	Comment	48
30.	Recognition	48
	Comment	49
31.	International Judicial Cooperation	49
	Comment	49

PRINCIPLES OF TRANSNATIONAL CIVIL PROCEDURE (with commentary), French Version 51

APPENDIX: REPORTERS' STUDY 99

RULES OF TRANSNATIONAL CIVIL PROCEDURE (with commentary) 100

Rule

A. Interpretation and Scope

1.	Standards of Interpretation	100
	Comment	100
2.	Disputes to Which These Rules Apply	100
	Comment	101

B. Jurisdiction, Joinder, and Venue

3.	Forum and Territorial Competence	103
	Comment	103
4.	Jurisdiction Over Parties	103
	Comment	104
5.	Multiple Claims and Parties; Intervention	105
	Comment	105
6.	*Amicus Curiae* Submission	106
	Comment	106
7.	Due Notice	107
	Comment	107
8.	Languages	108
	Comment	108

Rule

C. Composition and Impartiality of the Court

9.	Composition of the Court	108
	Comment	109
10.	Impartiality of the Court	109
	Comment	109

D. Pleading Stage

11.	Commencement of the Proceeding and Notice	110
	Comment	110
12.	Statement of Claim (Complaint)	111
	Comment	111
13.	Statement of Defense and Counterclaims	112
	Comment	113
14.	Amendments	114
	Comment	115
15.	Dismissal and Default Judgment	116
	Comment	116
16.	Settlement Offer	117
	Comment	118

E. General Authority of the Court

17.	Provisional and Protective Measures	120
	Comment	121
18.	Case Management	123
	Comment	124
19.	Early Court Determinations	125
	Comment	126
20.	Orders Directed to a Third Person	127
	Comment	128

F. Evidence

21.	Disclosure	128
	Comment	129
22.	Exchange of Evidence	130
	Comment	131
23.	Deposition and Testimony by Affidavit	134
	Comment	134
24.	Public Proceedings	136
	Comment	137

Rule

25.	Relevance and Admissibility of Evidence	137
	Comment	137
26.	Expert Evidence	139
	Comment	139
27.	Evidentiary Privileges	141
	Comment	141
28.	Reception and Effect of Evidence	143
	Comment	143
	G. Final Hearing	
29.	Concentrated Final Hearing	144
	Comment	144
30.	Record of the Evidence	147
	Comment	147
31.	Final Discussion and Judgment	147
	Comment	148
32.	Costs	148
	Comment	149
	H. Appellate and Subsequent Proceedings	
33.	Appellate Review	150
	Comment	151
34.	Rescission of Judgment	152
	Comment	153
35.	Enforcement of Judgment	153
	Comment	154
36.	Recognition and Judicial Assistance	155
	Comment	155

A Bibliography of Writings about the ALI/UNIDROIT Project 157

Index 163

INTRODUCTION

I. International "Harmonization" of Procedural Law

The human community of the world lives in closer quarters today than in earlier times. International trade is at an all-time high and is increasing steadily; international investment and monetary flows increase apace; businesses from the developed countries establish themselves all over the globe directly or through subsidiaries; business people travel abroad as a matter of routine; ordinary citizens in increasing numbers live temporarily or permanently outside their native countries. As a consequence, there are positive and productive interactions among citizens of different nations in the form of increased commerce and wider possibilities for personal experience and development. There are also inevitable negative interactions, however, including increased social friction, legal controversy, and litigation.

In dealing with these negative consequences, the costs and distress resulting from legal conflict can be mitigated by reducing differences in legal systems, so that the same or similar "rules of the game" apply no matter where the participants may find themselves. The effort to reduce differences among national legal systems is commonly referred to as "harmonization." Another method for reducing differences is "approximation," meaning the process of reforming the rules of various legal systems so that they approximate each other. Most endeavors at harmonization and approximation have addressed substantive law, particularly the law governing commercial and financial transactions. There is now in place a profusion of treaties and conventions governing these subjects as well as similar arrangements addressing personal rights such as those of employees, children, and married women.[1]

[1] See, for example, Convention on the Rights of the Child, November 20, 1989, 28 I.L.M. 1448; United States – Egypt Treaty Concerning the Reciprocal Encouragement and Protection of Investments, September 29, 1982, 21 I.L.M. 927; Convention on the Elimination of All

Harmonization of procedural law has made much less progress. Some conventions on civil and human rights contain fundamental procedural guaranties, such as equality before courts and the right to a fair, effective, public, and oral hearing or trial before an independent court. These guaranties are common international standards and a universally recognized basis of procedural harmonization.[2]

Further harmonization has been impeded by the assumption that national procedural systems are too different from each other and too deeply embedded in local political history and cultural tradition to permit reduction or reconciliation of differences among legal systems. There are, to be sure, some international conventions dealing with procedural law, notably the Hague Conventions on the Service Abroad and on the Taking of Evidence Abroad, the efforts of the Hague to frame a Convention on Jurisdiction and Judgments, and European conventions on recognition of judgments.[3] Thus far, the international conventions on procedural law have addressed the bases of personal jurisdiction and the mechanics for service of process to commence a lawsuit on one end of the litigation process, and recognition of judgments on the other end of the process.

Forms of Discrimination Against Women, December 18, 1979, 19 I.L.M. 33; International Covenant on Civil and Political Rights, December 16, 1966, 999 U.N.T.S. 171; Convention on the Settlement of Investment Disputes Between States and Nationals of Other States, March 16, 1965, 17 U.S.T. 1270, T.I.A.S. No. 6090, 575 U.N.T.S. 159.

2 See, for example, Article 47 of the Charter of Fundamental Rights of the European Union, OJ 2000 C 364/1; Article 7 of the African Charter on Human and People's Rights, June 27, 1981, 21 I.L.M. 58; Article 8 of the American Convention on Human Rights, November 22, 1969, 1144 U.N.T.S. 123; Article 14 of the International Covenant on Civil and Political Rights, December 16, 1966, 999 U.N.T.S. 171; Article 6 of the Convention for the Protection of Human Rights and Fundamental Freedoms, November 4, 1950, E.T.S. No. 5, as amended by Protocol No. 11, E.T.S. No. 155.

3 See Hague Convention on the Service Abroad of Judicial and Extra Judicial Documents in Civil and Commercial Matters, November 15, 1965, 20 U.S.T. 1361; 16 I.L.M. 1339; Hague Convention on the Taking of Evidence Abroad in Civil or Commercial Matters, March 18, 1970, 23 U.S.T. 2555, 8 I.L.M. 37; Brussels Convention on Jurisdiction and Enforcement of Judgments in Civil and Commercial Matters, September 27, 1968, 8 I.L.M. 229, reprinted as amended in 29 I.L.M. 1413, substantially replaced by the Council Regulation (EC) No. 44/2001 of December 22, 2000, on jurisdiction and the recognition and enforcement of judgments in civil and commercial matters, OJ 2011 L 12/1; Lugano Convention on Jurisdiction and Enforcement of Judgments in Civil and Commercial Matters, September 16, 1988, 28 I.L.M. 620. See also, for example, Catherine Kessedjian, Report, Hague Conference on Private International Law, Enforcement of Judgments, "International Jurisdiction and Foreign Judgments in Civil and Commercial Matters," Prel. Doc. No. 7 (April 1997).

However, the pioneering work of Professor Marcel Storme and his distinguished collaborators has demonstrated that harmonization is possible in such procedural matters as the formulation of claims, the development of evidence, and the decision procedure.[4] This project to develop Principles and Rules for transnational civil procedure has drawn extensively on the work of Professor Storme's group.

International arbitration often is a substitute for adjudication in national courts. However, the international conventions on arbitration have the same limited scope as the conventions dealing with international litigation in judicial forums. Thus, the international conventions on arbitration address aspects of commencement of an arbitration proceeding and the recognition to be accorded an arbitration award, but say little or nothing about the procedure in an international arbitration proceeding as such.[5] Instead, the typical stipulation concerning hearing procedure in international arbitration is that the procedural ground rules shall be as determined by negotiation or by the administering authority or the neutral arbitrator.[6]

This project endeavors to draft procedural principles and rules that a country could adopt for adjudication of disputes arising from international commercial transactions.[7] The project is inspired in part by the Approximation project led by Professor Storme, mentioned earlier; in part by The American Law Institute (ALI) project on Transnational Insolvency; and in part by the successful effort in the United States a half-century ago to unite many diverse jurisdictions under one system of procedural rules with the adoption of the Federal Rules of Civil Procedure. The Federal Rules established a single procedure to be employed in federal courts sitting in 48 different semisovereign States, each with its own procedural law, its own procedural culture, and its own bar. The Federal Rules thereby accomplished what many thoughtful observers thought impossible – a single system of procedure for

4 Marcel Storme, ed., *Approximation of Judiciary Law in the European Union* (Amsterdam, the Netherlands: Kluwer, 1994). See also Anteproyecto del Código Procesal Civil Modelo para Iberoamerica, Revista de Processo (Creating a Model Code of Civil Procedure for Ibero-america), vols. 52 and 53 (São Paulo: Editora Revista dos Tribunais, 1988 and 1989).

5 See New York Convention on the Recognition and Enforcement of Foreign Arbitral Awards, June 19, 1958, 21 U.S.T. 2517, T.I.A.S. No. 6997, 330 U.N.T.S. 38.

6 Alan S. Rau and Edward F. Sherman, Tradition and Innovation in International Arbitration Procedure, Texas International Law Journal, vol. 30 (Winter 1995), 89, 90.

7 See John J. Barceló, III, Introduction to Geoffrey C. Hazard, Jr., and Michele Taruffo, "Transnational Rules of Civil Procedure," *Cornell International Law Journal*, vol. 30, no. 2 (1997), 493, 493–494.

four dozen different legal communities. The project to establish Principles of Transnational Civil Procedure conjectures that a procedure for litigation across national boundaries is also worth the attempt.

II. UNIDROIT Partnership

In 2000, after a favorable report from Professor Rolf Stürner, the International Institute for the Unification of Private Law (UNIDROIT) joined the ALI in this project. Professor Stürner has been a Reporter, appointed by UNIDROIT, since 2001. It was at UNIDROIT's initiative that the preparation of Principles of Transnational Civil Procedure was undertaken. Since then, the project has primarily focused on the Principles.

A formulation of Principles generally appeals to the civil-law mentality. Common-law lawyers may be less familiar with this sort of generalization. Since the Principles and Rules have been developed simultaneously, the relation between generality and specification is illuminated more sharply. The Principles are interpretive guides to the Rules, which are a more detailed body of procedural law. The Principles could also be adopted as principles for interpretation of existing national codes of procedure. Correlatively, the Rules can be considered as an exemplification or implementation of the Principles, suitable either for adoption or for further adaptation in particular jurisdictions. Both can be considered as models for reform in domestic legislation.

The ALI/UNIDROIT Working Group has had four week-long meetings in the UNIDROIT headquarters in Rome in four years. The ALI Advisers and Members Consultative Group have had six meetings and drafts have been considered at five ALI Annual Meetings. Much additional discussion has also taken place by means of international conferences held in different countries and correspondence over the last seven years.

III. Fundamental Similarities in Procedural Systems

In undertaking international harmonization of procedural law, the Reporters have come to identify both fundamental similarities and fundamental differences among procedural systems. Obviously, it is the fundamental differences that present the difficulties. However, it is important to keep in mind that all modern civil procedural systems have fundamental similarities. These similarities result from the fact that a procedural system must respond to several inherent requirements. Recognition of these requirements makes easier the task of identifying functional similarities in diverse legal systems and, at the same time, puts into sharper perspective the ways in which procedural systems differ from one another.

The fundamental similarities among procedural systems can be summarized as follows:

- Standards governing assertion of personal jurisdiction and subject-matter jurisdiction
- Specifications for a neutral adjudicator
- Procedure for notice to defendant
- Rules for formulation of claims
- Explication of applicable substantive law
- Establishment of facts through proof
- Provision for expert testimony
- Rules for deliberation, decision, and appellate review
- Rules of finality of judgments

Of these, the rules of jurisdiction, notice, and recognition of judgments are sufficiently similar from one country to another that they have been susceptible to substantial resolution through international practice and formal conventions. Concerning jurisdiction, the United States is aberrant in that it has an expansive concept of "long-arm" jurisdiction, although this difference is one of degree rather than one of kind, and in that U.S. law governing authority of its constituent states perpetuates jurisdiction based on simple presence of the person ("tag" jurisdiction). Specification of a neutral adjudicator begins with realization that all legal systems have rules to assure that a judge or other adjudicator should be disinterested. Accordingly, in transnational litigation reliance generally can be placed on the local rules expressing that principle. Similarly, an adjudicative system requires a principle of finality. Therefore, the concept of "final" judgment is also generally recognized, although some legal systems permit the reopening of a determination more liberally than other systems do. The corollary concept of mutual recognition of judgments is also universally accepted.

IV. Differences Among Procedural Systems

The differences in procedural systems are, along one division, differences between the common-law systems and the civil-law systems. The common-law systems all derive from England and include Canada, Australia, New Zealand, South Africa, India, and the United States, as well as Israel, Singapore, and Bermuda. The civil-law systems originated on the European continent and include those derived from Roman law (the law of the Roman

Empire codified in the Justinian Code) and canon law (the law of the Roman Catholic Church, itself substantially derived from Roman law). The civil-law systems include those of France, Germany, Italy, Spain, and virtually all other European countries and, in a borrowing or migration of legal systems, those of Latin America, Africa, and Asia, including Brazil, Argentina, Mexico, Egypt, Russia, Japan, and China.

The significant differences between common-law and civil-law systems are as follows:

- The judge in civil-law systems, rather than the advocates in common-law systems, has primary responsibility for development of the evidence and articulation of the legal concepts that should govern decision. However, there is great variance among civil-law systems in the manner and degree to which this responsibility is exercised, and no doubt variance among the judges in any given system.
- Civil-law litigation in many systems proceeds through a series of short hearing sessions – sometimes less than an hour each – for reception of evidence, which is then consigned to the case file until an eventual final stage of analysis and decision. In contrast, common-law litigation has a preliminary or pretrial stage (sometimes more than one) and then a trial at which all the evidence is received consecutively.
- A civil-law judgment in the court of first instance is generally subject to more searching reexamination in the court of second instance than a common-law judgment. Reexamination in the civil-law systems extends to facts as well as law.
- The judges in civil-law systems typically serve a professional lifetime as judge, whereas the judges in common-law systems generally are selected from the ranks of the bar. Thus, most civil-law judges lack the experience of having been a lawyer, whatever effects that may have.

These are important differences, but they are not irreconcilable.

The American version of the common-law system has differences from other common-law systems that are of at least equal significance. The American system is unique in the following respects:

- Jury trial is a broadly available right in the American federal and state courts. No other country routinely uses juries in civil cases.
- American rules of discovery give wide latitude for exploration of potentially relevant information and evidence, including through oral deposition.

- The American adversary system generally affords the advocates far greater latitude in presentation of a case than is customary in other common-law systems.
- The American system operates through a cost rule under which each party ordinarily pays that party's own lawyer and cannot recover that expense from a losing opponent. In almost all other countries, except Japan and China, the winning party, whether plaintiff or defendant, recovers at least a substantial portion of litigation costs.[8]
- American judges are selected through a variety of ways in which political affiliation plays an important part. In most other common-law countries judges are selected on the basis of professional standards.

Most of the major differences between the United States and other common-law systems stem from the use of juries in American litigation. American proceedings conducted by judges without juries closely resemble their counterparts in other common-law countries.

V. Rules for Formulation of Claims (Pleading)

The rules governing formulation of claims are substantially similar in most legal systems. The pleading requirement in most common-law systems requires that the claimant state the claim with reasonable particularity as to facts concerning persons, place, time, and sequence of events involved in the relevant transaction. This pleading rule is essentially similar to the Code Pleading requirement that governed in most American states prior to adoption of the Federal Rules of Civil Procedure in 1938.[9] This rule was abandoned in federal courts in the United States in 1938 and replaced by Notice Pleading, which required a much less detailed pleading. The Principles and Rules require that pleading be in detail with particulars as to the basis of claim and that the particulars reveal a set of facts that, if proved, would entitle the claimant to a judgment.

[8] See, generally, James W. Hughes and Edward A. Snyder, "Litigation and Settlement under the English and American Rules: Theory and Evidence." *Journal of Law and Economics*, vol. 38, no. 1 (1995), 225, 225–250; A. Tomkins and T. Willging, Taxation of Attorney's Fees: Practices in English, Alaskan and Federal Courts (1986). See also, for example, A. Ehrenzweig, "Reimbursement of Counsel Fees and the Great Society." *California Law Review*, vol. 54 (1963), 792; T. Rowe, "The Legal Theory of Attorney Fee Shifting: A Critical Overview," *Duke Law Journal*, vol. 31 (1982), 651, 651–680.

[9] L. Tolman, "Advisory Committee's Proposals to Amend the Federal Rules of Civil Procedure," *ABA Journal*, vol. 40 (1954), 843, 844; F. James, G. Hazard, and J. Leubsdorf, Civil Procedure §§ 3.5, 3.6 (5th ed. 2001).

VI. Exchange of Evidence

The pleading rule requiring specific allegations of fact reduces the potential scope of discovery, because it provides for tightly framed claims and defenses from the very beginning of the proceeding. Moreover, the pleading rule contemplates that a party who has pleaded specific facts will be required to reveal, at a second stage of the litigation, the specific proof on which it intends to rely concerning these allegations, including documents, summary of expected testimony of witnesses, and experts' reports. The Principles and Rules require disclosure of these sources of proof before the plenary hearing. These requirements presuppose that a claimant properly may commence litigation only if the claimant has a provable case and not merely the hope or expectation of uncovering such a case through discovery from the opposing party.

The combination of strict rules of pleading and compulsory disclosure further reduces the necessity of additional exchange of evidence. A party generally must show its own cards, so to speak, rather than getting them from an opponent. Within that framework, the Rules attempt to define a limited right of document discovery and a limited right of deposition. These are regarded as improper in many civil-law systems. However, a civil-law judge has authority to compel presentation of relevant documentary evidence and testimony of witnesses. In a modern legal system, there is a growing practical necessity – if one is serious about justice – to permit document discovery to some extent and, at least in some cases, deposition of key witnesses.

In most common-law jurisdictions, pretrial depositions are unusual and, in some countries, are employed only when the witness will be unavailable for trial. Documents are subject to discovery only when relevant to the proceeding. Relevance for this purpose is defined by reference to the pleadings and, as noted earlier, the rules of pleading require full specification of claims and defenses.[10] In contrast, wide-ranging pretrial discovery is an integral part of contemporary American civil litigation, particularly in cases involving substantial stakes. The American Federal Rules of Civil Procedure were recently amended to restrict disclosure and discovery in certain respects, but the scope is still much broader than it is in other common-law countries. The Principles and Rules offer a compromise toward approximation in international litigation.

[10] See, generally, C. Platto, ed. *Pre-Trial and Pre-Hearing Procedures Worldwide* (London: Graham and Trotman and IBA, 1990).

The rules for document production in the common-law systems all derive from the English Judicature Acts of 1873 and 1875. In 1888 the standard for discovery was held in the leading *Peruvian Guano* decision to cover

> any document that relates to the matters in question in the action, which not only would be evidence upon any issue, but also which, it is reasonable to suppose, contains information which *may* – not which *must* – either directly or indirectly enable the party . . . either to advance his own case or to damage the case of his adversary . . . [A] document can properly be said to contain information which may enable the party requiring the affidavit either to advance his own case or to damage the case of his adversary, if it is a document which may fairly lead him to a train of inquiry, which may have either of these two consequences. . . . [11]

Under the civil law there is no discovery as such. However, a party has a right to request the court to interrogate a witness or to require the opposing party to produce a document. This arrangement is a corollary of the general principle in the civil-law system that the court rather than the parties is in charge of the development of evidence. In some civil-law systems, a party cannot be compelled to produce a document that will establish its own liability – something like a civil equivalent of a privilege against self-incrimination. However, in many civil-law systems a party may be compelled to produce a document when the judge concludes that the document is the only evidence concerning the point of issue. This result can also be accomplished by holding that the burden of proof as to the issue shall rest with the party having possession of the document. In any event, the standard for production under the civil law appears uniformly to be "relevance" in a fairly strict sense.

VII. Procedure at Plenary Hearing

Another difference between civil-law systems and common-law systems concerns presentation of evidence. It is well known that in the civil-law tradition the evidence is developed by the judge with suggestions from the advocates, while in the common-law tradition the evidence is presented by the advocates with supervision and supplementation by the judge. Furthermore, in many civil-law systems the evidence is usually taken in separate stages according to availability of witnesses, while in the common-law system

[11] *Compagnie Financière et Commerciale du Pacifique v. Peruvian Guano Co.*, 11 QBD 55, 63 (1882) (interpreting Order XXXI., rule 12, from the 1875 Rules of Supreme Court, which required production of documents "relating to any matters in question in the action").

it is usually taken in a consecutive hearing for which the witnesses must adjust their schedules. More fundamentally, the basic conception of the plenary hearing in the civil-law system has been that of an inquiry by the judge that is monitored by advocates on behalf of the parties, while the conception of a trial in the common-law systems is that of juxtaposed presentations to the court by the parties through their advocates.

In more pragmatic terms, the effectuation of these different conceptions of the plenary hearing requires different professional skills on the part of judge and advocates. An effective judge in the civil-law system must be able to frame questions and pursue them in an orderly series, and an effective advocate must give close attention to the judge's questioning and be alert to suggest additional directions or extensions of the inquiry. In the common-law system the required skills are more or less the opposite. The common-law advocate must be skillful at framing questions and pursuing them in orderly sequence, while the judge must be attentive to pursuing further development by supplemental questions. However, these differences are ones of degree, and the degrees of differences have diminished in the modern era.

VIII. Second-Instance Review and Finality

The Principles and Rules defer to the law of the forum concerning second-instance proceedings ("appeal"). The same is true for further review in a higher court, as is available in many systems. The Principles and Rules define conditions of finality that discourage the reopening of an adjudication that has been completed. An adjudication fairly conducted is the best approximation of true justice that human enterprise can afford. On that basis, an adjudication should be left at rest even when there may be some reason to think that a different result could be achieved, unless there is a showing of fraud in the proceeding or of conclusive evidence that was previously undisclosed and not reasonably discoverable at the time. The Principles and Rules adopt an approach to finality based on that philosophy.

IX. Recognition of the Principles and Rules

The Principles express basic concepts of fairness in resolution of legal disputes prevailing in modern legal systems. Most modern legal systems could implement the Principles by relatively modest modifications of their own codes of civil procedure. More substantial modification would be required in systems in which a party ordinarily has no opportunity to obtain evidence in its favor from an opposing party. The Rules, which are a model provided by the Reporters, but not formally adopted by UNIDROIT or the Institute, are a suggested implementation of the Principles, providing greater detail and illustrating concrete fulfillment of the Principles. Both Principles and Rules seek to combine the best elements of adversary procedure in the common-law tradition with the best elements of judge-centered procedure in the civil-law tradition. They are expressed in terminology and through concepts that can be assimilated in all legal traditions. The Principles and Rules could also be used in modified form in arbitration proceedings.

The implementation of these Principles and Rules is a matter of the domestic and international law of nation-states. They may be adopted by international convention or by legal authority of a national state for application in the courts of that state. In countries with a unitary legal system, that legal authority is vested in the national government. In federal systems, the allocation of that authority depends upon the terms of the particular federation. In a given federal system, these Principles and Rules might be adopted by the federal power to be used in the federal courts and by the state or provincial powers for use in the state or provincial courts. As used in the Principles and Rules, "state" refers to a national state and not to a province or state within a federal system.

These Principles and Rules could be adopted for use in the first-instance courts of general jurisdiction, in a specialized court, or in a division of the court of general jurisdiction having jurisdiction over commercial disputes. These Principles and Rules can also serve as models in the reform of various procedural systems.

X. Purpose of the Principles and Rules

The objective of the Principles and Rules is to offer a system of fair procedure for litigants involved in legal disputes arising from transnational commercial transactions. Appreciating that all litigation is unpleasant from the viewpoint of the litigants, the Principles and Rules seek to reduce the uncertainty and anxiety that particularly attend parties obliged to litigate in unfamiliar surroundings. The reduction of difference in legal systems, commonly called "harmonization" of law, is an aspect of achieving such fairness. However, a system of rules is only one aspect of fair procedure. Much more important, as a practical matter, are the competence, independence, and neutrality of judges and the competence and integrity of legal counsel. Nevertheless, rules of procedure are influential in the conduct of litigation.

These Principles and Rules seek to express, so far as such formulations can do so, the ideal of disinterested adjudication. In this regard, they also can provide terms of reference in matters of judicial cooperation, wherein the courts of different legal systems provide assistance to each other. By the same token, reference to the standards expressed herein can moderate the unavoidable tendency of practitioners in a legal system, both judges and lawyers, to consider their system from a parochial viewpoint.

The Principles and Rules, especially those prescribed for pleading, development and presentation of evidence and legal argument, and the final determination by the tribunal, may be adopted or referenced in proceedings not otherwise governed by these Rules, particularly arbitration. Also, a court could refer to the Principles and Rules as generally recognized standards of civil justice, when doing so is not inconsistent with its own organic or procedural law.

It is contemplated that, where adopted, the Principles and Rules would be a special form of procedure applicable to the disputes to which they are addressed, parallel to other specialized procedural rules that most nation-states have for such matters as bankruptcy, labor disputes, administration of decedent's estates, and civil claims against government agencies. Where permissible by forum law, with the consent of the court, the Rules could also be adopted through stipulation by parties to govern, in whole or in part, litigation between them. Such an implementation in substance would be a party stipulation to waive the otherwise governing rules of procedure in favor of these Rules.

XI. Revisions from Prior Drafts

Prior drafts of the Principles and Rules have been published in law reviews worldwide. See *Cornell International Law Journal*, vol. 30, no. 2 (1997), 493; *Texas International Law Journal*, vol. 33, no. 3 (1998), 499; and *New York University Journal of International Law and Politics*, vol. 33, no. 3 (2001), 769. These drafts, together with the ALI and UNIDROIT publications,[12] have elicited valuable criticism and comments from legal scholars and lawyers from both

[12] The most relevant ALI publications were Preliminary Draft Nos. 1–3 (1998, 2000, 2002); Interim Revision (1998); Council Draft Nos. 1–2 (2001, 2003); Discussion Draft Nos. 1–4 (1999, 2001, 2002, 2003); and Proposed Final Draft (2004). The most relevant UNIDROIT publications were Study LXXVI – Docs. 4–5 (2001, 2002) and 9–10 (2002, 2003), and Study LXXVI – Secretary's Report (2001, 2002, 2003, 2004). These publications were widely circulated worldwide, both in print and in electronic form.

civil- and common-law systems.[13] Comparison will demonstrate that many modifications have been adopted as a result of extensive discussions and deliberations following those previous publications. The net effect has been a new text with each new publication.

Earlier drafts of the Principles and Rules were translated into Russian by Nikolai Eliseev; into Arabic by Hossam Loutfi; into German by Gerhard Walter from Bern University and later by Stefan Huber from Heidelberg University; into Japanese by Koichi Miki from Keio University; into Greek by Flora Triantaphyllou; into French by Frédérique Ferrand from the University Jean Moulin and Gabriele Mecarelli from Paris University; into Chinese by Chi-Wei Huang and Chen Rong; into Italian by Francesca Cuomo and Valentina Riva from Pavia University; into Croatian by Eduard Kunštek; into Spanish by Lorena Bachmaier Winter from Universidad Complutense de Madrid, Evaluz Cotto from Puerto Rico University, Franciso Malaga from Pompeu Fabra University, Aníbal Quiroga León from Catholic University of Peru, Horácio Segundo Pinto from the Catholic University of Argentina, and Eduardo Oteiza from the National University of La Plata; and into Portuguese by Associate Reporter Antonio Gidi and later by Cassio Scarpinella Bueno. It is hoped that there will be translations into additional languages in the future.

The numerous revisions of the Principles and Rules emerged from discussions at several locations with Advisers and Consultants from various countries, including meetings in Stockholm, Sweden; Riga, Latvia; Athens, Greece; Iguassu Falls, Brazil; Buenos Aires, Argentina; Bologna and Rome, Italy; Freiburg and Heidelberg, Germany; Barcelona, Spain; Vancouver, Canada; San Francisco, Boston, Washington, D.C., and Philadelphia, United States; Vienna, Austria; Tokyo, Japan; Singapore; Paris and Lyon, France; Mexico City, Mexico; Beijing, China; Moscow, Russia; and London, England. Criticism and discussion also were conducted through correspondence.[14]

[13] See A Bibliography of Writings about the ALI/UNIDRCIT Project.

[14] In the seven years that the project remained open for public debate, we received written contributions from Lucio Cabrera Acevedo, Ricardo Almeida, Neil Andrews, Mathew Applebaum, Lorena Bachmaier Winter, Joaquim Barbosa, Robert Barker, Samuel Baumgartner, Allen Black, Robert Bone, Bennett Boskey, Ronald Brand, Edward Brown, Stephen Burbank, Robert Byer, Stephen Calkins, Aída Kemelmajer de Carlucci, Robert Casad, Gerhard Casper, Michael Cohen, Edward Cooper, Thomas F. Cope, Marco de Cristofaro, Sheldon Elsen, Enrique Falcón, Frédérique Ferrand, José Lebre de Freitas, Stephen Goldstein, Carl Goodman, Peter Gottwald, Jaime Greif, Trevor Hartley, Lars Heuman, Henry Hoffstot, Jr., Richard Hulbert, J. A. Jolowicz, Mary Kay Kane,

The project was the subject of extensive commentary and much candid and helpful criticism at an October 27, 2000, meeting of French proceduralists in the Université Panthéon-Assas (Paris II), in which participants included Judges Guy Canivet, Jacques Lemontey, and Jean Buffet, and Professors Bernard Audit, Georges Bolard, Loïc Cadiet, Philippe Fouchard, Hélène Gaudemet-Tallon, Serge Guinchard, Catherine Kessedjian, Pierre Mayer, Horatia Muir-Watt, Marie-Laure Niboyet, Jacques Normand, and Claude Reymond.[15]

On October 10 and 11, 2001, the project was presented at Renmin University in Beijing to a large group of Chinese law professors, judges, arbitrators, and practicing attorneys. On October 13, 2001, the project was also presented in Tokyo for the second time to a group of Japanese experts. On February 28, 2002, the project was presented at the Mexican Center for Uniform Law, and on March 1, 2002, at the UNAM Law School. The meetings in Mexico City were organized by Jorge A. Sánchez-Cordero Dávila and Carlos Sánchez-Mejorada y Velasco. On May 24, 2002, the project was presented in London, at a conference organized by Professor Neil Andrews and the British Institute of International and Comparative Law. On June 4, 2002, the project was presented in Moscow, at the Moscow State Institute of International Relations (MGIMO), at a conference organized by Professor Sergei Lebedev and Roswell Perkins.[16]

In 2003, the project was presented on May 16 and 17, in Bologna, Italy, at a conference organized by Professor Federico Carpi; on May 29, in Athens, Greece, at a conference organized by Professor Konstantinos Kerameus; on June 3, in Stockholm, Sweden, at a conference organized by Assistant Professor Patricia Shaughnessy; on June 6, in Riga, Latvia, at a conference organized by Professor John Burke; on June 10, in Heidelberg, Germany, at a conference organized by Professor Thomas Pfeiffer; on June 12, in Lyon, France, at a conference organized by Professor Frédérique Ferrand; on August 9, in

Dianna Kempe, Konstantinos Kerameus, Donald King, Faidonas Kozyris, John Leubsdorf, Houston Putnam Lowry, Luigia Maggioni, Richard Marcus, Stephen McEwen, Jr., James McKay, Jr., Gabriele Mecarelli, Tony Moussa, Ramón Mullerat-Balmaña, Lawrence Newman, Jacques Normand, Olakunle Olatawura, Ernesto Penalva, Thomas Pfeiffer, Lea Querzola, Hilmar Raeschke-Kessler, William Reynolds, Tom Rowe, Amos Shapira, Patricia Shaughnessy, Michael Stamp, Hans Rudolf Steiner, Louise Teitz, Laurel Terry, Natalie Thingelstad, Julius Towers, Spyros Vrellis, Janet Walker, Gerhard Walter, Garry Watson, Jack Weinstein, Ralph Whitten, Des Williams, Diane Wood, Pelayia Yessiou-Faltsi, Rodrigo Zamora, Joachim Zekoll, and others.

[15] See Philippe Fouchard, ed., *Vers un Procès Civil Universel? Les Règles Transnationales de Procédure Civile de l'American Law Institute* (Paris: Editions Panthéon-Assas, 2001).

[16] See *Moscow Journal of International Law* 252 (2002).

Iguassu Falls, Brazil, at a conference organized by Professors Luiz Rodrigues Wambier and Teresa Arruda Alvim Wambier; and on August 14, in Buenos Aires, Argentina, at a conference organized by Professors Roberto Berizonce and Eduardo Oteiza, and Justice Aída Kemelmajer de Carlucci.

It is hoped that this continuing dialogue has made the Principles and Rules more understandable and therefore more acceptable from both common-law and civil-law perspectives.

PRINCIPLES OF TRANSNATIONAL CIVIL PROCEDURE

(with commentary)

Scope and Implementation

These Principles are standards for adjudication of transnational commercial disputes. These Principles may be equally appropriate for the resolution of most other kinds of civil disputes and may be the basis for future initiatives in reforming civil procedure.

Comment:

P-A A national system seeking to implement these Principles could do so by a suitable legal measure, such as a statute or set of rules, or an international treaty. Forum law may exclude categories of matters from application of these Principles and may extend their application to other civil matters. Courts may adapt their practice to these Principles, especially with the consent of the parties to litigation. These Principles also establish standards for determining whether recognition should be given to a foreign judgment. See Principle 30. The procedural law of the forum applies in matters not addressed in these Principles.

P-B The adoptive document may include a more specific definition of "commercial" and "transnational." That task will necessarily involve careful reflection on local legal tradition and connotation of legal language. Transnational commercial transactions may include commercial contracts between nationals of different states and commercial transactions in a state by a national of another state. Commercial transactions may include sale, lease, loan, investment, acquisition, banking, security, property (including intellectual property), and other business or financial transactions, but do not necessarily include claims provided by typical consumer-protection statutes.

P-C Transnational disputes, in general, do not arise wholly within a state and involve disputing parties who are from the same state. For purposes of these Principles, an individual is considered a national both of a state of the person's citizenship and the state of the person's habitual residence. A jural entity (corporation, unincorporated association, partnership, or other organizational entity) is considered to be from both the state from which it has received its charter of organization and the state in which it has its principal place of business.

P-D In cases involving multiple parties or multiple claims, among which are ones not within the scope of these Principles, these Principles should apply when the court determines that the principal matters in controversy are within the scope of application of these Principles. However, these Principles are not applicable, without modification, to group litigation, such as class, representative, or collective actions.

P-E These Principles are equally applicable to international arbitration, except to the extent of being incompatible with arbitration proceedings, for example, the Principles related to jurisdiction, publicity of proceedings, and appeal.

1. Independence, Impartiality, and Qualifications of the Court and Its Judges

1.1 The court and the judges should have judicial independence to decide the dispute according to the facts and the law, including freedom from improper internal and external influence.

1.2 Judges should have reasonable tenure in office. Nonprofessional members of the court should be designated by a procedure assuring their independence from the parties, the dispute, and other persons interested in the resolution.

1.3 The court should be impartial. A judge or other person having decisional authority must not participate if there is reasonable ground to doubt such person's impartiality. There should be a fair and effective procedure for addressing contentions of judicial bias.

1.4 Neither the court nor the judge should accept communications about the case from a party in the absence of other parties, except for communications concerning proceedings without notice and for routine procedural administration. When communication between the court and a party occurs in the absence of another party, that party should be promptly advised of the content of the communication.

1.5 The court should have substantial legal knowledge and experience.

Comment:

P-1A Independence can be considered a more objective characteristic and impartiality a more subjective one, but these attributes are closely connected.

P-1B External influences may emanate from members of the executive or legislative branch, prosecutors, or persons with economic interests, and the like. Internal influence could emanate from other officials of the judicial system.

P-1C This Principle recognizes that typically judges serve for an extensive period of time, usually their entire careers. However, in some systems most judges assume the bench only after careers as lawyers and some judicial officials are designated for short periods. An objective of this Principle is to avoid the creation of ad hoc courts. The term "judge" includes any judicial or quasi-judicial official under the law of the forum.

P-1D A procedure for addressing questions of judicial bias is necessary only in unusual circumstances, but availability of the procedure is a reassurance to litigants, especially nationals of other countries. However, the procedure should not invite abuse through insubstantial claims of bias.

P-1E Proceedings without notice (*ex parte* proceedings) may be proper, for example, in initially applying for a provisional remedy. See Principles 5.8 and 8. Proceedings after default are governed by Principle 15. Routine procedural administration includes, for example, specification of dates for submission of proposed evidence.

P-1F Principle 1.5 requires only that judges for transnational litigation be familiar with the law. It does not require the judge to have special knowledge of commercial or financial law, but familiarity with such matters would be desirable.

2. Jurisdiction Over Parties

2.1 Jurisdiction over a party may be exercised:

2.1.1 By consent of the parties to submit the dispute to the tribunal;

2.1.2 When there is a substantial connection between the forum state and the party or the transaction or occurrence in dispute. A substantial connection exists when a significant part of the transaction or occurrence occurred in the forum state, when an individual defendant is a habitual resident of the forum state or a jural entity has received its charter of organization or has its principal place of business therein, or when property to which the dispute relates is located in the forum state.

2.2 Jurisdiction may also be exercised, when no other forum is reasonably available, on the basis of:

2.2.1 Presence or nationality of the defendant in the forum state; or

2.2.2 Presence in the forum state of the defendant's property, whether or not the dispute relates to the property, but the court's authority should be limited to the property or its value.

2.3 A court may grant provisional measures with respect to a person or to property in the territory of the forum state, even if the court does not have jurisdiction over the controversy.

2.4 Exercise of jurisdiction must ordinarily be declined when the parties have previously agreed that some other tribunal has exclusive jurisdiction.

2.5 Jurisdiction may be declined or the proceeding suspended when the court is manifestly inappropriate relative to another more appropriate court that could exercise jurisdiction.

2.6 The court should decline jurisdiction or suspend the proceeding, when the dispute is previously pending in another court competent to exercise jurisdiction, unless it appears that the dispute will not be fairly, effectively, and expeditiously resolved in that forum.

Comment:

P-2A Subject to restrictions on the court's jurisdiction under the law of the forum and subject to restrictions of international conventions, ordinarily a court may exercise jurisdiction upon the parties' consent. A court should not exercise jurisdiction on the basis of implied consent without giving the parties a fair opportunity to challenge jurisdiction. In the absence of the parties' consent, and subject to the parties' agreement that some other tribunal or forum has exclusive jurisdiction, ordinarily a court may exercise jurisdiction only if the dispute is connected to the forum, as provided in Principle 2.1.2.

P-2B The standard of "substantial connection" has been generally accepted for international legal disputes. Administration of this standard necessarily involves elements of practical judgment and self-restraint. That standard excludes mere physical presence, which within the United States is colloquially called "tag jurisdiction." Mere physical presence as a basis of jurisdiction within the American federation has historical justification that is inapposite in modern international disputes. The concept of "substantial connection" may be specified and elaborated in international conventions and in national laws. The scope of this expression might not be the same in all systems. However, the concept does not support general jurisdiction on the basis of "doing business" not related to the transaction or occurrence in dispute.

P-2C Principle 2.2 covers the concept of "forum necessitatis" – the forum of necessity whereby a court may properly exercise jurisdiction when no other forum is reasonably available.

P-2D Principle 2.3 recognizes that a state may exercise jurisdiction by sequestration or attachment of locally situated property, for example to secure a potential judgment, even though the property is not the object or subject of the dispute. The procedure with respect to property locally situated is called "quasi in rem jurisdiction" in some legal systems. Principle 2.3 contemplates that, in such a case, the merits of the underlying dispute might be adjudicated in some other forum. The location of intangible property should be ascribed according to forum law.

P-2E Party agreement to exclusive jurisdiction, including an arbitration agreement, ordinarily should be honored.

P-2F The concept recognized in Principle 2.5 is comparable to the common-law rule of *forum non conveniens*. In some civil-law systems, the concept is that of preventing abuse of the forum. This principle can be given effect by suspending the forum proceeding in deference to another tribunal. The existence of a more convenient forum is necessary for application of this Principle. This Principle should be interpreted in connection with the Principle of Procedural Equality of the Parties, which prohibits any kind of discrimination on the basis of nationality or residence. See Principle 3.2.

P-2G For the timing and scope of devices to stay other proceedings, such as lis pendens, see Principles 10.2 and 28.1.

3. Procedural Equality of the Parties

3.1 The court should ensure equal treatment and reasonable opportunity for litigants to assert or defend their rights.

3.2 The right to equal treatment includes avoidance of any kind of illegitimate discrimination, particularly on the basis of nationality or residence. The court should take into account difficulties that might be encountered by a foreign party in participating in litigation.

3.3 A person should not be required to provide security for costs, or security for liability for pursuing provisional measures, solely because the person is not a national or resident of the forum state.

3.4 **Whenever possible, venue rules should not impose an unreasonable burden of access to court on a person who is not a habitual resident of the forum.**

Comment:

P-3A The term "reasonable" is used throughout the Principles and signifies "proportional," "significant," "not excessive," or "fair," according to the context. It can also mean the opposite of arbitrary. The concept of reasonableness also precludes hypertechnical legal argument and leaves a range of discretion to the court to avoid severe, excessive, or unreasonable application of procedural norms.

P-3B Illegitimate discrimination includes discrimination on the basis of nationality, residence, gender, race, language, religion, political or other opinion, national or social origin, birth or other status, sexual orientation, or association with a national minority. Any form of illegitimate discrimination is prohibited, but discrimination on the basis of nationality or residence is a particularly sensitive issue in transnational commercial litigation.

P-3C Special protection for a litigant, through a conservatorship or other protective procedure such as a curator or guardian, should be afforded to safeguard the interests of persons who lack full legal capacity, such as minors. Such protective measures should not be abusively imposed on a foreign litigant.

P-3D Some jurisdictions require a person to provide security for costs, or for liability for provisional measures, in order to guarantee full compensation of possible future damages incurred by an opposing party. Other jurisdictions do not require such security, and some of them have constitutional provisions regarding access to justice or equality of the parties that prohibit such security. Principle 3.3 is a compromise between those two positions and does not modify forum law in that respect. However, the effective responsibility of a non-national or nonresident for costs or liability for provisional measures should be evaluated under the same general standards.

P-3E Venue rules of a national system (territorial competence) generally reflect considerations of convenience for litigants within the country. They should be administered in light of the principle of convenience of the forum stated in Principle 3.4. A venue rule that would impose substantial inconvenience within the forum state should not be given effect when there is another more convenient venue and transfer of venue within the forum state should be afforded from an unreasonably inconvenient location.

4. Right to Engage a Lawyer

4.1 A party has the right to engage a lawyer of the party's choice, including both representation by a lawyer admitted to practice in the forum and active assistance before the court of a lawyer admitted to practice elsewhere.

4.2 The lawyer's professional independence should be respected. A lawyer should be permitted to fulfill the duty of loyalty to a client and the responsibility to maintain client confidences.

Comment:

P-4A A forum may appropriately require that a lawyer representing a party be admitted to practice in the forum unless the party is unable to retain such a lawyer. However, a party should also be permitted the assistance of other lawyers, particularly its regular lawyer, who should be permitted to attend and actively participate in all hearings in the dispute.

P-4B A lawyer admitted to practice in the party's home country is not entitled by this Principle to be the sole representative of a party in foreign courts. That matter should be governed by forum law except that a foreign lawyer should at least be permitted to attend the hearing and address the court informally.

P-4C The attorney–client relationship is ordinarily governed by rules of the forum, including the choice-of-law rules.

P-4D The principles of legal ethics vary somewhat among various countries. However, all countries should recognize that lawyers in independent practice are expected to advocate the interests of their clients and generally to maintain the secrecy of confidences obtained in the course of representation.

5. Due Notice and Right to Be Heard

5.1 At the commencement of a proceeding, notice, provided by means that are reasonably likely to be effective, should be directed to parties other than the plaintiff. The notice should be accompanied by a copy of the complaint or otherwise include the allegations of the complaint and specification of the relief sought by plaintiff. A party against whom relief is sought should be informed of the procedure for response and the possibility of default judgment for failure to make timely response.

5.2 The documents referred to in Principle 5.1 must be in a language of the forum, and also a language of the state of an individual's habitual residence or a jural entity's principal place of business, or the language of the principal documents in the transaction. Defendant and other parties should give notice of their defenses and other contentions and requests for relief in a language of the proceeding, as provided in Principle 6.

5.3 After commencement of the proceeding, all parties should be provided prompt notice of motions and applications of other parties and determinations by the court.

5.4 The parties have the right to submit relevant contentions of fact and law and to offer supporting evidence.

5.5 A party should have a fair opportunity and reasonably adequate time to respond to contentions of fact and law and to evidence presented by another party, and to orders and suggestions made by the court.

5.6 The court should consider all contentions of the parties and address those concerning substantial issues.

5.7 The parties may, by agreement and with approval of the court, employ expedited means of communications, such as telecommunication.

5.8 An order affecting a party's interests may be made and enforced without giving previous notice to that party only upon proof of urgent necessity and preponderance of considerations of fairness. An *ex parte* order should be proportionate to the interests that the applicant seeks to protect. As soon as practicable, the affected party should be given notice of the order and of the matters relied upon to support it, and should have the right to apply for a prompt and full reconsideration by the court.

Comment:

P-5A The specific procedure for giving notice varies somewhat among legal systems. For example, in some systems the court is responsible for giving the parties notice, including copies of the pleadings, while in other systems that responsibility is imposed on the parties. The forum's technical requirements of notice should be administered in contemplation of the objective of affording actual notice.

P-5B The possibility of a default judgment is especially important in international litigation.

P-5C The right of a party to be informed of another party's contentions is consistent with the responsibility of the court stated in Principle 22.

P-5D According to Principle 5.5, the parties should make known to each other at an early stage the elements of fact upon which their claims or defenses are based and the rules of law that will be invoked, so that each party has timely opportunity to organize its case.

P-5E The standard stated in Principle 5.6 does not require the court to consider contentions determined at an earlier stage of the proceeding or that are unnecessary to the decision. See Principle 23, requiring that the written decision be accompanied by a reasoned explanation of its legal, evidentiary, and factual basis.

P-5F Forum law may provide for expedited means of communication without party approval or special court order.

P-5G Principle 5.8 recognizes the propriety of "*ex parte*" proceedings, such as a temporary injunction or an order for sequestration of property (provisional measures), particularly at the initial stage of litigation. Often such orders can be effective only if enforced without prior notice. An opposing party should be given prompt notice of such an order, opportunity to be heard immediately, and a right to full reconsideration of the factual and legal basis of such an order. An *ex parte* proceeding should be governed by Principle 8. See Principles 1.4 and 8.

6. Languages

6.1 The proceedings, including documents and oral communication, ordinarily should be conducted in a language of the court.

6.2 The court may allow use of other languages in all or part of the proceeding if no prejudice to a party will result.

6.3 Translation should be provided when a party or witness is not competent in the language in which the proceeding is conducted. Translation of lengthy or voluminous documents may be limited to portions, as agreed by the parties or ordered by the court.

Comment:

P-6A The court should conduct the proceeding in a language in which it is fluent. Ordinarily this will be the language of the state in which the court is situated. However, if the court and the parties have competence in a foreign language, they may agree upon or the judge may order that language for all or part of the proceeding, for example, the reception of a particular document or the testimony of a witness in the witness's native language.

P-6B Frequently in transnational litigation witnesses and experts are not competent in the language in which the proceeding is conducted. In such a case, translation is required for the court and for other parties. The testimony must be taken with the aid of an interpreter, with the party presenting the evidence paying the cost of the translation unless the court orders otherwise. Alternatively, the witness may be examined through deposition, upon agreement of the parties or by order of the court. The deposition can then be translated and submitted at the hearing.

7. Prompt Rendition of Justice

7.1 The court should resolve the dispute within a reasonable time.

7.2 The parties have a duty to cooperate and a right of reasonable consultation concerning scheduling. Procedural rules and court orders may prescribe reasonable time schedules and deadlines and impose sanctions on the parties or their lawyers for noncompliance with such rules and orders that is not excused by good reason.

Comment:

P-7A In all legal systems the court has a responsibility to move the adjudication forward. It is a universally recognized axiom that "justice delayed is justice denied." Some systems have specific timetables according to which stages of a proceeding should be performed.

P-7B Prompt rendition of justice is a matter of access to justice and may also be considered an essential human right, but it should also be balanced against a party's right of a reasonable opportunity to organize and present its case.

8. Provisional and Protective Measures

8.1 The court may grant provisional relief when necessary to preserve the ability to grant effective relief by final judgment or to maintain or otherwise regulate the status quo. Provisional measures are governed by the principle of proportionality.

8.2 A court may order provisional relief without notice only upon urgent necessity and preponderance of considerations of fairness. The applicant must fully disclose facts and legal issues of which

the court properly should be aware. A person against whom *ex parte* relief is directed must have the opportunity at the earliest practicable time to respond concerning the appropriateness of the relief.

8.3 **An applicant for provisional relief should ordinarily be liable for compensation of a person against whom the relief is issued if the court thereafter determines that the relief should not have been granted. In appropriate circumstances, the court must require the applicant for provisional relief to post a bond or formally to assume a duty of compensation.**

Comment:

P-8A "Provisional relief" embraces also the concept of "injunction," which is an order requiring or prohibiting the performance of a specified act, for example, preserving property in its present condition. Principle 8.1 authorizes the court to issue an order that is either affirmative, in that it requires performance of an act, or negative in that it prohibits a specific act or course of action. The term is used here in a generic sense to include attachment, sequestration, and other directives. The concept of regulation includes measures to ameliorate the underlying controversy, for example, supervision of management of a partnership during litigation among the partners. Availability of provisional remedies or interim measures, such as attachment or sequestration, should be determined by forum law, including applicable principles of international law. A court may also order disclosure of assets wherever located, or grant provisional relief to facilitate arbitration or enforce arbitration provisional measures.

P-8B Principle 5.8 and 8.2 authorize the court to issue an order without notice to the person against whom it is directed where doing so is justified by urgent necessity. "Urgent necessity," required as a basis for an *ex parte* order, is a practical concept, as is the concept of preponderance of considerations of fairness. The latter term corresponds to the common-law concept of "balance of equities." Considerations of fairness include the strength of the merits of the applicant's claim, relevant public interest if any, the urgency of the need for a provisional remedy, and the practical burdens that may result from granting the remedy. Such an injunction is usually known as an *ex parte* order. See Principle 1.4.

P-8C The question for the court, in considering an application for an *ex parte* order, is whether the applicant has made a reasonable and specific demonstration that such an order is required to prevent an irreparable deterioration in the situation to be addressed in the litigation, and that it would be imprudent to postpone the order until the opposing party has an opportunity to be heard. The burden is on the party requesting an *ex parte* order to justify its issuance. However, as soon as practicable, the opposing party or person to whom the order is addressed should be given notice of the order and of the matters relied upon to support it and should have the right to apply for a prompt and full reconsideration by the court. The party or person must have the opportunity for a *de novo* reconsideration of the decision, including opportunity to present evidence. See Principle 8.2.

P-8D Rules of procedure generally require that a party requesting an *ex parte* order make full disclosure to the court of all issues of law and fact that the court should legitimately take into account in granting the request, including those against the petitioner's interests and favorable to the opposing party. Failure to make such disclosure is a ground to vacate an order and may be a basis of liability for damages against the requesting party. In some legal systems, assessment of damages for an erroneously issued order does not necessarily reflect the proper resolution of the underlying merits.

P-8E After hearing those interested, the court may issue, dissolve, renew, or modify an order. If the court had declined to issue an order *ex parte*, it may nevertheless issue an order upon a hearing. If the court previously issued an order *ex parte*, it may dissolve, renew, or modify its order in light of the matters developed at the hearing. The burden is on the party seeking the order to show that it is justified.

P-8F Principle 8.3 authorizes the court to require a bond or other compensation, as protection against the disturbance and injury that may result from an order. The particulars of such compensation should be determined by the law of the forum. An obligation to compensate should be express, not merely by implication, and could be formalized through a bond underwritten by a third party.

P-8G An order under this Principle in many systems is ordinarily subject to immediate appellate review, according to the procedure of the forum. In some systems such an order is of very brief duration and subject to prompt reconsideration in the first-instance tribunal prior to the possibility of appellate review. The guarantee of a review is particularly necessary when the order has been issued *ex parte*. Review by a second-instance tribunal is regulated in different ways in various systems. However, it should also be recognized that such a review might entail a loss of time or procedural abuse.

9. Structure of the Proceedings

9.1 A proceeding ordinarily should consist of three phases: the pleading phase, the interim phase, and the final phase.

9.2 In the pleading phase the parties must present their claims, defenses, and other contentions in writing, and identify their principal evidence.

9.3 In the interim phase the court should if necessary:

9.3.1 Hold conferences to organize the proceeding;

9.3.2 Establish the schedule outlining the progress of the proceeding;

9.3.3 Address the matters appropriate for early attention, such as questions of jurisdiction, provisional measures, and statute of limitations (prescription);

9.3.4 Address availability, admission, disclosure, and exchange of evidence;

9.3.5 Identify potentially dispositive issues for early determination of all or part of the dispute; and

9.3.6 Order the taking of evidence.

9.4 In the final phase evidence not already received by the court according to Principle 9.3.6 ordinarily should be presented in a concentrated final hearing at which the parties should also make their concluding arguments.

Comment:

P-9A The concept of "structure" of a proceeding should be applied flexibly, according to the nature of the particular case. For example, if convenient a judge would have discretion to hold a conference in the pleading phase and to hold multiple conferences as the case progresses.

P-9B An orderly schedule facilitates expeditious conduct of the litigation. Discussion between the court and lawyers for the parties facilitates practical scheduling and orderly hearings. See Principle 14.2 and Comment *P-14A*.

P-9C Traditionally, courts in civil-law systems functioned through a sequence of short hearings, while those in common-law systems organized a proceeding around a final "trial." However, courts in modern practice in both systems provide for preliminary hearings and civil-law systems have increasingly come to employ a concentrated final hearing for most evidence concerning the merits.

P-9D In common-law systems, a procedure for considering potentially dispositive issues before final hearing is the motion for summary judgment, which can address legal issues, or the issue of whether there is genuine controversy about facts, or both such issues. Civil-law jurisdictions provide for similar procedures in the interim phase.

P-9E In most systems the objection of lack of jurisdiction over the person must be made by the party involved and at an early stage in the proceeding, under penalty of forfeiting the objection. In international litigation it is particularly important that questions of jurisdiction be addressed promptly.

10. Party Initiative and Scope of the Proceeding

10.1 The proceeding should be initiated through the claim or claims of the plaintiff, not by the court acting on its own motion.

10.2 The time of lodging the complaint with the court determines compliance with statutes of limitation, *lis pendens*, and other requirements of timeliness.

10.3 The scope of the proceeding is determined by the claims and defenses of the parties in the pleadings, including amendments.

10.4 A party, upon showing good cause, has a right to amend its claims or defenses upon notice to other parties, and when doing so does not unreasonably delay the proceeding or otherwise result in injustice.

10.5 The parties should have a right to voluntary termination or modification of the proceeding or any part of it, by withdrawal, admission, or settlement. A party should not be permitted unilaterally to terminate or modify the action when prejudice to another party would result.

Comment:

P-10A All modern legal systems recognize the principle of party initiative concerning the scope and particulars of the dispute. It is within the framework of party initiative that the court carries out its responsibility for just adjudication. See Principles 10.3 and 28.2. These Principles require the parties to provide details of fact and law in their contentions. See Principle 11.3. This practice contrasts with the more loosely structured system of "notice pleading" in American procedure.

P-10B All legal systems impose time limits for commencement of litigation, called statutes of limitation in common-law systems and prescription in civil-law systems. Service of process must be completed or attempted within a specified time after commencement of the proceeding, according to forum law. Most systems allow for an objection that service of process was not completed or attempted within a specified time after commencement of the proceeding.

P-10C The right to amend a pleading is very restricted in some legal systems. However, particularly in transnational disputes, the parties should be accorded some flexibility, particularly when new or unexpected evidence is confronted. Adverse effect on other parties from exercise of the right of amendment may be avoided or moderated by an adjournment or continuance, or adequately compensated by an award of costs.

P-10D The forum law may permit a claimant to introduce a new claim by amendment even though it is time-barred (statute of limitations or prescription), provided it arises from substantially the same facts as those that underlie the initial claim.

P-10E Most jurisdictions do not permit a plaintiff to discontinue an action after an initial phase of the proceeding over the objection of the defendant.

11. Obligations of the Parties and Lawyers

11.1 The parties and their lawyers must conduct themselves in good faith in dealing with the court and other parties.

11.2 The parties share with the court the responsibility to promote a fair, efficient, and reasonably speedy resolution of the proceeding. The parties must refrain from procedural abuse, such as interference with witnesses or destruction of evidence.

11.3 In the pleading phase, the parties must present in reasonable detail the relevant facts, their contentions of law, and the relief requested, and describe with sufficient specification the available evidence to be offered in support of their allegations. When a party shows good cause for inability to provide reasonable details of relevant facts or sufficient specification of evidence, the court should give due regard to the possibility that necessary facts and evidence will develop later in the course of the proceeding.

11.4 A party's unjustified failure to make a timely response to an opposing party's contention may be taken by the court, after warning the party, as a sufficient basis for considering that contention to be admitted or accepted.

11.5 Lawyers for parties have a professional obligation to assist the parties in observing their procedural obligations.

Comment:

P-11A A party should not make a claim, defense, motion, or other initiative or response that is not reasonably arguable in law and fact. In appropriate circumstances, failure to conform to this requirement may be declared an abuse of the court's process and subject the party responsible to cost sanctions and fines. The obligation of good faith, however, does not preclude a party from making a reasonable effort to extend an existing concept based on difference of circumstances. In appropriate circumstances, frivolous or vexatious claims or defenses may be considered an imposition on the court and may be subjected to default or dismissal of the case, as well as cost sanctions and fines.

P-11B Principle 11.3 requires the parties to make detailed statements of facts in their pleadings, in contrast with "notice pleading" permitted under the Federal Rules of Civil Procedure in the United States. The requirement of "sufficient specification" ordinarily would be met by identification of principal documents constituting the basis of a claim or defense and by concisely summarizing expected relevant testimony of identified witnesses. See Principle 16.

P-11C Failure to dispute a substantial contention by an opposing party ordinarily may be treated as an admission. See also Principle 21.3.

P-11D It is a universal rule that the lawyer has professional and ethical responsibilities for fair dealing with all parties, their lawyers, witnesses, and the court.

12. Multiple Claims and Parties; Intervention

12.1 A party may assert any claim substantially connected to the subject matter of the proceeding against another party or against a third person subject to the jurisdiction of the court.

12.2 A person having an interest substantially connected with the subject matter of the proceeding may apply to intervene. The court itself, or on motion of a party, may require notice to a person having such an interest, inviting intervention. Intervention may be permitted unless it would result in unreasonable delay or confusion of the proceeding or otherwise unfairly prejudice a party. Forum law may permit intervention in second-instance proceedings.

12.3 When appropriate, the court should grant permission for a person to be substituted for, or to be admitted in succession to, a party.

12.4 The rights and obligations of participation and cooperation of a party added to the proceeding are ordinarily the same as those of

the original parties. The extent of these rights and obligations may depend upon the basis, timing, and circumstances of the joinder or intervention.

12.5 The court may order separation of claims, issues, or parties, or consolidation with other proceedings, for fair or more efficient management and determination or in the interest of justice. The authority should extend to parties or claims that are not within the scope of these Principles.

Comment:

P-12A Principle 12.1 recognizes the right to assert claims available against another party related to the same transaction or occurrence.

P-12B There are differences in the rules of various countries governing jurisdiction over third parties. In some civil-law systems, a valid third-party claim is itself a basis of jurisdiction whereas in some common-law systems the third party must be independently subject to jurisdiction. Principle 12.1 requires an independent basis of jurisdiction.

P-12C Joinder of interpleading parties claiming the same property is permitted by this Principle, but the Principle does not authorize or prohibit class actions.

P-12D An invitation to intervene is an opportunity for the third person to do so. The effect of failure to intervene is governed by various rules of forum law. Before inviting a person to intervene, the court must consult with the parties.

P-12E Forum law provides for replacement or addition of parties, as a matter of substantive or procedural law, in various circumstances, such as death, assignment, merger of a corporation, bankruptcy, subrogation, and other eventualities. It may also permit participation on a limited basis, for example, with authority to submit evidence without becoming a full party.

P-12F In any event, the court has authority to sever claims and issues, and to consolidate them, according to their subject matter and the affected parties.

13. *Amicus Curiae* Submission

Written submissions concerning important legal issues in the proceeding and matters of background information may be received from third persons with the consent of the court, upon consultation with the parties. The court may invite such a submission. The parties must have the opportunity

to submit written comment addressed to the matters contained in such a submission before it is considered by the court.

Comment:

P-13A The "*amicus curiae* brief" is a useful means by which a nonparty may supply the court with information and legal analysis that may be helpful to achieve a just and informed disposition of the case. Such a brief might be from a disinterested source or a partisan one. Any person may be allowed to file such a brief, notwithstanding a lack of legal interest sufficient for intervention. Written submission may be supported by oral presentation at the discretion of the court.

P-13B It is in the court's discretion whether such a brief may be taken into account. The court may require a statement of the interest of the proposed *amicus*. A court has authority to refuse an *amicus curiae* brief when such a brief would not be of material assistance in determining the dispute. Caution should be exercised that the mechanism of the *amicus curiae* submission not interfere with the court's independence. See Principle 1.1. The court may invite a third party to present such a submission. An *amicus curiae* does not become a party to the case but is merely an active commentator. Factual assertions in an *amicus* brief are not evidence in the case.

P-13C In civil-law countries there is no well-established practice of allowing third parties without a legal interest in the merits of the dispute to participate in a proceeding, although some civil-law countries like France have developed similar institutions in their case law. Consequently, most civil-law countries do not have a practice of allowing the submission of *amicus curiae* briefs. Nevertheless, the *amicus curiae* brief is a useful device, particularly in cases of public importance.

P-13D Principle 13 does not authorize third persons to present written submissions concerning the facts in dispute. It permits only presentation of data, background information, remarks, legal analysis, and other considerations that may be useful for a fair and just decision of the case. For example, a trade organization might give notice of special trade customs to the court.

P-13E The parties must have opportunity to submit written comment addressed to the matters in the submission before it is considered by the court.

14. Court Responsibility for Direction of the Proceeding

14.1 Commencing as early as practicable, the court should actively manage the proceeding, exercising discretion to achieve disposition

of the dispute fairly, efficiently, and with reasonable speed. Consideration should be given to the transnational character of the dispute.

14.2 To the extent reasonably practicable, the court should manage the proceeding in consultation with the parties.

14.3 The court should determine the order in which issues are to be resolved and fix a timetable for all stages of the proceeding, including dates and deadlines. The court may revise such directions.

Comment:

P-14A Many court systems have standing orders governing case management. See Principle 7.2. The court's management of the proceeding will be fairer and more efficient when conducted in consultation with the parties. See also Comment *P-9A*.

P-14B Principle 14.3 is particularly important in complex cases. As a practical matter, timetables and the like are less necessary in simple cases, but the court should always address details of scheduling.

15. Dismissal and Default Judgment

15.1 Dismissal of the proceeding ordinarily must be entered against a plaintiff who, without justification, fails to prosecute the proceeding. Before entering such a dismissal, the court must give plaintiff a reasonable warning thereof.

15.2 Default judgment ordinarily must be entered against a defendant or other party who, without justification, fails to appear or respond within the prescribed time.

15.3 The court in entering a default judgment must determine that:

15.3.1 There is jurisdiction over the party against whom judgment is to be entered;

15.3.2 There has been compliance with notice provisions and that the party has had sufficient time to respond; and

15.3.3 The claim is reasonably supported by available facts and evidence and is legally sufficient, including the claim for damages and any claim for costs.

15.4 A default judgment may be no greater in monetary amount or in severity of other remedy than was demanded in the complaint.

15.5 A dismissal or a default judgment is subject to appeal or rescission.

15.6 A party who otherwise fails to comply with obligations to participate in the proceeding is subject to sanctions in accordance with Principle 17.

Comment:

P-15A Default judgment permits termination of a dispute if there is no contest. It is a mechanism for compelling a party to acknowledge the court's authority. For example, if the court lacked authority to enter a default judgment, a defendant could avoid liability simply by ignoring the proceeding and later disputing the validity of the judgment. A plaintiff's abandonment of prosecution of the proceeding is, in common-law terminology, usually referred to as "failure to prosecute" and results in "involuntary dismissal." It is the equivalent of a default. See Principles 11.4 and 17.3.

P-15B A party who appears after the time prescribed, but before judgment, may be permitted to enter a defense upon offering reasonable excuse, but the court may order compensation for costs resulting to the opposing party. In making its determination, the court should consider the reason why the party did not answer or did not proceed after having answered. For example, a party may have failed to answer because that party did not receive actual notice, or because the party was obliged by his or her national law not to appear by reason of hostility between the countries.

P-15C Reasonable care should be exercised before entering a default judgment because notice may not have been given to a defendant, or the defendant may have been confused about the need to respond. Forum procedure in many systems requires that, after a defendant has failed to respond, an additional notice be given to the defendant of the court's intention to enter default judgment.

P-15D The decision about whether the claim is reasonably supported by evidence and legally justified under Principle 15.3.3 does not require a full inquiry on the merits of the case. The judge must only determine whether the default judgment is consistent with the available facts or evidence and is legally warranted. For that decision, the judge must analyze critically the evidence supporting the statement of claims. The judge may request production of more evidence or schedule an evidentiary hearing.

P-15E Principle 15.4 limits a default judgment to the amount and kind demanded in the statement of claim. In civil-law systems, a restriction in a default judgment to the amount claimed in a complaint merely repeats a general restriction applicable even in contested cases (*ultra petita* or *extra petita* prohibition). In common-law systems, no such restriction applies in contested cases, but the restriction on default judgments is a generally recognized rule. The restriction permits a defendant to avoid the cost of defense without the risk of greater liability than demanded in the complaint.

P-15F Notice of a default judgment or a dismissal must be promptly given to the parties, according to Principle 5.3. If the requirements for a default judgment are not complied with, an aggrieved party may appeal or seek to set aside the judgment, according to the law of the forum. Every system has a procedure for invalidating a default judgment obtained without compliance with the rules governing default. In some systems, including most common-law systems, the procedure is initially pursued in the first-instance court, and in other systems, including some civil-law systems, it is through an appeal. This Principle defers to forum law.

P-15G The party who has defaulted should be permitted, within the limit of a reasonable time, to present evidence that the notice was materially deficient or other proper excuse.

16. Access to Information and Evidence

16.1 Generally, the court and each party should have access to relevant and nonprivileged evidence, including testimony of parties and witnesses, expert testimony, documents, and evidence derived from inspection of things, entry upon land, or, under appropriate circumstances, from physical or mental examination of a person. The parties should have the right to submit statements that are accorded evidentiary effect.

16.2 Upon timely request of a party, the court should order disclosure of relevant, nonprivileged, and reasonably identified evidence in the possession or control of another party or, if necessary and on just terms, of a nonparty. It is not a basis of objection to such disclosure that the evidence may be adverse to the party or person making the disclosure.

16.3 To facilitate access to information, a lawyer for a party may conduct a voluntary interview with a potential nonparty witness.

16.4 Eliciting testimony of parties, witnesses, and experts should proceed as customary in the forum. A party should have the right to conduct supplemental questioning directly to another party, witness, or expert who has first been questioned by the judge or by another party.

16.5 A person who produces evidence, whether or not a party, has the right to a court order protecting against improper exposure of confidential information.

16.6 The court should make free evaluation of the evidence and attach no unjustified significance to evidence according to its type or source.

Comment:

P-16A "Relevant" evidence is probative material that supports, contradicts, or weakens a contention of fact at issue in the proceeding. A party should not be permitted to conduct a so-called fishing expedition to develop a case for which it has no support, but an opposing party may properly be compelled to produce evidence that is under its control. These Principles thereby permit a measure of limited "discovery" under the supervision of the court. Nonparties are in principle also obliged to cooperate.

P-16B In some legal systems the statements of a party are not admissible as evidence or are accorded diminished probative weight. Principle 16.1 accords a party's testimony potentially the same weight as that of any other witness, but the court in evaluating such evidence may take into account the party's interest in the dispute.

P-16C Under Principle 16.2, the requesting party may be required to compensate a nonparty's costs of producing evidence.

P-16D In some systems, it is generally a violation of ethical or procedural rules for a lawyer to communicate with a potential witness. Violation of this rule is regarded as "tainting" the witness. However, this approach may impede access to evidence that is permitted in other systems and impair a good preparation of the presentation of evidence.

P-16E The physical or mental examination of a person may be appropriate when necessary and reliable and its probative value exceeds the prejudicial effect of its admission.

P-16F According to Principle 16.4, eliciting testimony of parties, witnesses, and experts should proceed as customary in the forum, either with the parties conducting the primary examination or with the judge doing so. In any event, a party should have the right to conduct supplemental questioning by directly addressing another party or witness. The right of a party to put questions directly to an adverse party or nonparty witness is of first importance and is now recognized in most legal systems. Similarly, a party should be permitted to address supplemental questions to a witness, including a party, who has initially been questioned by the court.

P-16G Principle 16.6 signifies that no special legal value, positive or negative, should be attributed to any kind of relevant evidence, for example, testimony of an interested witness. However, this Principle does not interfere with national laws that require a specified formality in a transaction, such as written documentation of a contract involving real property.

P-16H Sanctions may be imposed against the failure to produce evidence that reasonably appears to be within that party's control or access, or for a party's failure to cooperate in production of evidence as required by the rules of procedure. See Principles 17 and 21.3.

P-16I There are special problems in administering evidence in jury trials, not covered by these Principles.

17. Sanctions

17.1 The court may impose sanctions on parties, lawyers, and third persons for failure or refusal to comply with obligations concerning the proceeding.

17.2 Sanctions should be reasonable and proportionate to the seriousness of the matter involved and the harm caused and reflect the extent of participation and the degree to which the conduct was deliberate.

17.3 Among the sanctions that may be appropriate against parties are: drawing adverse inferences; dismissing claims, defenses, or allegations in whole or in part; rendering default judgment; staying the proceeding; and awarding costs in addition to those permitted under ordinary cost rules. Sanctions that may be appropriate against parties and nonparties include pecuniary sanctions, such as fines and *astreintes*. Among sanctions that may be appropriate against lawyers is an award of costs.

17.4 The law of the forum may also provide further sanctions including criminal liability for severe or aggravated misconduct by parties and nonparties, such as submitting perjured evidence or violent or threatening behavior.

Comment:

P-17A The sanctions a court is authorized to impose under forum law vary from system to system. These Principles do not confer authority for sanctions not permitted under forum law.

P-17B In all systems the court may draw adverse inferences from a party's failure to advance the proceeding or to respond as required. See

Principle 21.3. As a further sanction, the court may dismiss or enter a default judgment. See Principles 5.1 and 15. In common-law systems the court has authority under various circumstances to hold a party or lawyer in contempt of court. All systems authorize direct compulsory measures against third parties.

18. Evidentiary Privileges and Immunities

18.1 Effect should be given to privileges, immunities, and similar protections of a party or nonparty concerning disclosure of evidence or other information.

18.2 The court should consider whether these protections may justify a party's failure to disclose evidence or other information when deciding whether to draw adverse inferences or to impose other indirect sanctions.

18.3 The court should recognize these protections when exercising authority to impose direct sanctions on a party or nonparty to compel disclosure of evidence or other information.

Comment:

P-18A All legal systems recognize various privileges and immunities against being compelled to give evidence, such as protection from self-incrimination, confidentiality of professional communication, rights of privacy, and privileges of a spouse or family member. Privileges protect important interests, but they can impair establishment of the facts. The conceptual and technical bases of these protections differ from one system to another, as do the legal consequences of giving them recognition. In applying such rules choice-of-law problems may be presented.

P-18B The weight accorded to various privileges differs from one legal system to another and the significance of the claim of privilege may vary according to the context in specific litigation. These factors are relevant when the court considers drawing adverse inferences from the party's failure to produce evidence.

P-18C Principles 18.2 and 18.3 reflect a distinction between direct and indirect sanctions. Direct sanctions include fines, *astreintes*, contempt of court, or imprisonment. Indirect sanctions include drawing adverse inferences, judgment by default, and dismissal of claims or defenses. A court has discretionary authority to impose indirect sanctions on a party claiming a privilege, but a court ordinarily should not impose direct sanctions on a party or nonparty who refuses to disclose information protected by a privilege. A similar balancing approach may apply when blocking statutes hinder full cooperation by a party or nonparty.

P-18D In some systems, the court cannot recognize a privilege *sua sponte*, but may only respond to the initiative of the party benefited by the privilege. The court should give effect to any procedural requirement of the forum that an evidentiary privilege or immunity be expressly claimed. According to such requirements, a privilege or immunity not properly claimed in a timely manner may be considered waived.

19. Oral and Written Presentations

19.1 Pleadings, formal requests (motions), and legal argument ordinarily should be presented initially in writing, but the parties should have the right to present oral argument on important substantive and procedural issues.

19.2 The final hearing must be held before the judges who are to give judgment.

19.3 The court should specify the procedure for presentation of testimony. Ordinarily, testimony of parties and witnesses should be received orally, and reports of experts in writing; but the court may, upon consultation with the parties, require that initial testimony of witnesses be in writing, which should be supplied to the parties in advance of the hearing.

19.4 Oral testimony may be limited to supplemental questioning following written presentation of a witness's principal testimony or of an expert's report.

Comment:

P-19A Traditionally, all legal systems received witness testimony in oral form. However, in modern practice, the tendency is to replace the main testimony of a witness by a written statement. Principle 19 allows flexibility in this regard. It contemplates that testimony can be presented initially in writing, with orality commencing upon supplemental questioning by the court and opposing parties. Concerning the various procedures for interrogation of witnesses, see Principle 16.4 and Comment *P-16E*.

P-19B Forum procedure may permit or require electronic communication of written or oral presentations. See Principle 5.7.

P-19C In many civil-law systems, the primary interrogation is conducted by the court with limited intervention by the parties, whereas in most common-law systems, the roles of judge and lawyers are the reverse. In any event, the parties should be afforded opportunity to address questions directly to a witness. See Principle 16.4.

20. Public Proceedings

20.1 Ordinarily, oral hearings, including hearings in which evidence is presented and in which judgment is pronounced, should be open to the public. Following consultation with the parties, the court may order that hearings or portions thereof be kept confidential in the interest of justice, public safety, or privacy.

20.2 Court files and records should be public or otherwise accessible to persons with a legal interest or making a responsible inquiry, according to forum law.

20.3 In the interest of justice, public safety, or privacy, if the proceedings are public, the judge may order part of them to be conducted in private.

20.4 Judgments, including supporting reasons, and ordinarily other orders, should be accessible to the public.

Comment:

P-20A There are conflicting approaches concerning publicity of various components of proceedings. In some civil-law countries, the court files and records are generally kept in confidence although they are open to disclosure for justifiable cause, whereas in the common-law tradition they are generally public. One approach emphasizes the public aspect of judicial proceedings and the need for transparency, while the other emphasizes respect for the parties' privacy. These Principles express a preference for public proceedings, with limited exceptions. In general, court files and records should be public and accessible to the public and news media. Countries that have a tradition of keeping court files confidential should at least make them accessible to persons with a legal interest or making a responsible inquiry.

P-20B In some systems the court upon request of a party may grant privacy of all proceedings except the final judgment. Some systems have a constitutional guaranty of publicity in judicial proceedings, but have special exceptions for such matters as trade secrets, matters of national security, and so on. Arbitration proceedings are generally conducted in privacy.

21. Burden and Standard of Proof

21.1 Ordinarily, each party has the burden to prove all the material facts that are the basis of that party's case.

21.2 Facts are considered proven when the court is reasonably convinced of their truth.

21.3 When it appears that a party has possession or control of relevant evidence that it declines without justification to produce, the court may draw adverse inferences with respect to the issue for which the evidence is probative.

Comment:

P-21A The requirement stated in Principle 21.1 is often expressed in terms of the formula "the burden of proof goes with the burden of pleading." The allocation of the burden of pleading is specified by law, ultimately reflecting a sense of fairness. The determination of this allocation is often a matter of substantive law.

P-21B The standard of "reasonably convinced" is in substance that applied in most legal systems. The standard in the United States and some other countries is "preponderance of the evidence" but functionally that is essentially the same.

P-21C Principle 21.3 is based on the principle that both parties have the duty to contribute in good faith to the discharge of the opposing party's burden of proof. See Principle 11. The possibility of drawing adverse inferences ordinarily does not preclude the recalcitrant party from introducing other evidence relevant to the issue in question. Drawing such inferences can be considered a sanction, see Principle 17.3, or a shifting of the burden of proof, see Principle 21.1.

22. Responsibility for Determinations of Fact and Law

22.1 The court is responsible for considering all relevant facts and evidence and for determining the correct legal basis for its decisions, including matters determined on the basis of foreign law.

22.2 The court may, while affording the parties opportunity to respond:

22.2.1 Permit or invite a party to amend its contentions of law or fact and to offer additional legal argument and evidence accordingly;

22.2.2 Order the taking of evidence not previously suggested by a party; or

22.2.3 Rely upon a legal theory or an interpretation of the facts or of the evidence that has not been advanced by a party.

22.3 The court ordinarily should hear all evidence directly, but when necessary may assign to a suitable delegate the taking and preserving of evidence for consideration by the court at the final hearing.

22.4 The court may appoint an expert to give evidence on any relevant issue for which expert testimony is appropriate, including foreign law.

22.4.1 If the parties agree upon an expert, the court ordinarily should appoint that expert.

22.4.2 A party has a right to present expert testimony through an expert selected by that party on any relevant issue for which expert testimony is appropriate.

22.4.3 An expert, whether appointed by the court or by a party, owes a duty to the court to present a full and objective assessment of the issue addressed.

Comment:

P-22A It is universally recognized that the court has responsibility for determination of issues of law and of fact necessary for the judgment and that all parties have a right to be heard concerning applicable law and relevant evidence. See Principle 5.

P-22B Foreign law is a particularly important subject in transnational litigation. The judge may not be knowledgeable about foreign law and may need to appoint an expert or request submissions from the parties on issues of foreign law. See Principle 22.4.

P-22C The scope of the proceeding, and the issues properly to be considered, are determined by the claims and defenses of the parties in the pleadings. The judge is generally bound by the scope of the proceeding stated by the parties. However, the court in the interest of justice may order or permit amendment by a party, giving other parties a right to respond accordingly. See Principle 10.3.

P-22D Use of experts is common in complex litigation. Court appointment of a neutral expert is the practice in most civil-law systems and in some common-law systems. However, party-appointed experts can provide valuable assistance in the analysis of difficult factual issues. Fear that party appointment of experts will devolve into a "battle of experts" and thereby obscure the issues is generally misplaced. In any event, this risk is offset by the value of such evidence. Expert testimony may be received on issues of foreign law.

23. Decision and Reasoned Explanation

23.1 Upon completion of the parties' presentations, the court should promptly give judgment set forth or recorded in writing. The judgment should specify the remedy awarded and, in a monetary award, its amount.

23.2 The judgment should be accompanied by a reasoned explanation of the essential factual, legal, and evidentiary basis of the decision.

Comment:

P-23A A written decision not only informs the parties of the disposition, but also provides a record of the judgment, which may be useful in subsequent recognition proceedings. In several systems a reasoned opinion is required by constitutional provisions or is considered as a fundamental guarantee in the administration of justice. The reasoned explanation may be given by reference to other documents such as pleadings in case of a default judgment or the transcript of the instructions to the jury in case of a jury verdict. Forum law may specify a time limit within which the court must give judgment.

P-23B When a judgment determines less than all the claims and defenses at issue, it should specify the matters that remain open for further proceedings. For example, in a case involving multiple claims, the court may decide one of the claims (damages, for example) and keep the proceedings open for the decision of the other (injunction, for example).

P-23C In some systems, a judgment may be pronounced subject to subsequent specification of the monetary award or other terms of a remedy, for example an accounting to determine damages or a specification of the terms of an injunction.

P-23D See Principle 5.6, requiring that the court consider each significant contention of fact, evidence, and law.

24. Settlement

24.1 The court, while respecting the parties' opportunity to pursue litigation, should encourage settlement between the parties when reasonably possible.

24.2 **The court should facilitate parties' participation in alternative-dispute-resolution processes at any stage of the proceeding.**

24.3 **The parties, both before and after commencement of litigation, should cooperate in reasonable settlement endeavors. The court may adjust its award of costs to reflect unreasonable failure to cooperate or bad-faith participation in settlement endeavors.**

Comment:

P-24A The proviso "while respecting the parties' opportunity to pursue litigation" signifies that the court should not compel or coerce settlement among the parties. However, the court may conduct informal discussions of settlement with the parties at any appropriate times. A judge participating in settlement discussions should avoid bias. However, active participation, including a suggestion for settlement, does not impair a judge's impartiality or create an appearance of partiality.

P-24B Principle 24.3 departs from tradition in some countries in which the parties generally do not have an obligation to negotiate or otherwise consider settlement proposals from the opposing party. Forum law may appropriately provide settlement-offer procedure enforced by special cost sanctions for refusal to accept an opposing party's offer. Prominent examples of such procedures are the Ontario (Canada) civil-procedure rule and Part 36 of the new English procedural rules. Those are formal procedures whereby a party may make a definite offer of settlement and thereby oblige the opposing party to accept or refuse it on penalty of additional costs if that party does not eventually obtain a result more advantageous than the proposed settlement offer. See also Principle 25.2.

25. Costs

25.1 **The winning party ordinarily should be awarded all or a substantial portion of its reasonable costs. "Costs" include court filing fees, fees paid to officials such as court stenographers, expenses such as expert-witness fees, and lawyers' fees.**

25.2 **Exceptionally, the court may withhold or limit costs to the winning party when there is clear justification for doing so. The court may limit the award to a proportion that reflects expenditures for matters in genuine dispute and award costs against a winning party who has raised unnecessary issues or been otherwise unreasonably disputatious. The court in making cost decisions may take account of any party's procedural misconduct in the proceeding.**

Comment:

P-25A Award of attorneys' fees is the rule prevailing in most legal systems, although, for example, not in China, Japan, and the United States. In some systems, the amount of costs awarded to the prevailing party is determined by an experienced officer and often is less than the winning party is obligated to pay that party's lawyer. In some systems, the amount awarded to the prevailing party is governed by fee regulation. A fee-shifting rule is controversial in certain types of litigation but is generally considered appropriate in commercial litigation and is typically stipulated in commercial contracts.

P-25B According to Principle 25.2, exceptionally the court may decline to award any costs to a winning party, or award only part of the costs, or may calculate costs more generously or more severely than it otherwise would. The exceptional character of Principle 25.2 requires the judge to give reasons for the decision. See also Principle 24.3.

26. Immediate Enforceability of Judgments

26.1 The final judgment of the first-instance court ordinarily should be immediately enforceable.

26.2 The first-instance court or the appellate court, on its own motion or motion of a party, may in the interest of justice stay enforcement of the judgment pending appeal.

26.3 Security may be required from the appellant as a condition of granting a stay or from the respondent as a condition of denying a stay.

Comment:

P-26A The principle of finality is essential to effective adjudication. In some jurisdictions, immediate enforcement is available only for judgments of second-instance courts. However, the tendency is toward the practice of common-law and some civil-law countries that judgments of first-instance courts are accorded that effect by law or court order.

P-26B The fact that a judgment should be immediately enforceable upon becoming final does not prohibit a court from giving the losing party a period of time for compliance with the award. The judgment should be enforced in accordance with its own terms.

P-26C Under forum law, a partial judgment (dealing only with part of the controversy) may also be final and, therefore, immediately enforceable.

27. Appeal

27.1 Appellate review should be available on substantially the same terms as other judgments under the law of the forum. Appellate review should be concluded expeditiously.

27.2 The scope of appellate review should ordinarily be limited to claims and defenses addressed in the first-instance proceeding.

27.3 The appellate court may in the interest of justice consider new facts and evidence.

Comment:

P-27A Appellate procedure varies substantially among legal systems. The procedure of the forum therefore should be employed.

P-27B Historically, in common-law systems appellate review has been based on the principle of a "closed record," that is, that all claims, defenses, evidence, and legal contentions must have been presented in the first-instance court. In most modern common-law systems, however, the appellate court has a measure of discretion to consider new legal arguments and, under compelling circumstances, new evidence. Historically, in civil-law systems the second-instance court was authorized fully to reconsider the merits of the dispute, but there is variation from this approach in many modern systems. In a diminishing number of civil-law systems a proceeding in the court of second instance can be essentially a new trial and is routinely pursued. In many systems the decision of the court of first instance can be reversed or amended only for substantial miscarriage of justice. This Principle rejects both of these extremes. However, reception of new evidence at the appellate level should be permitted only when required by the interest of justice. If a party is permitted such an opportunity, other parties should have a correlative right to respond. See Principle 22.2.

P-27C In some systems, the parties must preserve their objections in the first-instance tribunal and cannot raise them for the first time on appeal.

28. *Lis Pendens* and *Res Judicata*

28.1 In applying the rules of *lis pendens*, the scope of the proceeding is determined by the claims in the parties' pleadings, including amendments.

28.2 In applying the rules of claim preclusion, the scope of the claim or claims decided is determined by reference to the claims and defenses in the parties' pleadings, including amendments, and the court's decision and reasoned explanation.

28.3 The concept of issue preclusion, as to an issue of fact or application of law to facts, should be applied only to prevent substantial injustice.

Comment:

P-28A This Principle is designed to avoid repetitive litigation, whether concurrent (*lis pendens*) or successive (*res judicata*).

P-28B Some systems have strict rules of *lis pendens* whereas others apply them more flexibly, particularly having regard to the quality of the proceeding of both forums. The Principle of *lis pendens* corresponds to Principle 10.3, concerning the scope of the proceeding, and Principle 2.6, concerning parallel proceedings.

P-28C Some legal systems, particularly those of common law, employ the concept of issue preclusion, sometimes referred to as collateral estoppel or issue estoppel. The concept is that a determination of an issue as a necessary element of a judgment generally should not be reexamined in a subsequent dispute in which the same issue is also presented. Under Principle 28.3, issue preclusion might be applied when, for example, a party has justifiably relied in its conduct on a determination of an issue of law or fact in a previous proceeding. A broader scope of issue preclusion is recognized in many common-law systems, but the more limited concept in Principle 28.3 is derived from the principle of good faith, as it is referred to in civil-law systems, or estoppel in pais, as the principle is referred to in common-law systems.

29. Effective Enforcement

Procedures should be available for speedy and effective enforcement of judgments, including money awards, costs, injunctions, and provisional measures.

Comment:

P-29A Many legal systems have archaic and inefficient procedures for enforcement of judgments. From the viewpoint of litigants, particularly the winning party, effective enforcement is an essential element of justice. However, the topic of enforcement procedures is beyond the scope of these Principles.

30. Recognition

A final judgment awarded in another forum in a proceeding substantially compatible with these Principles must be recognized and enforced unless

substantive public policy requires otherwise. A provisional remedy must be recognized in the same terms.

Comment:

P-30A Recognition of judgments of another forum, including judgments for provisional remedies, is especially important in transnational litigation. Every legal system has firm rules of recognition for judgments rendered within its own system. International conventions prescribe other conditions concerning recognition of foreign judgments. Many jurisdictions limit the effect of most kinds of provisional measures to the territory of the issuing state and cooperate by issuing parallel injunctions. However, the technique of parallel provisional measures is less acceptable than direct recognition and enforcement. See also Principle 31.

P-30B According to Principle 30, a judgment given in a proceeding substantially compatible with these Principles ordinarily should have the same effect as judgments rendered after a proceeding under the laws of the recognizing state. Principle 30 is therefore a principle of equal treatment. The Principles establish international standards of international jurisdiction, sufficient notice to the judgment debtor, procedural fairness, and the effects of *res judicata*. Consequently most traditional grounds for nonrecognition, such as lack of jurisdiction, insufficient notice, fraud, unfair foreign proceedings, or conflict with another final judgment or decision, do not arise if the foreign proceeding meets the requirements of these Principles. Reciprocity is no longer a prerequisite of recognition in many countries, but it will be also fulfilled if the law of the forum accepts these Principles and especially Principle 30. Only the limited exception for nonrecognition based on substantive public policy is allowed when the foreign proceedings were conducted in substantial accordance with these Principles.

31. International Judicial Cooperation

The courts of a state that has adopted these Principles should provide assistance to the courts of any other state that is conducting a proceeding consistent with these Principles, including the grant of protective or provisional relief and assistance in the identification, preservation, and production of evidence.

Comment:

P-31A International judicial cooperation and assistance supplement international recognition and, in modern context, are equally important.

P-31B Consistent with rules concerning communication outside the presence of parties or their representatives (*ex parte* communications), judges should, when necessary, establish communication with judges in other jurisdictions. See Principle 1.4.

P-31C For the significance of the term "evidence," see Principle 16.

PRINCIPLES OF TRANSNATIONAL CIVIL PROCEDURE

(with commentary)
French Version

UNIDROIT
INSTITUT INTERNATIONAL POUR L'UNIFICATION DU DROIT PRIVE

LISTE DES ETATS PARTICIPANTS

Afrique du Sud
Allemagne
Argentine
Australie
Autriche
Belgique
Bolivie
Bresil
Bulgarie
Canada
Chili
Chine
Chypre
Colombie
Croatie
Cuba
Danemark
Egypte
Espagne
Estonie
Etats-unis d'Amerique
Federation de Russie
Finlande
France
Grece
Hongrie
Inde
Iran
Iraq
Irlande
Israel
Italie
Japon
Luxembourg
Malte
Mexique
Nicaragua
Nigeria
Norvege
Pakistan
Paraguay
Pays-bas
Pologne
Portugal
Republique de Coree
Republique tcheque
Roumanie
Royaume-Uni
Saint-marin
Saint-Siege
Serbie et Montenegro
Slovaquie
Slovenie
Suede
Suisse
Tunisie
Turquie
Uruguay
Venezuela

Mars 2004

LE CONSEIL DE DIRECTION D'UNIDROIT (2004–2008)

Berardino Libonati	Président d'UNIDROIT
Martin Adensamer	Autriche
Tuğrul Arat	Turquie
Antonio Boggiano	Argentine
Hans-Georg Bollweg	Allemagne
Sergio Carbone	Italie
Michael Bendik Elmer	Danemark
Henry Deeb Gabriel	Etats-Unis d'Amérique
Ian Govey	Australie
Attila Harmathy	Hongrie
Arthur S. Hartkamp	Pays-Bas
Gerard William Hogan	Irlande
Kiyoshi Hosokawa	Japon
Anthony Inglese	Royaume-Uni
Alexander S. Komarov	Fédération de Russie
Lyou Byung-Hwa	République de Corée
Didier Opertti Badán	Uruguay
Jorge A. Sánchez-Cordero Dávila	Mexique
Biswanath B. Sen	Inde
Stanislaw J. Soltysinski	Pologne
Bruno Sturlese	France
Anne-Marie Trahan	Canada
Evelio Verdera y Tuells	Espagne
Ioannis Voulgaris	Grèce
Pierre Widmer	Suisse
Zhang Yuqing	République populaire de Chine

LA DIRECTION d'UNIDROIT

BERARDINO LIBONATI, Président
HERBERT KRONKE, Secrétaire Général
WALTER RODINO, Secrétaire Général adjoint

CONTENTS

PRINCIPLES OF TRANSNATIONAL CIVIL PROCEDURE (with commentary), French Version — *page* 51

Principe

	Champ d'application et transposition en droit interne	61
	Commentaire	61
1.	Indépendance, impartialité et qualification du tribunal et de ses membres	62
	Commentaire	63
2.	Compétence à l'égard des parties	64
	Commentaire	65
3.	Égalité procédurale des parties	66
	Commentaire	66
4.	Droit pour les parties d'être assistées par un avocat	67
	Commentaire	68
5.	Notification et droit d'être entendu	68
	Commentaire	69
6.	Langue de la procédure	70
	Commentaire	70
7.	Célérité de la justice	71
	Commentaire	71
8.	Mesures provisoires et conservatoires	71
	Commentaire	72
9.	Déroulement du procès	74
	Commentaire	74
10.	Principe dispositif	75
	Commentaire	76
11.	Devoirs des parties et de leurs avocats	76
	Commentaire	77
12.	Jonction d'instance et intervention	78
	Commentaire	78

Principe

13. Avis d'un *amicus curiae* 79
Commentaire 79
14. L'office du juge dans la conduite de l'instance 80
Commentaire 80
15. Jugement de rejet et jugement par défaut 81
Commentaire 81
16. Accès aux éléments d'information et à la preuve 83
Commentaire 84
17. Sanctions 85
Commentaire 86
18. Confidentialité et immunité 86
Commentaire 86
19. Dépositions écrites et orales 87
Commentaire 88
20. Publicité de la procédure 88
Commentaire 89
21. Charge de la preuve et conviction du juge 89
Commentaire 90
22. Devoir du juge et des parties dans la détermination des éléments de fait et de droit 90
Commentaire 91
23. Jugement et motivation 92
Commentaire 92
24. Transaction et conciliation 92
Commentaire 93
25. Frais et dépens 93
Commentaire 94
26. Caractère immédiatement exécutoire du jugement 94
Commentaire 95
27. Appel 95
Commentaire 95
28. Litispendance et chose jugée 96
Commentaire 96
29. Exécution effective 97
Commentaire 97
30. Reconnaissance 97
Commentaire 97
31. Coopération judiciaire internationale 98
Commentaire 98

PRINCIPES ALI-UNIDROIT DE PROCEDURE CIVILE TRANSNATIONALE

(avec commentaires)

Champ d'application et transposition en droit interne

Les présents Principes sont destinés au règlement des litiges transnationaux en matière commerciale. Ils peuvent être également appropriés pour la solution de la plupart des autres litiges de nature civile et peuvent constituer le fondement de futures réformes des règles nationales de procédure.

Commentaire:

P-A Un système national souhaitant transposer les présents Principes peut le faire par un acte normatif, tel qu'une loi ou un ensemble de règles, ou un traité international. La loi du for peut décider que certaines catégories de litiges seront exclues du champ d'application des présents Principes, ou décider que l'application de ces derniers sera étendue à d'autres litiges civils. Les tribunaux peuvent adapter leur pratique aux présents Principes, en particulier si les parties à l'instance y sont favorables. Par ailleurs, les Principes fixent des *standards* permettant la reconnaissance, dans l'État du for, des jugements étrangers. V. le Principe 30. Les règles de procédure du for sont appliquées dans les litiges non soumis aux présents Principes.

P-B L'acte transposant les présents Principes pourra préciser les notions de ⟪commercial⟫ ou de ⟪transnational⟫, en prenant nécessairement en compte les traditions juridiques ainsi que la terminologie nationales. La notion d'opérations commerciales transnationales peut inclure les contrats commerciaux conclus entre ressortissants de différents États ou conclus, dans un État, entre un ressortissant national et un autre, d'un État étranger. De telles opérations commerciales peuvent inclure les ventes, les baux, les emprunts, les investissements, les acquisitions, les opérations bancaires, les sûretés, les droits réels, la propriété intellectuelle ou toutes autres opérations commerciales ou financières, mais non nécessairement le droit de la consommation.

P-C Un différend ne peut être considéré comme transnational lorsqu'il concerne uniquement un État et des parties ressortissantes de ce même État. Pour les besoins de ces Principes, une personne physique est considérée comme ressortissante d'un État en raison de sa nationalité ou de sa résidence habituelle. Une personne morale (société commerciale, une association ou tout autre personne morale ou entité ayant capacité à agir) sont réputées être ressortissantes de l'État où elles ont été immatriculées et de celui où se trouve leur centre principal d'activités.

P-D Dans les litiges qui concernent une pluralité de parties ou de demandes, parmi lesquelles certaines ne relèveraient pas du champ d'application des présents Principes, ces derniers peuvent être néanmoins appliqués lorsque le tribunal considère que l'objet principal du litige relève de leur champ d'application. Toutefois, les Principes ne sont pas applicables, sans modifications, aux actions qui concernent un intérêt collectif, telles que les *class actions*, ou les actions en représentation conjointe, ou aux procédures collectives.

P-E Ces Principes sont également applicables aux procédures d'arbitrage international, sauf incompatibilité avec de telles procédures (comme par exemple, en ce qui concerne les Principes relatifs à la compétence, la publicité du procès et aux voies de recours).

1. Indépendance, impartialité et qualification du tribunal et de ses membres

1.1 Le tribunal et ses membres doivent disposer d'une indépendance leur permettant de résoudre le différend au regard des faits et des moyens de droit. Le tribunal doit être exempt d'influences intérieures et extérieures injustifiées.

1.2 Les juges bénéficient d'une permanence raisonnable. Les membres non professionnels du tribunal doivent être nommés à l'issue d'une procédure qui garantit leur indépendance par rapport aux parties, au litige et à toute personne intéressée au litige.

1.3 Le tribunal doit être impartial. Un juge ou toute personne ayant le pouvoir de prendre une décision ne doit pas participer aux activités du tribunal, dès lors qu'il existe des motifs raisonnables de mettre en doute son impartialité. Le droit du for doit prévoir des moyens équitables et efficaces pour contester l'impartialité.

1.4 Ni le tribunal ni le juge ne doivent accepter les communications relatives au litige faites par une partie en l'absence des autres parties, à l'exception des communications concernant une procédure non contradictoire ou la gestion ordinaire de l'instance. Si une telle communication a lieu, la partie absente doit être promptement informée du contenu de celle-ci.

1.5 Le tribunal doit avoir des connaissances juridiques solides et de l'expérience.

Commentaire:

P-1A L'indépendance doit être considérée comme une notion plus objective, et l'impartialité comme plus subjective, mais les deux qualités sont étroitement liées.

P-1B Des influences extérieures peuvent être exercées par des membres du pouvoir exécutif ou législatif; les influences internes peuvent provenir d'autres membres du pouvoir judiciaire.

P-1C Ce Principe reconnaît que les juges exercent leurs fonctions pendant une longue période, et généralement pendant toute leur carrière. Toutefois, dans certains systèmes juridiques, les juges bénéficient d'une expérience préalable en tant qu'avocats et certains magistrats sont nommés pour une courte période. Un des objectifs de ces Principes est d'éviter la création de tribunaux *ad hoc*. Le terme ⟪juge⟫ désigne tout magistrat judiciaire ou quasi-judiciaire, selon la loi du for.

P-1D Même si l'existence d'une procédure permettant de contester l'impartialité du juge n'est nécessaire que dans des circonstances exceptionnelles, la possibilité d'accéder à une telle procédure renforce la confiance des parties, spécialement lorsqu'elles sont ressortissantes d'un autre État. Toutefois, l'existence d'une telle procédure ne doit pas conduire à des abus, par l'introduction de contestations infondées.

P-1E Le recours à des procédures non contradictoires (procédures *ex parte*) peut être justifié, notamment pour l'obtention de mesures provisoires. Voir les Principes 5.8 et 8. La procédure par défaut est soumise au Principe 15. La gestion de l'instance comprend, par exemple, la fixation du calendrier pour la présentation des éléments de preuve allégués.

P-1F Le Principe 1.5 exige seulement que les juges chargés d'un litige transnational aient des connaissances juridiques. Il n'exige pas qu'ils aient des connaissances spécifiques en droit des affaires ou en droit financier. Toutefois, la connaissance de ces domaines serait souhaitable.

2. Compétence à l'égard des parties

2.1 La compétence du tribunal peut s'exercer à l'égard d'une partie

2.1.1 Lorsque les parties décident de soumettre le litige au tribunal;

2.1.2 Lorsqu'il existe un lien substantiel entre l'État du for et la partie, l'opération ou les circonstances du litige. Un tel lien existe lorsqu'une partie essentielle de l'opération ou des circonstances du litige s'est réalisée dans l'État du for, lorsque le défendeur a sa résidence habituelle, s'il s'agit d'une personne physique, ou bien le centre principal de ses activités ou le lieu où il a été immatriculé dans l'État du for, s'il s'agit d'une personne morale. Ce lien existe également si les biens qui font l'objet du litige sont situés dans l'État du for.

2.2 La compétence peut être étendue si aucune autre juridiction étrangère n'apparaît raisonnablement compétente

2.2.1 A l'égard d'un défendeur qui se trouve dans l'État du for ou qui a la nationalité de ce dernier.

2.2.2 En cas de situation d'un bien du défendeur dans l'État du for, que le litige porte ou non sur ce bien; dans ce cas, la compétence du tribunal doit être limitée à ce bien ou à sa valeur.

2.3 Des mesures provisoires peuvent être prononcées à l'encontre d'une personne ou de biens situés dans l'État du for, même si les tribunaux d'un autre État sont compétents pour connaître du litige.

2.4 Le tribunal saisi décline généralement sa compétence en présence d'une clause attributive de juridiction par laquelle les parties reconnaissent compétence exclusive à un autre tribunal.

2.5 Le tribunal peut décliner sa compétence ou surseoir à statuer, lorsqu'il apparaît que la compétence du tribunal serait manifestement inadéquate et que la compétence d'un autre tribunal serait plus appropriée.

2.6 Le tribunal décline sa compétence ou surseoit à statuer, si le litige est pendant devant les juridictions compétentes d'un autre État, à moins qu'il n'apparaisse que le litige ne sera pas équitablement, efficacement et rapidement tranché devant ces juridictions.

Commentaire:

P-2A Sous réserve des règles de compétence prévues par la loi du for ou par le droit international, généralement le tribunal peut être compétent en vertu de l'accord des parties. Un tribunal ne peut se déclarer compétent sur le fondement d'un consentement tacite des parties sans donner à celles-ci une possibilité équitable de contester cette compétence. A défaut d'accord des parties, et dans le respect de la volonté des parties de considérer qu'un autre tribunal ou un autre pays auront une compétence exclusive, un tribunal est compétent uniquement s'il existe un lien substantiel entre le litige et le for, selon les dispositions du Principe 2.1.2.

P-2B Le principe du «lien substantiel» est généralement accepté dans le contentieux transnational. La mise en œuvre de ce standard implique nécessairement des considérations de nature pratique et une certaine retenue de la part du tribunal Ce principe exclut la simple présence physique, appelée familièrement aux États-Unis la «*tag jurisdiction*». Bien que fondé d'un point de vue historique dans la fédération américaine, le critère de la simple présence physique est inadapté au contentieux international moderne. Le concept de «lien substantiel» peut être précisé et dégagé à partir du droit conventionnel et de la loi nationale. La portée de cette expression peut ne pas être la même dans tous les systèmes. Toutefois, ce concept ne peut justifier que la compétence du tribunal soit fondée sur des relations d'affaires non liées à l'opération ou encore aux circonstances du litige.

P-2C Le Principe 2.2 couvre le concept de «*forum necessitatis*»- le for nécessaire- selon lequel le tribunal peut se considérer compétent lorsque aucun autre tribunal n'est accessible.

P-2D Le Principe 2.3 reconnaît qu'un État peut étendre la compétence de ses tribunaux par la saisie de biens situés sur son territoire, par exemple pour garantir l'efficacité d'un éventuel jugement, même lorsque la propriété de ces biens ne constitue pas l'objet du différend. La procédure est dans ce cas appelée «*quasi in rem jurisdiction*» dans certains systèmes juridiques. Le Principe 2.3 envisage que, dans ce cas, le fond du litige puisse être tranché par un autre tribunal. La question de la localisation des bien immatériels est soumise à la loi du for.

P-2E Les clauses attributives de juridiction ainsi que les clauses compromissoires doivent en principe être respectées.

P-2F Le concept reconnu dans le Principe 2.5 est comparable à la règle du *forum non conveniens* des pays de *common law*. Dans certains systèmes de droit civil, le concept tend à prévenir les abus de procédure fondés sur la compétence. La volonté de rendre ce Principe efficace peut aboutir à la suspension de l'instance dans le for, par égards envers un autre tribunal. L'existence d'un tribunal plus approprié est nécessaire à l'application de ce Principe. Ce Principe doit être interprété à la lumière du principe de l'égalité procédurale des parties, qui interdit tout type de discrimination fondée sur la nationalité ou la résidence. Voir principe 3.2.

P-2G Pour les délais et la portée des mécanismes permettant de suspendre d'autres procédures, comme la litispendance, voir les Principes 10.2 et 28.1.

3. Égalité procédurale des parties

3.1 Le tribunal assure aux parties, en demande et en défense, les mêmes garanties procédurales.

3.2 Ce droit s'oppose à toute discrimination non justifiée, de quelque sorte que ce soit, et notamment sur le fondement de leur nationalité ou de leur résidence. Le tribunal prend en compte les difficultés rencontrées par une partie étrangère pour pouvoir participer au procès.

3.3 Aucune caution ou garantie des frais de procédure ou, en cas d'une demande de mesures provisoires, dans l'éventualité où elle serait condamnée au fond, ne doit être exigée d'une personne sur le seul fondement de sa nationalité étrangère ou de son absence de résidence habituelle dans l'État du for.

3.4 Dans la mesure du possible, les règles de compétence territoriale ne doivent pas imposer à la partie n'ayant pas sa résidence habituelle dans l'État du for des frais déraisonnables pour accéder au tribunal.

Commentaire:

P-3A Le terme «raisonnable» est utilisé à plusieurs reprises dans les Principes, dans le sens, selon le contexte, de «proportionnel», «significatif», «non excessif», ou «équitable». Il peut aussi être employé par opposition à «arbitraire». La référence au concept de raisonnable s'oppose aussi à une interprétation trop technique et reconnaît une marge de discrétion au tribunal, afin d'éviter une application trop stricte, excessive et déraisonnable des règles de procédure.

P-3B Les discriminations interdites peuvent se fonder sur la nationalité, le sexe, la race, la langue, la religion, les opinions politiques ou autres, les origines nationales ou sociales, la naissance ou tout autre état, les orientations sexuelles, ou l'appartenance à une minorité nationale. Toute forme de discrimination est interdite, mais les discriminations fondées sur la nationalité ou le lieu de résidence représentent un point particulièrement sensible dans le contentieux transnational.

P-3C Une protection particulière doit être assurée à une partie, telle qu'un mineur, n'ayant pas une pleine capacité juridique, pour la protection de ses intérêts, comme la nomination d'un tuteur ou d'un curateur. De telles mesures de protection ne peuvent être imposées de façon abusive à une partie étrangère.

P-3D Certains systèmes juridiques exigent qu'une personne fournisse une caution, ou une garantie en cas de demande de mesures provisoires, dans l'éventualité où elle serait condamnée au fond, pour garantir l'entier dédommagement pour les éventuels préjudices subis par l'autre partie. D'autres, au contraire, n'exigent pas de telles cautions ou garanties, ou les interdisent, par des dispositions constitutionnelles concernant l'accès à la justice ou l'égalité des parties. Le Principe 3.3 constitue un compromis entre ces deux positions, sans pour autant modifier, sur ce point, la loi du for. Toutefois, l'obligation pour une partie étrangère ou n'ayant pas sa résidence habituelle dans l'État du for de fournir une caution ou une garantie, dans le cas de mesures provisoires ou conservatoires, doit être appréciée selon les mêmes principes généraux.

P-3E Les règles nationales de compétence territoriale prennent en compte des considérations relatives à la facilité d'accès au tribunal à l'intérieur du pays. Elles devraient être appliquées à la lumière du principe de la facilité d'accès au tribunal prévue par le Principe 3.4. Une règle de compétence qui imposerait des difficultés essentielles pour l'accès au tribunal à l'intérieur de l'État du for ne devrait pas être appliquée dès lors qu'il existe un autre tribunal dont l'accès serait plus aisé; de même, le procès devrait être transféré dans l'État du for dès lors que les règles de compétence désignent un tribunal dont l'accès est particulièrement difficile.

4. Droit pour les parties d'être assistées par un avocat

4.1 Chaque partie a le droit d'être assistée par un avocat de son choix. Elle doit pouvoir être représentée par un avocat admis à exercer dans l'État du for et assistée activement par un avocat exerçant ailleurs.

4.2 L'indépendance professionnelle de l'avocat doit être respectée. L'avocat doit être mis en mesure de respecter son devoir de loyauté envers son client et la confidentialité de ses échanges avec ce dernier.

Commentaire:

P-4A La loi du for peut exiger que l'avocat représentant une partie soit admis à exercer dans l'État du for, et interdire, si tel n'est pas le cas, que la partie puisse être représentée par lui. Toutefois, une partie devrait pouvoir être assistée par un autre avocat (et plus particulièrement par son avocat habituel) qui devrait être autorisé à assister et à participer activement à toutes les audiences.

P-4B Un avocat admis à exercer dans le pays d'une des parties n'est pas autorisé par ces Principes à représenter seul cette partie devant les tribunaux étrangers. Cette question est soumise à la loi du for; toutefois, l'avocat étranger doit au moins être autorisé à assister aux audiences et à s'adresser, de façon informelle, au tribunal.

P-4C Les relations entre l'avocat et son client sont généralement soumises à la loi du for, y compris le choix des règles de droit applicables.

P-4D Les principes relatifs à la déontologie varient quelque peu selon les différents pays. Toutefois, tous les pays devraient reconnaître que les avocats, lors de l'exercice indépendant de leur mission, sont tenus à la défense des intérêts de leurs clients et à la protection du secret de la confidentialité des informations obtenus par eux.

5. Notification et droit d'être entendu

5.1 L'acte introductif d'instance doit faire l'objet d'une notification à toutes les parties qui ne sont pas demandeurs. Cette notification initiale doit être effectué par des moyens raisonnablement efficaces et contenir une copie de la demande introductive d'instance, ou comprendre sous quelque autre forme les allégations du demandeur ainsi que la solution requise. Une partie à l'encontre de laquelle une prétention est formulée doit être informée des moyens qui lui sont offerts pour répondre, ainsi que de la possibilité que soit rendu un jugement par défaut s'il s'abstient de répondre dans les délais requis.

5.2 La notification des documents précisés dans le Principe 5.1 doit être faite dans la langue de l'État du for ou bien dans une langue de l'État dans lequel le destinataire, s'il est une personne physique, a sa résidence habituelle ou, s'il est une personne morale, a le centre principal de ses activités ou bien encore dans la langue dans laquelle les principaux documents de l'opération litigieuse sont rédigés. Le défendeur et les autres parties doivent notifier leurs réponses et autres explications et requêtes dans la langue du procès, selon les dispositions du Principe 6.

5.3 Les parties reçoivent, au cours du procès, notification dans un bref délai de tous les actes des autres parties, ainsi que des décisions du tribunal.

5.4 Les parties ont le droit d'alléguer les faits et les moyens de droit pertinents, ainsi que de présenter des éléments de preuve.

5.5 Chaque partie doit avoir la possibilité, de façon équitable et dans un délai raisonnable, de répondre aux moyens de fait et de droit et aux preuves présentées par la partie adverse, ainsi qu'aux ordonnances et suggestions du tribunal.

5.6 Le tribunal doit prendre en considération tous les moyens de fait et de droit qui sont invoqués par les parties, et répondre à ceux qui sont essentiels.

5.7 Les parties ont le droit, d'un commun accord et avec l'autorisation du tribunal, d'avoir recours à des moyens rapides de communication tels que les moyens de télécommunication.

5.8 Une ordonnance affectant les intérêts d'une partie sans que celle-ci en ait reçu préalablement notification ne peut être rendue et exécutée que sur preuve d'une nécessité urgente et après considération des exigences d'équité. Une ordonnance rendue *ex parte* doit être proportionnelle aux intérêts dont le requérant demande la protection. Dès que possible, la partie doit recevoir notification de l'ordonnance ainsi que de ses motifs, afin qu'elle puisse la déférer au tribunal pour qu'il la réexamine dans sa totalité dans un délai bref.

Commentaire:

P-5A Les procédures de notification varient quelque peu selon les systèmes juridiques. Par exemple, dans certains systèmes le tribunal a la charge de procéder à la notification, y compris de l'acte introductif d'instance, alors que dans d'autres pays cette obligation incombe aux parties. Les modalités techniques requises par le droit du for doivent être respectées, afin de fournir une notification précise.

P-5B La possibilité qu'un jugement par défaut puisse être rendu revêt une importance particulière dans le contentieux international.

P-5C Le droit pour une partie d'être informée des moyens de fait et de droit de son adversaire est en accord avec les devoirs du tribunal, tels que définis au Principe 22.

P-5D Selon le Principe 5.5, les parties devraient notifier rapidement les éléments de faits sur lesquels reposent leurs demandes et défenses, ainsi que les règles de droit qui seront invoquées, afin que leur adversaire puisse préparer sa défense.

P-5E Le standard défini dans le Principe 5.6 n'exige pas que le tribunal prenne en considération des moyens de faits et de droit déjà appréciés dans une phase précédente de la procédure ou non nécessaires à la solution du litige. Voir le Principe 23, qui exige que la décision écrite soit accompagnée d'une motivation en fait et en droit.

P-5F Le droit du for peut prévoir l'emploi de moyens rapides de communication, sans que l'accord des parties, ou un ordre spécial du tribunal soit nécessaire.

P-5G Le Principe 5.8 autorise le recours à des procédures *ex parte*, telle q'une ordonnance ou une mesure provisoire ou conservatoire, en particulier dans la première phase de l'instance. L'efficacité de ces mesures dépend souvent de la possibilité de les exécuter sans notification préalable. La partie à l'encontre de laquelle une telle mesure a été ordonnée doit en être rapidement informée, pouvoir être immédiatement entendue et pouvoir la faire réexaminer en fait et en droit. Une procédure *ex parte* doit être conduite conformément au Principe 8. Voir les Principes 1.4 et 8.

6. Langue de la procédure

6.1 La procédure doit être conduite généralement dans la langue du tribunal; il en va de même des documents présentés et des communications orales.

6.2 Le tribunal peut autoriser l'emploi d'autres langues pour toute ou partie de la procédure à condition qu'il ne soit causé de grief à aucune des parties.

6.3 Une traduction doit être prévue lorsqu'une partie ou un témoin ne parle pas suffisamment la langue dans laquelle se déroule la procédure. La traduction de documents longs ou volumineux peut être limitée à des passages sélectionnés par les parties ou choisies par le tribunal.

Commentaire:

P-6A Le tribunal doit conduire le procès dans une langue qu'il maîtrise couramment. Il s'agira généralement de la langue de l'État où il siège. Toutefois, si le tribunal et les parties parlent une langue étrangère, elles peuvent choisir, ou le tribunal peut ordonner l'usage de cette langue pour tout ou partie du procès. Cela peut concerner l'examen par le tribunal d'un document particulier ou l'audition d'un témoin dans sa langue maternelle.

P-6B Souvent, lors d'un litige transnational, les témoins et les experts ne parlent pas la langue dans laquelle la procédure se déroule. Dans un tel cas, la traduction est nécessaire au tribunal et aux autres parties. Les témoignages peuvent être présentés par écrit à l'aide d'un traducteur, dont la partie qui a présenté le témoignage prend en charge les honoraires, à moins que le tribunal n'en décide autrement. Ou bien le témoin peut être interrogé au moment de sa déposition, sur accord des parties ou sur ordre du tribunal. La déposition peut alors être traduite et soumise au tribunal lors de l'audience.

7. Célérité de la justice

7.1 Le tribunal tranche le litige dans un délai raisonnable.

7.2 A cette fin, les parties doivent coopérer avec le tribunal et ont le droit d'être raisonnablement consultées pour l'établissement du calendrier de la procédure. Les règles de procédure et les ordonnances du tribunal peuvent fixer le calendrier prévisionnel et impartir des délais; des sanctions peuvent être prévues à l'encontre des parties ou de leurs avocats qui, sans motif légitime, ne respecteraient pas de telles obligations.

Commentaire:

P-7A Dans tous les systèmes juridiques le tribunal a le devoir d'avancer vers la solution du différend. Ce principe est généralement évoqué par la formule: ⟪*justice delayed is justice denied*⟫. Certains systèmes prévoient un calendrier précisant les différentes étapes de la procédure.

P-7B La possibilité de pouvoir obtenir rapidement une décision judiciaire est un aspect de l'accès à la justice; il est aussi considéré comme un droit fondamental; il doit toutefois être compatible avec le droit pour une partie de pouvoir organiser et présenter sa défense.

8. Mesures provisoires et conservatoires

8.1 Le tribunal peut accorder une mesure provisoire lorsque cela est nécessaire pour assurer l'efficacité de la décision à intervenir, ou pour protéger ou régler la situation présente La mesure provisoire est prononcée dans le respect du principe de proportionnalité.

8.2 Un tribunal peut accorder une mesure provisoire sans notification préalable uniquement si l'urgence et de prépondérantes raisons d'équité l'exigent. Le demandeur doit communiquer tous les éléments de faits et moyens de droit que le juge doit équitablement prendre en considération. Une personne à l'encontre de laquelle

une telle ordonnance *ex parte* a été rendue doit pouvoir contester dans les délais les plus brefs possibles le bien-fondé de l'ordonnance.

8.3 **Le requérant qui a sollicité du juge l'octroi d'une mesure provisoire est tenu d'indemniser l'adversaire contre lequel a été rendue l'ordonnance si le tribunal considère par la suite que l'ordonnance n'était pas fondée. Lorsque cela lui paraît nécessaire, le tribunal peut exiger du requérant qu'il dépose une garantie ou qu'il assume de façon formelle une telle obligation d'indemnisation.**

Commentaire:

P-8A L'expression «mesure provisoire» inclut le concept d' «ordonnance», ou d' «*injunction*», à savoir l'ordre du tribunal de faire ou de ne pas faire, comme par exemple, l'obligation de préserver la propriété du bien en l'état. Le Principe 8.1 autorise ainsi les ordonnances de faire (qui exigent l'accomplissement d'un acte) ou de ne pas faire (qui interdisent un acte spécifique ou une série d'actions). Cette expression est utilisée dans une acception large, qui inclut les saisies-arrêt et les saisies conservatoires, et toute autre directive du tribunal. L'expression «régler», inclut la possibilité d'améliorer le différend sous-jacent. C'est le cas par exemple des mesures de gestion d'une société pendant l'instance qui oppose deux associés. La possibilité, pour le tribunal, d'accorder des mesures telles que les saisies, s'apprécie d'après le droit du for ainsi que les principes de droit international applicable. Le tribunal peut accorder des mesures provisoires pour faciliter le déroulement d'une procédure arbitrale, ou pour faire exécuter une mesure provisoire accordée par un arbitre, ou exiger que la partie visée par l'ordonnance communique la localisation et la composition de son patrimoine.

P-8B Les Principes 5.8 et 8.2 autorisent le tribunal à rendre une ordonnance sans notification préalable à la personne contre laquelle celle-ci a été rendue, lorsqu'une «nécessité urgente» l'exige. Cette «nécessité urgente», qui constitue la justification des ordonnances *ex parte*, est un concept qui est utilisé dans une acception concrète, tout comme celui de la prépondérance de considérations d'équité. Cette dernière expression correspond, dans le langage des pays de *common law*, au concept de «*balance of equities*». L'appréciation des éléments d'équité doit prendre en compte le poids des arguments du demandeur, l'intérêt public le cas échéant, l'urgence du besoin d'une protection provisoire, et les charges pratiques qui découleraient de l'octroi d'une telle mesure. Une telle ordonnance est généralement connue sous le nom d'ordonnance *ex parte*. Voir le Principe 1.4.

P-8C Lors de l'examen de la demande d'une partie, qui sollicite l'octroi d'une mesure *ex parte*, le tribunal est appelé à apprécier si le demandeur a, de façon raisonnable et spécifique, démontré qu'une telle mesure est sollicitée pour prévenir un dommage irréparable dans la situation faisant l'objet du litige, et qu'il serait imprudent que le tribunal entende le défendeur avant de l'octroyer. C'est à la partie qui sollicite la délivrance d'une ordonnance sur requête de prouver que de telles conditions sont réunies. Toutefois, dès que possible, l'autre partie ou la personne à l'encontre de laquelle l'ordonnance a été délivrée doit recevoir une notification de l'ordonnance et avoir la possibilité d'exiger le réexamen dans un bref délai de la mesure accordée, ainsi que la possibilité de présenter de nouveaux éléments de preuve. Voir le Principe 8.2.

P-8D Les règles de procédure exigent généralement que la partie qui sollicite la délivrance d'une mesure *ex parte* fournisse au tribunal tous les éléments de droit et de fait sur lesquelles elle fonde sa demande, que le tribunal prendra en compte, y compris les éléments qui ne soutiennent pas ses intérêts et qui sont favorables à son adversaire. Le défaut de communiquer ces éléments constitue un motif valable pour refuser la délivrance d'une telle mesure et pour engager la responsabilité de la partie requérante. Dans certains systèmes, le fait pour le tribunal d'accorder des dommages-intérêts en raison d'une ordonnance rendue de façon infondée ne reflète pas nécessairement la solution du litige au fond.

P-8E Après avoir entendu les intéressés, le tribunal peut accorder, annuler, renouveler, ou modifier une ordonnance. Si le tribunal a refusé de délivrer une ordonnance *ex parte*, il peut néanmoins délivrer une ordonnance à l'issue d'une audience. Si le tribunal a préalablement délivré une ordonnance *ex parte*, il peut renouveler ou modifier son ordonnance à la lumière des arguments développés lors de l'audience. La charge de prouver que l'ordonnance est justifiée repose sur la partie qui la sollicite.

P-8F Le Principe 8.3 autorise le tribunal à exiger le dépôt d'une garantie ou toute autre indemnisation, pour garantir les troubles ou le préjudice découlant d'une ordonnance. Les détails d'une telle indemnisation devraient être déterminés par la loi du for. Une telle obligation d'indemniser devrait être expresse et non simplement présumée, et pourrait être formalisée par un cautionnement accordé par un tiers.

P-8G À l'encontre d'une ordonnance délivrée selon ce Principe, il est possible de présenter, dans certains systèmes juridiques, un appel immédiat, selon les règles de procédure du for. Dans certains pays, une telle ordonnance a une durée limitée et son réexamen doit être effectué par le tribunal de première instance, avant un éventuel recours en appel. La garantie de la possibilité d'un réexamen est particulièrement nécessaire lorsqu'il s'agit d'une mesure *ex parte*. L'appel, devant la juridiction de deuxième degré, se déroule de façon différente suivant les systèmes juridiques. Toutefois, il faudrait aussi tenir compte du fait qu'un tel réexamen peut entraîner une perte de temps ou des abus de procédure.

9. Déroulement du procès

9.1 Le procès est normalement organisé en trois phases: la phase introductive, la phase intermédiaire et la phase finale.

9.2 Lors de la phase introductive, les parties doivent présenter dans les écritures leurs demandes, défenses et autres affirmations et faire état de leurs principaux éléments de preuve.

9.3 Dans la phase intermédiaire, le tribunal, si nécessaire

9.3.1 Détermine, lors de conférences, le déroulement de la procédure;

9.3.2 Établit le calendrier de déroulement de la procédure;

9.3.3 Apprécie les questions qui se prêtent à un examen préalable, telles que les questions de compétence, de mesures provisoires ou de prescription;

9.3.4 Apprécie les questions d'accessibilité, d'admission, de communication et d'échange des moyens de preuve;

9.3.5 Identifie les questions pouvant faire l'objet d'une décision préalable;

9.3.6 Ordonne l'administration de la preuve.

9.4 Lors de la phase finale, les éléments de preuve qui n'ont pas encore été communiqués au tribunal selon les modalités du Principe 9.3.6 sont généralement présentés dans une audience finale concentrée au cours de laquelle les parties présentent leurs conclusions finales.

Commentaire:

P-9A La notion de «déroulement» d'une procédure doit faire l'objet d'une application souple en fonction de la nature de chaque espèce. Ainsi par exemple, si cela est utile, le juge a le pouvoir discrétionnaire de tenir une conférence lors de la phase introductive et d'en tenir plusieurs au fur et à mesure de la progression de l'affaire.

P-9B Un calendrier méthodique facilite le déroulement rapide du litige. Un dialogue entre le tribunal et les avocats des parties facilite l'adoption d'un calendrier concret et des auditions méthodiques. Voir Principe 14.2 et Commentaire *P-14A*.

P-9C Traditionnellement, les juridictions des pays de droit civil avaient recours à une suite de courtes audiences, alors que celles des pays de *common law* organisaient la procédure avec une audience «finale». Cependant, dans la pratique moderne, les tribunaux des deux systèmes de droit organisent des audiences préliminaires, et les systèmes de droit civil ont de plus en plus recours à une audience finale concentrée pour la plupart des moyens de preuve concernant le bien fondé de la demande.

P-9D Dans les systèmes de *common law*, une procédure permettant de parvenir à des solutions préalables est la requête de «*summary judgment*», qui peut concerner des questions purement factuelles ou juridiques. Les tribunaux de droit civil connaissent des procédures similaires, lors de la phase intermédiaire.

P-9E Dans la plupart des systèmes l'exception d'incompétence doit être soulevée par la partie concernée, au début de l'instance, sous peine de forclusion. Il est important, d'un point de vue pratique, que dans un litige international les questions de compétence soient soulevées rapidement.

10. Principe dispositif

10.1 L'instance est introduite par la demande d'un plaideur; le tribunal ne peut se saisir d'office.

10.2 Le dépôt de la demande auprès du tribunal constitue le moment déterminant le calcul des délais de prescription, la litispendance et les autres délais.

10.3 L'objet du litige est déterminé par les demandes et défenses des parties, telles que présentées dans l'acte introductif d'instance et dans les conclusions en défense, y compris dans les modifications qui leur sont apportées.

10.4 Si elle justifie de motifs sérieux, une partie a le droit de modifier ses demandes ou défenses, en le notifiant aux autres parties. Cette modification ne doit pas retarder de façon déraisonnable la procédure ni avoir pour conséquence quelque autre injustice.

10.5 Les parties ont le droit de mettre volontairement un terme à l'instance ou de la modifier, par désistement, acquiescement, admission, ou accord amiable. Une partie ne peut mettre unilatéralement

un terme à son action ou la modifier si cela cause un préjudice à son adversaire.

Commentaire:

P-10A Tous les systèmes juridiques modernes reconnaissent le principe selon lequel ce sont les parties qui définissent le champ du litige et ses éléments factuels. C'est dans le cadre défini par les parties que le tribunal exerce sa responsabilité de statuer correctement sur le litige. Voir Principes 10.3 et 28.2. Les Principes exigent des parties qu'elles fournissent des moyens de fait et de droit détaillés dans leurs conclusions. Voir Principe 11.3. Cette pratique est contraire au système américain du ⟪*notice pleading*⟫.

P-10B Tous les systèmes juridiques prévoient une date limite pour l'introduction de l'instance, dans le cadre des règles appelées ⟪*statutes of limitation*⟫ dans les systèmes de *common law* et délais de prescription dans les pays de droit civil. La notification doit être effectuée, ou du moins tentée, dans le délai prévu par le droit du for. La plupart des systèmes permettent aux parties de soulever une exception devant le tribunal, si la notification n'a pas été effectuée dans un tel délai.

P-10C Le droit de modifier ses prétentions est extrêmement limité dans certains systèmes juridiques. Toutefois, et particulièrement dans les litiges transnationaux, il convient d'accorder une certaine flexibilité aux parties, notamment en présence d'éléments de preuve nouveaux ou inattendus. Les conséquences défavorables que le droit de modifier ses prétentions peut avoir sur les autres parties peuvent être évitées ou limitées par un renvoi ou un ajournement; elles peuvent aussi être compensées de façon adéquate par un remboursement de frais et dépens.

P-10D La loi du for peut autoriser le demandeur à introduire une nouvelle demande par modification de la première même si les délais sont expirés (prescription) à condition toutefois que cette nouvelle demande découle substantiellement des mêmes faits que ceux qui fondent la demande initiale.

P-10E La plupart des systèmes ne permettent pas au demandeur de se désister, après la phase initiale, si le défendeur s'y oppose.

11. Devoirs des parties et de leurs avocats

11.1 Les parties et leurs avocats doivent se conduire loyalement dans leurs relations avec le tribunal et les autres parties.

11.2 Les parties partagent avec le tribunal la charge de favoriser une solution du litige équitable, efficace et raisonnablement rapide. Les parties doivent s'abstenir de tout abus de procédure, comme

le fait d'influencer les témoins ou de détruire des éléments de preuve.

11.3 **Dans la phase introductive, les parties doivent présenter, de façon raisonnablement détaillée, les faits allégués et les moyens de droit, la mesure demandée, en décrivant de façon suffisamment précise les moyens de preuve disponibles qui les soutiennent. Lorsque des motifs sérieux justifient l'incapacité pour une partie de fournir des détails raisonnables sur les faits qu'elle invoque ou des précisions suffisantes sur ses moyens de preuve, le tribunal prend en considération la possibilité que des faits ou preuves nécessaires soient produits ultérieurement au cours de l'instance.**

11.4 **En l'absence de contestation en temps utile par une partie d'un moyen soulevé par la partie adverse, le tribunal peut considérer que ledit moyen a été admis ou accepté.**

11.5 **Les avocats des parties sont tenus professionnellement d'aider leurs clients à respecter leurs obligations procédurales.**

Commentaire:

P-11A Une partie ne doit pas formuler de demande, défense, requête, réponse ou toute autre initiative qui ne serait pas susceptible d'être soutenue en fait et en droit. Dans certaines circonstances, l'absence de respect de cette exigence peut être considérée comme un abus de procédure et conduire à des sanctions et amendes à l'encontre de la partie responsable de cette violation. Toutefois, l'obligation de bonne foi n'empêche pas une partie de faire des efforts raisonnables en vue d'étendre un concept existant à des circonstances différentes. Dans certaines situations, une demande ou défense futile ou vexatoire peut être considérée comme un abus envers le tribunal et peut entraîner un jugement par défaut à l'encontre du demandeur ou du défendeur, de même que des sanctions et amendes.

P-11B Le Principe 11.3 exige des parties qu'elle détaillent dans leurs conclusions leurs moyens de fait, contrairement à la procédure de ⟪*notice pleading*⟫ admise dans les Règles fédérales de Procédure civile des États-Unis. L'exigence de ⟪décrire de façon suffisante⟫ consiste généralement dans l'obligation d'identifier les principaux documents sur lesquels se fonde la demande ou la défense, et de présenter de façon synthétique les témoignages attendus.Voir le Principe 16.

P-11C Le fait, pour une partie, de ne pas contester les allégations de la partie adverse permet généralement de considérer qu'elle les admet. Voir aussi le Principe 21.3.

P-11D Il est universellement admis que l'avocat a des responsabilités professionnelles et déontologiques en ce qui concerne les rapports loyaux avec toutes les parties, leurs avocats, les témoins et le tribunal.

12. Jonction d'instance et intervention

12.1 Une partie peut formuler toutes demandes à l'encontre de son adversaire ou d'un tiers soumis à l'autorité du tribunal, à condition que la demande présente un lien substantiel avec l'objet initial du litige.

12.2 Toute personne justifiant d'un intérêt présentant un lien substantiel avec l'objet du litige a la faculté d'intervenir. Le tribunal, d'office ou à la demande d'une partie, peut informer une partie justifiant d'un tel intérêt en l'invitant à intervenir. Une intervention peut être autorisée par le tribunal à moins qu'elle n'ait pour conséquence de retarder ou de compliquer la procédure de façon excessive ou ne cause inéquitablement tout autre préjudice à une partie. La loi du for peut autoriser une intervention en appel.

12.3 Lorsque cela lui paraît justifié, le tribunal peut autoriser une personne à se substituer à une partie ou à continuer l'action en cours d'instance.

12.4 En principe, une partie qui se joint à la procédure bénéficie des mêmes droits et est soumise aux mêmes obligations de participation et de coopération que les parties initiales. L'étendue de ces droits et obligations peut dépendre du fondement, du moment et des circonstances de l'intervention ou de la jonction d'instances.

12.5 Le tribunal peut ordonner la disjonction de demandes, questions ou parties, ou les joindre à d'autres instances dans un souci d'équité ou afin d'améliorer l'efficacité de l'organisation de la procédure et de la décision, ou encore dans l'intérêt de la justice. Cette compétence s'étend aux parties ou aux demandes qui ne relèvent pas du champ d'application des présents Principes.

Commentaire:

P-12A Le Principe 12.1 reconnaît le droit très large de formuler toute demande possible à l'encontre d'une autre partie, si les prétentions se rapportent à la même opération commerciale ou au même événement.

P-12B Les règles relatives à la compétence à l'égard des tiers sont très variables selon les pays. Dans les pays de droit civil, une prétention valable émanant d'un tiers constitue en soi-même un fondement de compétence, alors que dans certains pays de *common law*, le tiers doit relever de la compétence du tribunal de façon autonome. Le Principe 12.1 exige un fondement autonome de compétence du tribunal.

P-12C Le Principe autorise les jonctions d'instance concernant des parties revendiquant le même bien; il ne permet ni n'interdit les 《*class actions*》 (actions de groupe).

P-12D L'invitation à intervenir constitue pour un tiers une opportunité de rejoindre l'instance. Les effets d'un éventuel refus sont régis par la loi du for. Avant d'inviter un tiers à intervenir, le tribunal doit consulter les parties.

P-12E La loi du for est compétente pour régler les questions de remplacement ou d'adjonction d'une partie, au titre du droit matériel ou processuel du for, dans plusieurs circonstances telles que le décès, la cession de créance, la fusion de société, la faillite, la subrogation. La participation peut être accordée de façon limitée, comme par exemple la possibilité de présenter un élément de preuve sans pour autant devenir une partie à part entière.

P-12F En toute hypothèse, le tribunal est habilité à diviser les demandes et questions à traiter ou à les rassembler en fonction de leur objet et des parties concernées.

13. Avis d'un *amicus curiae*

Le tribunal, après consultation des parties, peut accepter de recevoir de tierces personnes des avis écrits relatifs à des questions juridiques importantes du procès et des informations sur le contexte général du litige. Le tribunal peut également solliciter un tel avis. Avant que le tribunal prenne en compte l'avis de l' *amicus curiae*, les parties doivent avoir la possibilité de soumettre au tribunal leurs observations écrites sur le contenu de cet avis.

Commentaire:

P-13A L'avis d'un *amicus curiae* est un moyen utile par lequel un tiers fournit au tribunal des informations et une analyse juridique qui peuvent faciliter une solution juste et bien fondée du litige. Un tel avis peut émaner d'une personne n'ayant aucun intérêt dans le litige ou au contraire d'une personne plus partisane. Toute personne peut être autorisée à formuler un tel avis, nonobstant l'absence d'un intérêt juridique suffisant pour une intervention en cause. L'avis écrit peut être complété, à la libre appréciation du tribunal, par une présentation orale devant ce dernier.

P-13B Le tribunal apprécie librement si l'avis doit être pris en compte. Il peut exiger que soit énoncé l'intérêt de l'*amicus curiae* proposé. Le tribunal peut refuser qu'un avis soit donné si celui-ci ne facilite matériellement en aucune façon la résolution du litige. Une vigilance doit être exercée afin que le mécanisme de l'*amicus curiae* n'interfère pas avec l'indépendance du tribunal. Voir Principe 1.1. Le tribunal peut inviter un tiers à présenter son avis. L'*amicus curiae* ne devient pas partie au litige; il est seulement un commentateur actif. Des affirmations de fait contenues dans l'avis de l'*amicus curiae* ne constituent pas des éléments probatoires dans le litige.

P-13C Dans les pays de droit civil, il n'existe pas de pratique établie permettant à des tiers sans intérêt juridique à la solution du litige de participer à la procédure, bien que la jurisprudence de certains pays tels que la France ait développé des institutions similaires. Par voie de conséquence, la plupart des pays de droit civil n'ont aucune pratique admettant la présentation au tribunal d'avis d'*amici curiae*. Néanmoins, un tel avis est un instrument utile, notamment dans les litiges présentant une grande importance publique.

P-13D Le Principe 13 n'autorise pas les tiers à présenter des déclarations écrites relatives à des faits du litige. Il ne concerne que la présentation de données, d'informations sur le contexte général du litige, de remarques, analyses juridiques ou toutes autres considérations pouvant s'avérer utiles en vue d'une solution correcte et équitable du litige. Ainsi par exemple, une organisation commerciale pourrait donner au tribunal des informations sur des usages spéciaux des affaires.

P-13E Les parties doivent bénéficier de la possibilité de soumettre des observations écrites relatives aux questions abordées dans l'avis de l'*amicus curiae*, avant que cet avis puisse être pris en compte par le tribunal.

14. L'office du juge dans la conduite de l'instance

14.1 Le tribunal conduit activement l'instance le plut tôt possible dans la procédure. Il exerce un pouvoir d'appréciation afin de pouvoir mettre fin au litige loyalement, de façon efficace et dans un délai raisonnable. Le caractère transnational du litige doit être pris en compte.

14.2 Dans la limite du raisonnable, le tribunal conduit l'instance en collaboration avec les parties.

14.3 Le tribunal détermine l'ordre dans lequel les questions doivent être traitées et établit un calendrier comprenant dates et délais pour chaque étape de la procédure. Le tribunal peut modifier ces dispositions.

Commentaire:

P-14A De nombreux systèmes juridictionnels possèdent des règles relatives à la direction de l'instance. Voir Principe 7.2. La conduite de l'instance par le tribunal sera plus équitable et efficace si elle se fait après consultation des parties. Voir également le commentaire P-9A.

P-14B Le Principe 14.3 est particulièrement important dans les affaires complexes. En pratique, des calendriers et autres mesures sont moins nécessaires dans les affaires simples; le tribunal doit néanmoins toujours préciser les détails du déroulement de la procédure.

15. Jugement de rejet et jugement par défaut

15.1 Un jugement de rejet est en principe rendu à l'encontre du demandeur qui, sans motif légitime, ne poursuit pas la procédure qu'il a engagée. Avant de prononcer un tel jugement, le tribunal doit raisonnablement en avertir le demandeur.

15.2 Un jugement par défaut est en principe rendu à l'encontre du défendeur ou d'une autre partie qui, sans motif légitime, s'abstient de comparaître ou de répondre dans les délais prescrits.

15.3 Avant de prononcer un jugement par défaut, le tribunal doit vérifier que:

15.3.1 Le tribunal est compétent à l'égard de la partie à l'encontre de laquelle la décision doit être rendue;

15.3.2 Les règles de notification ont bien été respectées et que la partie a bénéficié d'un délai suffisant pour répondre.

15.3.3 La demande est raisonnablement soutenue par des faits et des preuves disponibles et est juridiquement fondée, y compris une demande en dommages-intérêts ainsi que toute demande en matière de frais de procédure.

15.4 Un jugement par défaut ne peut accorder des sommes supérieures ou prononcer des sanctions plus sévères que ce qui était demandé dans l'acte introductif d'instance.

15.5 Tout jugement de rejet ou par défaut peut faire l'objet d'un appel ou d'un recours en annulation.

15.6 Toute partie qui, de quelque autre manière que ce soit, ne respecte pas son obligation de participer à la procédure peut faire l'objet de sanctions conformément au Principe 17.

Commentaire:

P-15A Un jugement par défaut permet de mettre fin au différend en l'absence de contestation. Il s'agit d'un mécanisme destiné à contraindre une partie à reconnaître l'autorité du tribunal. Si le tribunal n'était pas habilité à rendre un jugement par défaut, un défendeur pourrait échapper à ses responsabilités simplement en s'abstenant de participer au procès et en contestant par la suite la validité du jugement. Le désistement du demandeur, qui s'abstient de poursuivre l'instance, est connu, dans la terminologie des pays de *common law*, comme défaut de poursuite de l'instance (《*failure to prosecute*》) et conduit à une décision de rejet de la demande (《*involuntary dismissal*》) qui est équivalent à un jugement par défaut. Voir les Principes 11.4 et 17.3.

P-15B Une partie qui comparaît après l'expiration des délais prescrits, mais avant le prononcé du jugement, peut être autorisée, en cas d'excuse justifiée, à présenter sa défense, mais le tribunal peut ordonner une compensation des coûts que ce retard a occasionnés à son adversaire. En prenant une telle décision, le tribunal doit prendre en compte les motifs avancés par la partie, qui ont provoqué son défaut de comparution ou son défaut de participation à la procédure après avoir répondu. Ainsi par exemple, une partie peut ne pas avoir participé au procès, faute d'avoir reçu véritablement notification, ou bien parce que son droit national l'a empêchée de comparaître en raison d'une hostilité entre les deux États.

P-15C Avant de prononcer un jugement par défaut, le tribunal doit faire preuve d'une attention particulière, puisque le défendeur aurait pu ne pas recevoir notification de l'instance, ou se méprendre quant à la nécessité de répondre. Plusieurs procédures nationales imposent qu'à défaut de comparution du défendeur, ce dernier reçoive notification de l'intention du tribunal de prononcer un jugement par défaut.

P-15D Lorsque le tribunal apprécie si la demande est raisonnablement soutenue par des preuves disponibles et est juridiquement fondée au sens du Principe 15.3.3, il n'est pas tenu d'examiner de façon exhaustive le fond du litige. Le juge doit simplement décider si un jugement par défaut serait conciliable avec les faits et les preuves disponibles et légalement justifié. Pour ce faire, le juge doit apprécier de façon critique les preuves au soutien de la demande. Le juge peut exiger la production de preuves supplémentaires ou prévoir une audience dédiée à l'examen des éléments probatoires.

P-15E Le Principe 15.4 limite le jugement par défaut au montant et à la sanction demandés dans l'acte introductif d'instance. Dans les systèmes de droit civil, une telle restriction ne fait que reprendre celle, générale, qui est applicable dans tout litige même lorsque toutes les parties comparaissent (prohibition de l'*infra* et de l'*ultra petita*). Dans les systèmes de *common law*, une telle restriction ne s'applique pas dans les procédures où toutes les parties comparaissent; elle est en revanche reconnue de façon générale en cas de défaut. Cette restriction permet au défendeur de se dispenser des coûts de la défense sans prendre le risque de voir sa responsabilité plus lourdement engagée que cela n'avait été demandé dans l'acte introductif d'instance.

P-15F En vertu du Principe 5.3, le jugement par défaut ou le jugement de rejet doit être signifié sans délai aux parties. Si les conditions permettant au tribunal de prononcer un jugement par défaut ne sont pas réunies, la partie subissant un grief peut former un appel ou demander que le jugement soit infirmé, selon le droit du for. Chaque système prévoit des moyens pour former un recours à l'encontre d'un jugement par défaut délivré en violation des règles en matière de défaut. Dans certains systèmes juridiques, y compris dans la plupart des systèmes de *common law*, un tel recours est d'abord formé devant la juridiction de première instance; dans d'autres, y compris dans certains systèmes de droit civil, devant la juridiction d'appel. Les présents Principes renvoient sur ce point à la loi du for.

P-15G La partie défaillante doit pouvoir, dans un délai raisonnable, prouver l'absence de notification préalable ou tout autre motif légitime justifiant sa conduite.

16. Accès aux éléments d'information et à la preuve

16.1 Le tribunal et chaque partie ont en règle générale un accès aux preuves pertinentes pour le litige et non couvertes par une obligation de confidentialité. Font partie de ces preuves les déclarations des parties et les déclarations des témoins, le rapport des experts, les preuves documentaires et les preuves qui résultent de l'examen d'objets, de leur placement sous main de justice ou, dans certains cas, de l'examen physique ou mental d'une personne. Les parties ont le droit de présenter des déclarations ayant une valeur probatoire.

16.2 Si une partie en fait la demande en temps utile, le tribunal ordonne la production de toutes preuves pertinentes, non couvertes par des règles de confidentialité et raisonnablement identifiées qui se trouvent en possession ou sous le contrôle d'une partie ou – si cela apparaît nécessaire et justifié – d'un tiers. La production d'un élément de preuve ne peut être écartée au motif qu'elle serait défavorable à une partie ou à la personne requise.

16.3 Afin de faciliter l'accès aux informations, l'avocat d'une partie peut recueillir la déposition spontanée d'un tiers susceptible de témoigner.

16.4 Les parties, les témoins et les experts sont entendus selon les règles de l'État du for. Une partie a le droit de poser directement des questions additionnelles à une autre partie, à un témoin ou à un expert si le juge ou l'adversaire procède à l'audition en premier.

16.5 Une personne qui produit des éléments de preuve dont elle dispose, qu'elle soit partie ou non à l'instance, peut requérir du tribunal qu'il empêche par ordonnance une révélation abusive d'informations confidentielles.

16.6 Le tribunal apprécie librement les éléments de preuve sans tenir compte de façon injustifiée de leur nature ou de leur origine.

Commentaire:

P-16A La preuve ⟪*pertinente*⟫ est un élément probatoire qui soutient, contredit ou affaiblit une affirmation de fait contestée dans la procédure. Une partie ne doit pas être autorisée à conduire des ⟪*fishing expeditions*⟫ afin de développer un litige qui ne se fonde sur aucun élément; en revanche, la partie adverse peut se voir enjoindre de produire une preuve qui est sous son contrôle. Les Principes permettent ainsi une ⟪*discovery*⟫ (communication) limitée sous le contrôle du tribunal. Les tiers sont en principe également tenus de coopérer.

P-16B Dans certains systèmes juridiques, les déclarations d'une partie ne sont pas admises comme preuve ou bien se voient accorder une valeur probatoire réduite. Le Principe 16.1 reconnaît aux déclarations des parties la même valeur probatoire potentielle qu'à celles de tous témoins, mais le tribunal, pour apprécier ce mode de preuve, peut prendre en compte les intérêts de la partie dans le litige.

P-16C Au regard du Principe 16.2, la partie demandant la production de pièces peut être tenue de compenser les frais du tiers résultant de cette production.

P-16D Dans certains systèmes juridiques, le fait pour un avocat de communiquer avec un témoin potentiel constitue en principe une violation de règles déontologiques ou procédurales. La violation d'une telle règle est considérée comme ⟪*entachant*⟫ le témoignage. Toutefois, cette façon de voir peut entraver l'accès à des preuves qui sont admises dans d'autres systèmes juridiques et porter atteinte à une bonne préparation de la production des preuves.

P-16E L'examen physique ou mental d'une personne peut être opportun, s'il est nécessaire et fiable et si sa valeur probatoire excède les effets préjudiciables de l'admission de cette preuve.

P-16F Conformément au Principe 16.4, l'audition des parties, des témoins et des experts se déroule selon les règles de l'État du for, l'interrogatoire étant conduit d'abord soit par les parties, soit par le juge. En tout cas, une partie a le droit de poser des questions additionnelles en s'adressant directement à la partie adverse ou au témoin. Le droit d'une partie de poser directement des questions à une partie adverse ou à un témoin qui n'est pas partie à l'instance, est d'importance centrale et est aujourd'hui reconnu dans la plupart des systèmes juridiques. De façon similaire, une partie doit être admise à poser des questions additionnelles à un témoin (y compris à une partie) qui aurait été initialement interrogé par le tribunal.

P-16G Le Principe 16.6 signifie qu'aucune valeur juridique particulière, qu'elle soit positive ou négative, ne saurait être attribuée à quelque mode de preuve que ce soit (par exemple au témoignage d'un témoin intéressé au litige). Toutefois, ce Principe n'interfère pas avec les lois nationales qui exigent des formes particulières pour certains actes juridiques, telles qu'un écrit pour un contrat portant sur un immeuble.

P-16H Des sanctions peuvent être prononcées en cas de défaut de production d'une preuve apparaissant raisonnablement comme étant sous le contrôle d'une partie ou en sa possession, ou bien en cas d'absence de coopération d'une partie dans l'administration de la preuve telle que requise par les règles de procédure. Voir Principes 17 et 21.3.

P-16I Les problèmes spécifiques d'administration de la preuve concernant les procès avec jury ne sont pas couverts par ces Principes.

17. Sanctions

17.1 Le tribunal peut sanctionner les parties, leurs avocats ou les tiers qui s'abstiennent ou refusent de déférer aux injonctions du tribunal concernant l'instance.

17.2 Les sanctions, qui doivent être raisonnables et proportionnées à l'importance de la question concernée ainsi qu'au dommage causé, tiennent compte de l'étendue de la participation et de l'intention manifeste des personnes impliquées.

17.3 Peuvent être considérées comme des sanctions appropriées à l'encontre des parties: le fait de tirer des conséquences défavorables, le rejet total ou partiel de la demande ou de la défense, le jugement par défaut, la suspension de l'instance, la condamnation aux frais et dépens au delà de celle prévue par les règles normalement applicables. Les sanctions qui peuvent être appropriées à l'encontre de parties ou de tiers comprennent les sanctions pécuniaires

telles que les amendes ou les astreintes. Les avocats peuvent notamment se voir condamner aux frais de la procédure.

17.4 **Le droit du for peut prévoir des sanctions supplémentaires, telles que la responsabilité pénale d'une partie ou d'un tiers ayant commis une faute grave, par exemple en cas de faux témoignage, de violence ou de tentative d'intimidation.**

Commentaire:

P-17A Les sanctions qu'un tribunal est autorisé à prononcer selon la loi du for varient selon les systèmes juridiques. Les présents Principes ne conduisent pas à autoriser des sanctions que la loi du for n'admettrait pas.

P-17B Dans tous les systèmes juridiques, le tribunal peut tirer des conséquences défavorables du défaut d'une partie à faire progresser la procédure ou à répondre de la manière requise. Voir Principe 21.3. Il peut en outre, à titre de sanction supplémentaire, rejeter la demande ou rendre un jugement par défaut. Voir Principes 5.1 et 15. Dans les pays de *common law*, le tribunal peut, dans diverses circonstances, placer une partie ou son avocat sous «*contempt of court*». Tous les systèmes juridiques prévoient des mesures coercitives directes à l'encontre des parties.

18. **Confidentialité et immunité**

18.1 **En matière de divulgation des preuves ou d'autres informations doivent être respectés le devoir de confidentialité qui incombe aux parties et aux tiers, les immunités dont ils bénéficient ainsi que les autres règles protectrices similaires.**

18.2 **Lorsqu'il décide de tirer des conséquences défavorables à une partie ou d'imposer d'autres sanctions indirectes, le tribunal vérifie si ces protections peuvent justifier l'absence de production de preuve par cette partie.**

18.3 **Le tribunal reconnaît ces protections lorsqu'il use de son pouvoir de prononcer des sanctions directes pour imposer à une partie ou un tiers la divulgation de preuves ou d'autres informations.**

Commentaire:

P-18A Tous les systèmes juridiques reconnaissent divers devoirs de confidentialité et immunités permettant de ne pas être contraint à fournir une preuve: il en va ainsi du droit de ne pas s'auto-incriminer, du secret professionnel, du respect de la vie privée ainsi que des droits des époux ou des membres de la famille d'être dispensés de déposer. De telles règles protègent des intérêts importants, mais elles peuvent faire obstacle à l'établissement des faits. Les bases dogmatiques et techniques de ces protections varient selon les systèmes juridiques, de même que les conséquences légales de la reconnaissance de ces devoirs et immunités. Lors de l'application de telles règles, des difficultés de choix de la loi peuvent se présenter.

P-18B La valeur accordée à différents droits ou devoirs de confidentialité varie selon les systèmes juridiques; la portée de leur invocation peut également varier selon le contexte spécifique du litige. Ces éléments jouent un rôle lorsque le tribunal envisage de tirer des conséquences défavorables de l'absence de production de preuve par une partie.

P-18C Les Principes 18.2 et 18.3 traduisent une distinction entre sanctions directes et sanctions indirectes. Les sanctions directes comprennent les amendes, les astreintes, le *contempts of court* ou l'emprisonnement. Les sanctions indirectes incluent le fait de tirer des conséquences défavorables, le jugement par défaut et le rejet de la demande ou de la défense. Le tribunal apprécie souverainement s'il y a lieu d'imposer des sanctions indirectes à une partie invoquant devoir de confidentialité ou immunité, mais il ne doit en principe pas prononcer de sanctions directes à l'encontre d'une partie ou d'un tiers refusant de divulguer des informations protégées par la confidentialité ou une immunité. Une approche similaire de pesée des intérêts peut être adoptée lorsque des dispositions légales mettent obstacle à la coopération pleine et entière d'une partie ou d'un tiers.

P-18D Dans certains systèmes juridiques, le tribunal ne peut pas reconnaître un droit de confidentialité de sa propre initiative, mais doit seulement y faire droit lorsque la partie en bénéficiant l'invoque. Le tribunal doit suivre toute exigence procédurale de la loi du for qui imposerait que le droit ou devoir de confidentialité soit expressément invoqué. Au regard de telles exigences, un droit de confidentialité ou une immunité qui n'aurait pas été invoqué régulièrement dans les délais requis peut être considéré comme ayant fait l'objet d'une renonciation.

19. Dépositions écrites et orales

19.1 Les conclusions, mémoires et moyens de droit sont en principe présentés initialement par écrit. Les parties peuvent toutefois présenter oralement des moyens supplémentaires sur des questions importantes de fond ou de procédure.

19.2 L'audience finale doit se dérouler devant les juges chargés de rendre le jugement.

19.3 Le tribunal fixe les modalités procédurales pour l'administration des preuves testimoniales. En général, les dépositions des parties et des témoins sont reçues oralement, et les rapports des experts par écrit. Le tribunal peut toutefois exiger, après avoir consulté les parties, que la déposition initiale des témoins sera consignée dans un écrit qui devra être communiqué aux parties avant l'audience.

19.4 La déposition orale peut être limitée aux questions additionnelles à la déposition écrite d'un témoin ou au rapport d'un expert.

Commentaire:

P-19A Traditionnellement, tous les systèmes juridiques recevaient les témoignages sous forme orale. La pratique moderne a toutefois tendance à remplacer le témoignage principal d'un témoin par une déclaration écrite. Le Principe 19 permet une souplesse sur ce point. Il envisage que le témoignage puisse être présenté initialement sous forme écrite, la phase orale débutant par les questions additionnelles du tribunal et de la partie adverse. Sur les différentes procédures en matière d'interrogation des témoins, voir Principe 16.4 et le commentaire *P-16E*.

P-19B Les règles de procédure du for peuvent permettre ou exiger la communication électronique des dépositions écrites ou orales. Voir Principe 5.7.

P-19C Dans de nombreux pays de droit civil, l'interrogatoire initial est conduit par le tribunal et les interventions des parties sont limitées, alors que dans les systèmes de *common law*, les rôles du juge et des avocats sont inversés. En tout état de cause, les parties doivent être en mesure de poser directement des questions à un témoin. Voir Principe 16.4.

20. Publicité de la procédure

20.1 En règle générale, les audiences, y compris celles qui sont consacrées à l'administration de la preuve et au prononcé du jugement, sont ouvertes au public. Après consultation des parties, le tribunal peut toutefois ordonner que certaines audiences ou parties d'audience auront lieu à huis clos dans l'intérêt de la justice, de l'ordre public ou du respect de la vie privée.

20.2 Les dossiers du tribunal et les enregistrements réalisés sont publics, ou accessibles de quelque autre façon aux personnes faisant état d'un intérêt légitime ou formulant une demande justifiée de renseignements et ce dans les conditions de la loi du for.

20.3 Dans l'intérêt de la justice, de l'ordre public ou du respect de la vie privée, lorsque la procédure est publique, le juge peut ordonner qu'une partie de celle-ci se déroule à huis clos.

20.4 Les jugements, leurs motifs ainsi que toute autre décision du tribunal sont accessibles au public.

Commentaire:

P-20A La publicité de divers éléments de la procédure fait l'objet d'approches opposées. Dans certains pays de droit civil, les dossiers et registres du tribunal sont en général confidentiels, même si leur accès peut être autorisé en cas de motif légitime. Dans la tradition de *common law* au contraire, les registres sont en général publics. Cette approche insiste sur l'aspect public des procédures judiciaires et la nécessité de transparence, alors que la première met en exergue le droit des parties au respect de leur vie privée. Les présents Principes expriment une préférence pour une procédure publique, avec des exceptions limitées. En règle générale, les dossiers du tribunal et les enregistrements doivent être publics et accessibles au public ainsi qu'aux médias. Les pays dont la tradition est de garder ces dossiers confidentiels devraient au moins permettre aux personnes ayant un intérêt justifié ou formulant une demande justifiée de renseignement, d'y avoir accès.

P-20B Dans certains systèmes juridiques, le tribunal, à la demande d'une partie, peut décider que toute la procédure se déroulera à huis clos, à l'exception du jugement final. Certains systèmes juridiques garantissent constitutionnellement le droit à la publicité de la procédure, tout en prévoyant certaines dérogations pour les domaines tels que le secret des affaires, la sécurité nationale etc. Les procédures arbitrales se déroulent en règle générale à huis clos.

21. Charge de la preuve et conviction du juge

21.1 En principe, il incombe à chaque partie de prouver les faits allégués au soutien de sa prétention.

21.2 Les faits sont prouvés si le tribunal est raisonnablement convaincu de leur véracité.

21.3 Lorsqu'une partie a en sa possession ou sous son contrôle un élément de preuve pertinent que, sans justification, elle refuse de produire, le tribunal peut tirer toute conséquence défavorable de ce refus au regard de la question concernée par l'élément de preuve non produit.

Commentaire:

P-21A L'exigence posée dans le Principe 21.1 est souvent exprimée par la formule «la charge de la preuve suit la charge de l'allégation». La charge de l'allégation est déterminée par la loi, qui traduit en fin de compte l'idée d'équité. La détermination de cette charge relève souvent du droit matériel.

P-21B Le degré contenu dans l'expression «raisonnablement convaincu» est en substance celui qui est retenu dans la plupart des systèmes juridiques. Aux États-Unis et dans certains autres pays, le standard retenu est celui de «*preponderance of the evidence*» (de la probabilité prépondérante) qui fonctionnellement a le même sens.

P-21C Le Principe 21.3 repose sur la règle selon laquelle les deux parties ont le devoir de contribuer de bonne foi à décharger la partie adverse de la charge de la preuve. Voir Principe 11. La possibilité de tirer des conséquences défavorables n'empêche en général pas la partie récalcitrante de produire d'autres éléments de preuve pertinents pour la question concernée. Le fait de tirer de telles conséquences défavorables peut être considéré comme une sanction, voir Principe 17.3; ce peut également être un renversement de la charge de la preuve, voir Principe 21.1.

22. Devoir du juge et des parties dans la détermination des éléments de fait et de droit

22.1 Le tribunal a le devoir de prendre en compte tous les faits et éléments probatoires pertinents pour déterminer le fondement juridique de sa décision, y compris les questions à trancher selon la loi étrangère.

22.2 En donnant aux autres parties l'occasion de présenter leurs observations, le tribunal peut

22.2.1 Permettre à une partie ou l'inviter à modifier ses allégations de fait ou de droit et à présenter en conséquence des moyens de droit ou des preuves additionnels.

22.2.2 Ordonner l'administration d'une preuve qui n'a pas été préalablement suggérée par une partie.

22.2.3 Se fonder sur une analyse juridique ou une interprétation des faits ou des preuves qui n'a pas été proposée par une partie.

22.3 En principe, le tribunal reçoit directement tous les éléments de preuve. Si nécessaire, l'administration et la sauvegarde de la preuve

peuvent toutefois être confiées à un délégué approprié. La preuve sera ensuite prise en compte par le tribunal lors de l'audience finale.

22.4 Lorsqu'une expertise paraît utile, le tribunal peut procéder à la nomination d'un expert dont la mission pourra concerner toute question pertinente, y compris la teneur du droit étranger.

22.4.1 Si les parties conviennent de la nomination d'un expert déterminé, le tribunal doit en principe procéder à sa nomination.

22.4.2 Sur toute question pertinente pour laquelle une expertise paraît indiquée, chaque partie a le droit de produire le rapport d'un expert choisi par elle.

22.4.3 Un expert nommé par le tribunal ou par une partie, doit présenter un rapport complet et objectif sur la question qui lui a été soumise.

Commentaire:

P-22A Il est universellement admis que le tribunal a le devoir de déterminer les questions de droit et de fait nécessaires pour le jugement, et que toutes les parties ont le droit d'être entendues au sujet de la loi applicable et des preuves pertinentes. Voir Principe 5.

P-22B La loi étrangère est une question particulièrement importante dans les litiges transnationaux. Il est possible que le juge ne connaisse pas la teneur de la loi étrangère et doive désigner un expert ou demander aux parties de présenter des observations sur les aspects de droit étranger. Voir Principe 22.4.

P-22C L'objet du litige et les questions à prendre en compte sont déterminés par les demandes et défenses des parties telles que formulées dans leurs écritures. En principe, le juge est tenu par l'objet du litige tel que déterminé par les parties. Cependant, le tribunal, dans l'intérêt de la justice, peut ordonner ou autoriser à une partie des modifications, tout en donnant à la partie adverse un droit de réponse. Voir Principe 10.3.

P-22D L'appel à des experts est usuel dans les litiges complexes. La désignation par le tribunal d'un expert neutre est la pratique dans la plupart des pays de droit civil et de certains systèmes de *common law*. Toutefois, des experts désignés par les parties peuvent également apporter une aide précieuse lors de l'analyse de questions de fait difficiles. Il n'y a en général pas lieu de craindre que la désignation d'experts par les parties ne conduise à une «bataille d'experts» qui rendrait encore plus confuses les questions à trancher. Un tel risque serait de toute façon compensé par la valeur d'une telle preuve. L'expertise peut porter sur des questions de droit étranger.

23. Jugement et motivation

23.1 A l'issue des débats, le tribunal rend dans les plus brefs délais un jugement écrit ou retranscrit par écrit. Le jugement doit préciser la mesure prononcée et, en cas de condamnation pécuniaire, le montant accordé.

23.2 Le jugement doit comprendre les motifs essentiels de fait, de droit et probatoires qui soutiennent la décision.

Commentaire:

P-23A La décision écrite informe les parties de ce qui a été décidé; elle permet également un enregistrement du jugement qui peut être utile lors d'une procédure de reconnaissance ultérieure. Dans divers systèmes juridiques, une motivation est requise par la Constitution nationale ou est considérée comme une garantie fondamentale de l'administration de la justice. Les motifs peuvent consister en des renvois à d'autres documents tels que les conclusions du demandeur en cas de jugement par défaut, ou la transcription des instructions du jury si le verdict émane d'un tel jury. La loi du for peut imposer au tribunal un délai pour rendre son jugement.

P-23B Lorsqu'un jugement ne statue pas sur toutes les demandes et défenses des parties, il doit préciser quelles questions demeurent susceptibles de faire l'objet d'un nouveau procès. Ainsi par exemple, en cas de litige contenant plusieurs demandes, le tribunal peut statuer sur une des demandes (les dommages-intérêts par exemple) et maintenir la procédure ouverte pour trancher les autres questions (par exemple celle d'une injonction).

P-23C Dans certains systèmes juridiques, il est possible de prononcer un jugement avec fixation postérieure du montant pécuniaire ou de tout autre remède accordé, par exemple un calcul pour déterminer le montant des dommages-intérêts ou une précision des termes d'une injonction.

P-23D Voir Principe 5.6, qui impose au tribunal d'examiner toute affirmation de fait ou de droit ainsi que tout élément de preuve qui semblent essentiels.

24. Transaction et conciliation

24.1 Le tribunal, tout en respectant le droit des parties de poursuivre le procès, encourage la transaction et la conciliation lorsqu'elles apparaissent raisonnablement possibles.

24.2 Le tribunal favorise à tout stade de la procédure la participation des parties à des modes alternatifs de résolution du litige.

24.3 Les parties, avant et après le début du procès, coopèrent à toute tentative raisonnable de conciliation ou transaction. Dans sa décision sur les frais de procédure, le tribunal peut tenir compte du refus déraisonnable d'une partie de coopérer ou de son comportement de mauvaise foi lors des tentatives de conciliation ou transaction.

Commentaire:

P-24A La formule «en respectant le droit des parties de poursuivre le procès» signifie que le tribunal ne saurait imposer une transaction aux parties ou les y contraindre. Il peut en revanche, à tout moment approprié, entamer des discussions informelles avec les parties à propos d'une éventuelle transaction ou conciliation. Le juge qui participe à des négociations en vue d'une solution amiable doit éviter de favoriser une partie. Une participation active du juge, comprenant même une proposition d'accord amiable, ne porte toutefois pas atteinte à son impartialité ni ne crée une apparence de partialité.

P-24B Le Principe 24.3 s'écarte de la tradition de certains pays dans lesquels les parties n'ont en général aucune obligation de négocier ou de prendre en compte de quelque autre façon les propositions de transaction de la partie adverse. Le droit du for peut prévoir une procédure amiable pouvant conduire à des sanctions en matière de frais de procédure à l'encontre de la partie qui aura refusé la proposition de transaction de son adversaire. De telles procédures se trouvent par exemple dans les règles procédurales de la province Ontario (Canada) ou encore dans la Part 36 des nouvelles règles anglaises de procédure civile. Il s'agit là de procédures formelles au cours desquelles une partie peut faire une offre définitive de transaction et ainsi obliger la partie adverse à accepter ou à décliner cette offre sous menace de condamnation à des frais additionnels si cette partie n'obtient pas en fin de compte un résultat plus avantageux que l'offre de transaction qui lui avait été faite. Voir également Principe 25.2.

25. Frais et dépens

25.1 La partie gagnante a en principe droit au remboursement de la totalité ou au moins d'une partie substantielle des frais raisonnablement engagés. Le terme «frais» comprend les frais de justice, du personnel judiciaire tels que des greffiers, les frais relatifs par exemple à l'expertise et les honoraires d'avocat.

25.2 A titre exceptionnel, et en présence de motifs évidents, le tribunal peut refuser ou limiter le remboursement des frais accordés à la partie gagnante. Le tribunal peut limiter ce remboursement aux dépenses qui auraient dû être engagées dans un tel litige et sanctionner une partie gagnante qui a soulevé des questions non pertinentes ou qui s'est rendue coupable d'un quelconque abus de procédure. Lorsqu'il prend des décisions concernant les frais, le tribunal peut tenir compte les fautes commises par les parties au cours de l'instance.

Commentaire:

P-25A Le remboursement des frais d'avocat est la règle qui prévaut dans la plupart des systèmes juridiques; elle ne s'applique toutefois pas en Chine, au Japon ni aux États-Unis. Dans certains systèmes juridiques, le montant des frais accordés à la partie gagnante est fixé par un officier judiciaire expérimenté et est souvent inférieur aux honoraires que la partie gagnante doit verser à son avocat. Dans d'autres systèmes, le montant accordé à la partie gagnante est déterminé par les règles en matière d'honoraires. Dans certains types de litiges, la règle de répartition des honoraires est contestée, mais elle est en général considérée comme appropriée dans les différends commerciaux et est en général stipulée dans les contrats commerciaux.

P-25B En vertu du Principe 25.2, le tribunal peut, à titre exceptionnel, refuser tout remboursement de frais à une partie gagnante, ou ne lui accorder qu'un remboursement partiel, ou encore calculer les frais de façon plus généreuse ou plus sévère qu'il ne le ferait en temps normal. Le caractère exceptionnel du Principe 25.2 impose au juge de motiver sa décision sur ce point. Voir également Principe 24.3.

26. Caractère immédiatement exécutoire du jugement

26.1 Le jugement définitif de première instance est en principe immédiatement exécutoire.

26.2 Le tribunal de première instance ou la juridiction d'appel, d'office ou à la demande d'une partie, peut suspendre l'exécution d'un jugement faisant l'objet d'un appel, si cela s'avère nécessaire dans l'intérêt de la justice.

26.3 Le tribunal peut exiger la consignation d'une garantie de la part de l'appelant pour accorder une suspension de l'exécution forcée, ou de la part de l'intimé pour refuser une telle suspension.

Commentaire:

P-26A Le principe selon lequel le jugement est définitif est essentiel en vue d'une décision effective. Dans certains États, l'exécution immédiate n'est possible que pour les décisions des juridictions de deuxième instance. La tendance est toutefois, comme c'est le cas en *common law* ou dans certains pays de droit civil, au caractère immédiatement exécutoire du jugement de première instance par la loi même ou par décision du tribunal.

P-26B Le fait qu'un jugement doive être exécutoire immédiatement lorsqu'il est définitif n'empêche pas le tribunal d'accorder à la partie adverse un délai pour exécuter la condamnation. Le jugement doit être exécuté en conformité avec ses propres termes.

P-26C La loi du for peut également déclarer définitif et donc immédiatement exécutoire un jugement seulement partiel (c'est-à-dire ne tranchant qu'une partie du litige).

27. Appel

27.1 **L'appel est recevable selon des modalités équivalentes à celles qui sont prévues par la loi du for pour les autres jugements. L'instance d'appel doit se terminer dans des délais brefs.**

27.2 **L'appel est en principe limité aux demandes et défenses présentées en première instance.**

27.3 **Dans l'intérêt de la justice, la juridiction d'appel peut prendre en considération de nouveaux faits et de nouvelles preuves.**

Commentaire:

P-27A Les procédures d'appel sont très différentes selon les systèmes juridiques. Il convient donc de renvoyer à l'application de la loi du for.

P-27B Historiquement, dans les systèmes de *common law*, l'appel était fondé sur le principe de «*closed record*», ce qui signifiait que toutes les demandes, défenses, moyens de preuve et moyens de droit devaient avoir été présentés devant la juridiction de première instance. Toutefois, dans la plupart des systèmes modernes de *common law*, la juridiction d'appel peut apprécier s'il y a lieu de prendre en compte de nouveaux moyens de droit et, en cas de circonstances majeures, de nouvelles preuves. Historiquement, dans les pays de droit civil, la juridiction de seconde instance était autorisée à réexaminer entièrement les éléments du litige, mais de nombreux systèmes juridiques modernes se sont éloignés de cette approche. Ce n'est plus que dans un nombre de plus en plus faible de pays de droit civil que la procédure devant la juridiction d'appel peut être un procès entièrement nouveau et est couramment engagée. Dans de nombreux systèmes juridiques au contraire, la décision de la juridiction de première instance ne peut être infirmée ou modifiée qu'en cas d'erreur grave. Le Principe 27 rejette ces deux solutions extrêmes. Toutefois, la production de nouvelles preuves au cours de l'instance d'appel devrait être autorisée uniquement lorsqu'elle est dans l'intérêt de la justice. Si une partie bénéficie d'une telle autorisation, les autres parties doivent se voir accorder un droit de réponse correspondant. Voir les Principes 22.2.

P-27C Dans certains systèmes juridiques, les parties doivent faire valoir leurs objections devant la juridiction de première instance et ne peuvent les soulever pour la première fois en appel.

28. Litispendance et chose jugée

28.1 Pour l'application des règles sur la litispendance, l'objet du litige est déterminé par les demandes et défenses des parties telles que formulées dans l'acte introductif d'instance et dans les conclusions en défense, et par leurs éventuelles modifications.

28.2 Pour l'application des règles sur l'autorité de la chose jugée, le domaine de cette autorité est déterminé par les demandes et défenses des parties, telles que contenues dans l'acte introductif d'instance, les conclusions en défense, dans leurs modifications ainsi que dans le dispositif et les motifs du jugement.

28.3 Le concept d'autorité de la chose implicitement jugée, qu'il s'agisse d'une question de fait ou de l'application de la loi aux faits, ne doit être appliqué qu'en vue de prévenir une injustice grave.

Commentaire:

P-28A Ce Principe est destiné à éviter les litiges répétés, qu'ils soient concurrents (litispendance) ou successifs (chose jugée).

P-28B Certains systèmes juridiques ont des règles strictes en matière de litispendance, alors que d'autres appliquent des règles plus flexibles, en tenant notamment compte de la qualité de la procédure dans les deux fors. Le Principe de litispendance correspond au Principe 10.3 relatif à l'objet du litige et au Principe 2.6 concernant les procédures parallèles.

P-28C Certains systèmes juridiques, notamment ceux de *common law*, emploient le concept de chose implicitement jugée (*issue preclusion, collateral estoppel* ou *issue estoppel*). Selon ce concept, la solution judiciaire d'une question qui constitue un élément nécessaire du jugement ne peut en principe pas faire l'objet d'un nouvel examen lors d'un litige postérieur au cours duquel la même question est abordée. Le Principe 28.3 peut conduire à l'application de l'autorité de chose implicitement jugée lorsque, par exemple, une partie s'est légitimement fondée, dans la procédure, sur la solution d'une question de fait ou de droit dans une procédure antérieure. De nombreux systèmes de *common law* reconnaissent un champ plus large à l'autorité de chose implicitement jugée. La conception plus limitée retenue par le Principe 28.3 découle du principe de loyauté tel que le connaissent les systèmes de droit civil, et de l'*estoppel in pais* des systèmes de *common law*.

29. Exécution effective

Les parties doivent pouvoir avoir accès à des procédures qui permettent une exécution rapide et effective des jugements, y compris des condamnations pécuniaires, des condamnations aux frais, des ordonnances et des mesures provisoires.

Commentaire:

P-29A De nombreux systèmes juridiques possèdent des procédures archaïques et inefficaces d'exécution des jugements. Du point de vue des parties au litige, et notamment de la partie gagnante, une exécution effective est un élément essentiel de justice. Toutefois, la question des voies d'exécution n'entre pas dans le champ des présents Principes.

30. Reconnaissance

Les jugements définitifs prononcés au cours ou à l'issue d'un procès conduit à l'étranger selon une procédure substantiellement compatible avec les présents Principes, doivent être reconnus et exécutés sauf en cas d'exigence contraire de l'ordre public matériel. Les mesures provisoires sont reconnues dans les mêmes conditions.

Commentaire:

P-30A La reconnaissance de jugements rendus dans un autre for, y compris les jugements ordonnant des mesures provisoires, est particulièrement importante pour les litiges transnationaux. Tout droit national possède des règles strictes de reconnaissance pour les jugements rendus au sein de son propre système juridique. Les conventions internationales prévoient d'autres conditions relatives à la reconnaissance des jugements étrangers. De nombreux pays limitent l'effet de la plupart des mesures provisoires au territoire de l'État des juridictions duquel elles émanent et coopèrent en émettant des ordonnances parallèles. Toutefois, la technique des mesures provisoires parallèles est moins acceptable que la reconnaissance et l'exécution directes. Voir également Principe 31.

P-30B En vertu du Principe 30, un jugement rendu à l'issue d'une procédure substantiellement conforme aux présents Principes doit en principe avoir les mêmes effets qu'un jugement prononcé à l'issue d'une procédure qui s'est déroulée selon la loi de l'État de reconnaissance. Le Principe 30 consacre donc un principe de traitement égalitaire. Les présents Principes établissent des critères internationaux de compétence, de notification suffisante au débiteur selon le jugement, d'équité procédurale et d'effet de la chose jugée. En conséquence, la plupart des motifs traditionnels de non reconnaissance, tels que défaut de compétence, notification insuffisante, fraude, procédure étrangère inéquitable ou encore inconciliabilité avec une autre décision définitive, ne peuvent se produire si la procédure étrangère remplit les exigences des Principes. La réciprocité n'est plus, dans de nombreux pays, un pré-requis pour la reconnaissance, mais elle sera quand même réalisée si la loi du for adopte ces Principes, notamment le Principe 30. Seul sera ainsi admis le motif de non reconnaissance fondé sur l'ordre public matériel, dès lors que la procédure étrangère aura été conduite en respect des Principes.

31. Coopération judiciaire internationale

Les tribunaux d'un État qui a adopté les présents Principes prêtent leur assistance aux juridictions de tout État étranger devant lesquelles se déroule un procès conformément aux présents Principes. Ceci comprend l'octroi de mesures provisoires et conservatoires, ainsi que la coopération à l'identification, à la préservation ou à la production de preuves.

Commentaire:

P-31A La coopération et l'assistance judiciaires internationales complètent la reconnaissance internationale et sont tout aussi importantes dans le contexte moderne.

P-31B En compatibilité avec les règles relatives aux communications hors la présence des parties ou de leurs représentants (*ex parte*), les juges établissent, si nécessaire, des communications avec des magistrats d'autres États. Voir Principe 1.4.

P-31C Sur la signification du terme ⟪*preuve*⟫, voir Principe 16.

APPENDIX

Reporters' Study

Introductory Note: The following Rules of Transnational Civil Procedure have not been formally adopted by UNIDROIT or the ALI but are the Reporters' model implementation of the Principles, providing greater detail and illustrating concrete fulfillment of the Principles. These Rules may be considered either for adoption or for further adaptation in various legal systems, and along with the Principles can be considered as a model for reform in domestic legislation.

RULES OF TRANSNATIONAL CIVIL PROCEDURE

(with commentary)

A. Interpretation and Scope

1. Standards of Interpretation

1.1 These Rules are to be interpreted in accordance with the Principles of Transnational Civil Procedure and applied with consideration of the transnational nature of the dispute.

1.2 The procedural law of the forum governs matters not addressed in these Rules.

Comment:

R-1A Rule 1.2 does not authorize use of local concepts to interpret these Rules. The Transnational Rules should develop an autonomous mode of interpretation, consistent with the principles and concepts by which they are guided.

R-1B The Transnational Rules of Civil Procedure are not a comprehensive "code" in the civil-law sense of the word. They are a set of rules to supersede inconsistent forum law and to be supplemented by forum law whenever forum law is not inconsistent with the Transnational Rules.

2. Disputes to Which These Rules Apply

2.1 Subject to domestic constitutional provisions, and statutory provisions not superseded by these Rules, these Rules apply to disputes arising from transnational commercial transactions, if the dispute:

2.1.1 Is between parties from different states, determined by the habitual residence of an individual and by the principal place of business of a jural entity;

2.1.2 Concerns property located in the forum state (including movable property and intangible property), to which a party

from a different state claims an interest, whether of ownership, lien, security, or otherwise; or

2.1.3 Is governed by an arbitration agreement providing that these Rules apply.

2.2 In a proceeding involving multiple claims or multiple parties, some of which are not within the scope of this Rule, the court must determine which are the principal matters in dispute.

2.2.1 If the principal matters in dispute are within the scope of these Rules, the Rules apply to all parties and all claims. Otherwise, the rules of the forum apply.

2.2.2 The court may separate the proceeding and then apply Rule 2.2.1.

2.3 The forum state may exclude categories of matters from application of these Rules and may extend application of these Rules to other civil and commercial matters.

Comment:

R-2A Rule 2.1 defines the matters governed by these Rules. The Rules apply to contract disputes and disputes arising from contractual relations; injuries to property, including immovable (real property), movable (personal property), and intangible property such as copyright, trademark, and patent rights; and injuries resulting from breach of obligations and commercial torts in business transactions. They do not apply to claims for personal injury or wrongful death. The term "transnational commercial transactions" includes a series of related events, such as repeated interference with property.

R-2B The scope of application of these Rules is limited to commercial disputes as a matter of comity and public policy, not because the Rules are inappropriate for other types of legal disputes. In many countries, for example, disputes arising from employment relationships are governed by special procedures in specialized courts. The same is true of domestic-relations matters.

Commercial disputes include disputes involving a government or government agency acting in a proprietary capacity. The court should apply the definition of "proprietary capacity" established in forum law.

R-2C The term "dispute" as used in Rule 2.1 may have different connotations in various legal systems. For example, under Rule 20 of the Federal Rules of Civil Procedure in the United States, the term dispute would be interpreted in accordance with the broad concept of "transaction or occurrence." In civil-law systems, the term dispute would be interpreted in accordance with the narrower concept of dispute as framed by the plaintiff's claim.

R-2D Under Rule 2.1.1, these Rules apply when a plaintiff and a defendant are from different states, determined by habitual residence or principal place of business. Thus, these Rules would apply in a dispute between a Japanese on one side and a Japanese and a Canadian on the other side. The habitual residence of an individual and the principal place of business of a jural entity are determined by general principles of private international law.

R-2E Rule 2.1.2 provides that these Rules apply in a dispute concerning property located in one state as to which a claim is made by a plaintiff or a defendant who is from another state. Whether a legal claim concerns property and whether it is a claim of ownership or of a security or other interest is determined by general principles of private international law.

R-2F Rule 2.1.3 provides that these Rules apply by contractual option, in case of arbitration. Some Rules are not applicable to arbitration disputes, such as Rules 3, 4, 5, 9, 10, and 17.

R-2G Legal disputes may involve claims asserted on multiple substantive legal bases, one of which is under these Rules but another of which is not. The court may entertain both the claim under these Rules and the other claim or claims and apply the Rules as provided in Rule 2.2.

R-2H A case may be one not governed by Rule 2 at the outset of the litigation, but a claim or a party may later be joined that would justify application of these Rules. For example, in a claim based on contract by A against B, B could implead C on the basis of an indemnity obligation. If A and C or B and C are from different states, and the claim between them did not arise wholly within the forum state, these Rules would apply. Rule 2.2 confers authority on the court to determine whether the principal matters in dispute are within these Rules and thereupon to direct that the dispute be governed by these Rules or forum law, according to that determination.

R-2I For the purposes of these Rules, "Party" includes plaintiff, defendant, and a third party; "Person" includes a jural entity (corporation or other organization such as a société anonyme, partnership, and an unincorporated association); and "Witness" includes third persons, expert witnesses, and may include the parties themselves.

R-2J Rule 2.3 recognizes that the forum law may adopt provisions that enlarge or restrict the scope of application of the Rules.

B. Jurisdiction, Joinder, and Venue

3. Forum and Territorial Competence

3.1 **Proceedings under these Rules should be conducted in a court of specialized jurisdiction for commercial disputes or in the forum state's first-instance courts of general jurisdiction.**

3.2 **Appellate jurisdiction of a proceeding under these Rules must be in the court having jurisdiction over the first-instance court.**

3.3 **Whenever possible, territorial competence should be established, either originally or by transfer of the proceeding, at a place in the forum state that is reasonably convenient to a defendant.**

Comment:

R-3A Territorial competence is the equivalent of "venue" in some common-law systems.

R-3B Typically it would be convenient that a specialized court or division of court be established in a principal commercial city, such as Milan in Italy or London in the United Kingdom. Committing disputes under these rules to specialized courts would facilitate development of a more uniform procedural jurisprudence.

4. Jurisdiction Over Parties

4.1 **Jurisdiction is established over a plaintiff by the plaintiff's commencement of a proceeding or over a person who intervenes by the act of intervention.**

4.2 **Jurisdiction may be established over another person as follows:**

4.2.1 **By consent of that person to the jurisdiction of the court;**

4.2.2 **Over an individual who is a habitual resident of the forum;**

4.2.3 **Over a jural entity that has received its charter of organization from the forum state or maintains its principal place of business or administrative headquarters in the state; or**

4.2.4 **Over a person who has:**

4.2.4.1 **Provided goods or services in the forum state, or agreed to do so, when the proceeding concerns such goods or services; or**

4.2.4.2 Committed tortious conduct in the forum state, or conduct having direct effect in the forum state, when the proceeding concerns such conduct.

4.3 Jurisdiction may be exercised over a person who claims an interest (of ownership, lien, security, or otherwise) in property located in the forum state with respect to that interest.

4.4 Jurisdiction may be exercised, when no other forum is reasonably available, on the basis of:

4.4.1 Presence or nationality of the defendant in the forum state; or

4.4.2 Presence in the forum state of the defendant's property, whether or not the dispute relates to the property, but the court's authority is limited to the property or its value.

4.5 A court may grant provisional measures with respect to a person or to property in the territory of the forum state, even if the court does not have jurisdiction over the controversy.

4.6 The forum should decline to exercise jurisdiction or suspend the proceeding, if:

4.6.1 Another forum was validly designated by the parties as exclusive;

4.6.2 The forum is manifestly inappropriate relative to another forum that could exercise jurisdiction; or

4.6.3 The dispute is previously pending in another court.

4.7 The forum may nevertheless exercise its jurisdiction or reinstate the proceeding when it appears that the dispute cannot otherwise be effectively and expeditiously resolved or there are other compelling reasons for doing so.

Comment:

R-4A The standard of "substantial connection" has been generally accepted for international legal disputes. That standard excludes mere physical presence, which within the United States is colloquially called "tag jurisdiction." Mere physical presence as a basis of jurisdiction within the American federation has historical justification but is inappropriate in international disputes. But see Rule 4.4.1.

R-4B The concept of "jural entity" includes a corporation, société anonyme, unincorporated association, partnership, or other organization recognized as a jural entity by forum law.

R-4C Rule 4.4.2 recognizes that when no other forum is reasonably available a state may exercise jurisdiction by sequestration or attachment of locally situated property, even though the property is not the object or subject of the dispute. The procedure is called "quasi in rem jurisdiction" in some legal systems.

R-4D The concept recognized in Rule 4.6.2 corresponds in common-law systems to the rule of *forum non conveniens*.

5. Multiple Claims and Parties; Intervention

5.1 A party may assert any claim substantially connected to the subject matter of the proceeding against another party or against a third person subject to the jurisdiction of the court.

5.2 A third person made a party as provided in Rule 5.1 should be summoned as provided in Rule 7.

5.3 A person having an interest substantially connected with the subject matter of the proceeding may apply to intervene. The court itself or on motion of a party may require notice to a party having such an interest, inviting intervention. Intervention may be permitted unless it will unduly delay, introduce confusion into the proceeding, or otherwise unfairly prejudice a party.

5.4 A party added to the proceeding ordinarily has the same rights and obligations of participation and cooperation as the original parties. The extent of these rights and obligations should be adjusted according to the basis, timing, and circumstances of the joinder or intervention.

5.5 When appropriate, the court should grant permission for a person to be substituted for or to be admitted in succession to a party.

5.6 The court may order separation of claims, issues, or parties, or consolidation with other proceedings, for a fair or more efficient management and determination or in the interest of justice. That authority should extend to parties or claims that are not within the scope of these Rules.

Comment:

R-5A Rule 5 recognizes the right afforded in many legal systems to assert any claim available against another party that is substantially connected to the subject matter of the proceeding. The court has authority to sever claims and issues, and to consolidate them, according to their subject matter and the affected parties.

R-5B Rule 5.3 states the concept of intervention by a third party. The precise definition of intervention varies somewhat among legal systems. However, in general a person (whether individual or jural entity) who has some interest that could be affected by the proceedings, and who seeks to participate, should be allowed to do so. Some systems also allow intervention when there exists between the intervenor and one or more of the parties to the proceeding a question of law or fact in common with one or more of the questions in issue in the proceeding. The scope and terms of intervention may be limited by the court to avoid confusion, delay, or prejudice.

6. *Amicus Curiae* Submission

Any person or jural entity may present a written submission to the court containing data, information, remarks, legal analysis, and other considerations that may be useful for a fair and just decision of the case. The court may refuse such a submission. The court may invite a nonparty to present such a submission. The parties must have an opportunity to submit written comment addressed to the matters in the submission before it is considered by the court.

Comment:

R-6A The "*amicus curiae* brief" is a useful means by which a nonparty may supply the court with information and legal analysis that may be helpful to achieve a just and informed disposition of the case. Therefore, any person may be allowed to file such a brief, notwithstanding a lack of legal interest sufficient for intervention. It is in the court's discretion whether such a brief may be taken into account. An *amicus curiae* does not become a party to the case but is merely an active commentator. Factual assertions in an *amicus* brief are not evidence in the case.

R-6B In civil-law countries there is no well-established practice of allowing third parties without a legal interest in the merits of the dispute to participate in a proceeding, although some civil-law countries such as France have developed similar institutions in their decisional law. Consequently, most civil-law countries do not have a practice of allowing the submission of *amicus curiae* briefs. Nevertheless, the *amicus curiae* brief is an important device, particularly in cases of public significance.

7. Due Notice

7.1 A party must be given formal notice of the proceeding commenced against that party, provided in accordance with forum law by means reasonably likely to be effective.

7.2 The notice must:

7.2.1 Contain a copy of the statement of claim;

7.2.2 Advise that plaintiff invokes these Rules;

7.2.3 Specify the time within which response is required and state that a default judgment may be entered against a party who does not respond within that time; and

7.2.4 Be in a language of the forum and also in a language of the state of an individual's habitual residence or of a jural entity's principal place of business, or in the language of the principal documents in the transaction.

7.3 All parties must have prompt notice of claims, defenses, motions, and applications of other parties, and of determinations and suggestions by the court. Parties must have a fair opportunity and reasonably adequate time to respond.

Comment:

R-7A Responsibility for giving notice in most civil-law systems and some common-law systems is assigned to the court. In other common-law systems it is assigned to the parties. In most systems the notice (called a summons in common-law terminology) must be accompanied by a copy of the complaint, which itself contains detailed notice about the dispute. Many systems require a recital of advice as to how to respond. The warning about default is especially important. See Comment *R-11B*.

R-7B Concerning the language of the notice, the court ordinarily will assume that its own language is appropriate. The parties therefore may have responsibility to inform the court when that assumption is inaccurate. The requirement that notice be in a language of the state of the person to whom it is addressed establishes an objective standard for specification of language.

R-7C In all systems, after the complaint has been transmitted and the defendant has responded, communications among the court and the parties ordinarily are conducted through the parties' lawyers.

8. Languages

8.1 The proceedings, including documents and oral communication, ordinarily should be conducted in a language of the court.

8.2 The court may allow use of other languages in all or part of the proceeding if no prejudice to a party will result.

8.3 Translation must be provided when a document is not written, or a party or witness is not competent in a language in which the proceeding is conducted. Translation must be made by a neutral translator selected by the parties or appointed by the court. The cost must be paid by the party presenting the pertinent witness or document unless the court orders otherwise. Translation of lengthy or voluminous documents may be limited to relevant portions, as agreed by the parties or ordered by the court.

Comment:

R-8A The language in which the proceeding is conducted should be that in which the court is fluent. Ordinarily this will be the language of the state in which the court is situated. However, if the court and the parties have competence in a foreign language, they may agree upon or the judge may order some other language for all or part of the proceeding, for example, the reception of a particular document or the testimony of a witness in the witness's native language.

R-8B In transnational litigation, it happens frequently that witnesses and experts are not fluent in the language in which the proceeding is conducted, ordinarily that of the country where the case is tried. In such a case, translation is required for the court and for other parties. The testimony must be taken with the aid of an interpreter, with the party presenting the evidence paying the cost of the translation unless the court decides otherwise.

R-8C A second possibility is examining the witness by way of deposition, as provided in Rule 23.1, under agreement of the parties or by order of the court. The deposition can then be translated and submitted at the hearing. The procedure and cost of the deposition are determined according to Rule 23.

C. Composition and Impartiality of the Court

9. Composition of the Court

The court is constituted as follows: [---].

Comment:

R-9A Rule 9 contemplates that the forum state, when implementing these Rules, may constitute a court of special jurisdiction to adjudicate disputes governed by these Rules.

R-9B In most legal systems today, the courts of first instance consist of a single judge. However, many civil-law systems normally use three judges in courts of general authority. In some legal systems the composition of the court may be one or three judges, according to various criteria.

R-9C Jury trial is a matter of constitutional right under various circumstances in some countries, notably the United States. Where jury trial is of right, the parties may waive the right or these Rules can apply with the use of a jury. See Rule 2.1 (subjecting these Rules to domestic constitutional provisions). Jury trial requires special rules of evidence, for example, concerning hearsay and prejudicial evidence, that preserve the integrity of the decision-making process.

10. Impartiality of the Court

10.1 A judge or other person having decisional authority must not participate if there are reasonable grounds to doubt such person's impartiality.

10.2 A party must have the right to make reasonable challenge of the impartiality of a judge, referee, or other person having decisional authority. A challenge must be made promptly after the party has knowledge of the basis for challenge.

10.3 A challenge of a judge must be heard and determined either by a judge other than the one so challenged or, if by the challenged judge, under procedure affording immediate appellate review or reconsideration by another judge.

10.4 The court may not accept communications about the case from a party or from anyone else in the absence of other parties, except for communications concerning routine procedural administration and communications in proceedings without notice as provided in Rule 17.2.

Comment:

R-10A All legal systems require judges to be impartial. In many systems, however, there is no recognized procedure by which a party to litigation can challenge a judge's impartiality. The absence of such a procedure means the problem itself is not sufficiently acknowledged. A procedure for challenge is essential to give reality to the concept.

R-10B Other persons having "decisional authority" include a lay member of the court, such as jurors, and an expert appointed by the court under Rule 26.

R-10C A challenge to a judge's impartiality should be made only on substantial grounds and must be made promptly. Otherwise, the challenge procedure can be abused as a device for attacking unfavorable rulings.

R-10D The prohibition on *ex parte* communications or proceedings (i.e., without notice to the person adversely interested) should extend not only to communications from the parties and the lawyers but also to communications from other government officials. There have been instances in which improper influence has been attempted by other judges in a court system.

D. Pleading Stage

11. Commencement of the Proceeding and Notice

11.1 The plaintiff shall submit to the court a statement of claim, as provided in Rule 12. The court shall thereupon give notice of the proceeding, as provided in Rule 7.

11.2 The time of lodging of the complaint with the court determines compliance with statutes of limitations, lis pendens, and other requirements of timeliness, subject to compliance with requirements of timely notice to the party affected thereby.

Comment:

R-11A Rule 11 specifies the rule for commencement of suit for purposes of determining the competence of the court, lis pendens, interruption of statutes of limitations, and other purposes as provided by the forum law.

R-11B Rule 11 also provides for giving notice of the proceeding to the defendant, or "service of process" as it is called in common-law procedure. The Hague Service Convention specifies rules of notice that govern proceedings in countries signatory to that Convention. When judicial assistance from the courts of another country is required in order to effect notice, the procedure for obtaining such assistance should be followed. In any event, the notice must include a copy of the statement of claim, a statement that the proceeding is conducted under these Rules, and a warning that default judgment may be taken against a defendant that does not respond. See Rule 7.2.

Beyond these requirements, the rules of the forum govern the mechanisms and formalities for giving notice of the proceeding. In some states it is sufficient to mail the notice; some states require that notice, such as a summons, be delivered by an officer of the court.

12. Statement of Claim (Complaint)

12.1 The plaintiff must state the facts on which the claim is based, describe the evidence to support those statements, and refer to the legal grounds that support the claim, including foreign law, if applicable.

12.2 The reference to legal grounds must be sufficient to permit the court to determine the legal validity of the claim.

12.3 The statement of facts must, so far as reasonably practicable, set forth detail as to time, place, participants, and events.

12.4 A party who is justifiably uncertain of a fact or legal grounds may make statements about them in the alternative. In connection with an objection that a pleading lacks sufficient detail, the court should give due regard to the possibility that necessary facts and evidence will develop in the course of the proceeding.

12.5 If plaintiff is required to have first resorted to arbitration or conciliation procedure, or to have made a demand concerning the claim, or to have complied with another condition precedent, the complaint must allege compliance therewith.

12.6 The complaint must state the remedy requested, including the monetary amount demanded and the terms of any other remedy sought.

Comment:

R-12A Rule 12.1 requires the plaintiff to state the facts upon which the claim is based. Rule 12.3 calls for particularity of statement, such as that required in most civil-law and most common-law jurisdictions. In contrast, some American systems, notably those employing "notice pleading" as under the Federal Rules of Civil Procedure, permit very general allegations. In these Rules, the facts pleaded in the statements of claim and defense establish the standard of relevance for exchange of evidence, which is limited to matters relevant to the facts of the case as stated in the pleadings. See Rule 25.2.

R-12B Under Rules 12.1 and 12.2, the complaint must refer to the legal grounds on which the plaintiff relies to support the claim. Reference to such grounds is a common requirement in many legal systems and is especially appropriate when the transaction may involve the law of more than one legal system and present problems of choice of law. Rules of procedure in many national systems require a party's pleading to set forth foreign law when the party intends to rely on that law. However, according to Principle 22.1, the court has responsibility for determining the correct legal basis for its decisions.

R-12C According to Rule 7.2.2, the notice must advise that plaintiff invokes these Rules. The court or a defendant or other party may challenge that application, or demand application of these Rules if plaintiff has not done so.

R-12D Some systems require that a claim or demand be made against a prospective defendant before commencing litigation, for example, claims against public agencies or insurance companies.

R-12E Rule 12.6 requires a statement of the amount of money demanded and, if injunctive or declaratory relief is sought, the nature and terms of the requested remedy. If the defendant defaults, the court may not award a judgment in an amount greater or in terms more severe than demanded in the complaint, so that the defendant can calculate on an informed basis whether to dispute the claim. See Rule 15.4. It is an important requirement that a default judgment may be entered only when the plaintiff has offered sufficient proof of the claims for which judgment is awarded. See Rule 15.3.3.

13. Statement of Defense and Counterclaims

13.1 A defendant must, within [60] consecutive days from the date of service of notice, answer the complaint. The time for answer may be extended for a reasonable time by agreement of the parties or by court order.

13.2 A defendant in the answer must admit, admit with explanations, or allege an alternative statement of facts, and deny allegations defendant wishes to controvert. Failure explicitly to deny an allegation is considered an admission for purposes of the proceeding and obviates proof thereof, except as provided in Rule 15 concerning default judgment.

13.3 The defendant may state a counterclaim seeking relief from a plaintiff, or a claim against a co-defendant or a third person. Such a claim must be answered by the party to whom it is addressed as provided in this Rule.

13.4 **The requirements of Rule 12 concerning the detail of statements of claims apply to the answer, affirmative defenses, counterclaims, and third-party claims.**

13.5 **Objections referred to in Rule 19.1.1 and 19.1.2 may be presented in a motion before the answer but such a motion does not extend the time in which to answer unless the court so orders or the parties agree.**

Comment:

R-13A Forum law should specify the time within which a defendant's response is required. The specification should take into account the transnational character of the dispute.

R-13B Rule 13.2 requires that the defendant's statement of defense address the allegations of the complaint, denying or admitting with explanation those allegations that are to be controverted. Allegations not so controverted are admitted for purposes of the litigation. The defendant may assert an "alternative statement of facts," which is simply a different narrative of the circumstances that the defendant presents in order to clarify the dispute. Whether an admission in a proceeding under these Rules has effect in other proceedings is determined by the law governing such other proceedings. An "affirmative defense" is the allegation of additional facts or contentions that avoids the legal effect of the facts and contentions raised by the plaintiff, rather than contradict them directly. An example is the defense that an alleged debt has previously been discharged in bankruptcy. A "negative defense" is the denial.

R-13C These Rules generally do not specify the number of days within which a specific procedural act should be performed. A transnational proceeding must be expeditious, but international transactions often involve severe problems of communications. It is generally understood that the time should be such as to impose an obligation of prompt action, but should not be so short as to create unfair risk of prejudice. Therefore, a period of 60 days in which to respond generally should be sufficient. However, if the defendant is at a remote location, additional time may be necessary and should be granted as of course. In any event, the forum state should prescribe time limits, and the basis on which they are calculated, in its adoption of the Rules.

R-13D Rule 13.4 applies to the defendant's answer the same rules of form and content as Rule 12 provides with respect to the statement of claim. Thus, additional facts stated by the defendant, by way of affirmative defense or alternative statement, must be in the same detail as required by Rule 12.3. If a counterclaim is asserted, the defendant must make a demand for judgment as required by Rule 12.6.

R-13E Rule 13.3 permits the defendant to assert a counterclaim, third-party claim, or cross-claim. Such a claim may be for indemnity or contribution. In most civil-law systems, a counterclaim is permitted only for a claim arising from the dispute addressed in the plaintiff's complaint. See Comment *R-2C* for reference to the civil-law concept of "dispute." In common-law systems a wider scope for counterclaims is generally permitted, including a "set off" based on a different transaction or occurrence. Compare United States Federal Rules of Civil Procedure, Rule 13. These Rules adopt the broader scope but do not provide for compulsory counterclaims, so that omission to interpose a counterclaim does not result in preclusion. See Principles 10.3 and 28.2.

Rule 13.3 requires a plaintiff, third party, or co-defendant to submit an answer to a counterclaim, third-party claim, or cross-claim. No such response is required to an affirmative defense or other allegations in the answer that are not counterclaims or other claims.

R-13F Rule 13.5 authorizes a defendant to make objections referred to in Rules 19.1.1 and 19.1.2 either by a motion pursuant to those Rules or by answer to the complaint.

14. Amendments

14.1 A party, upon showing good cause to the court and notice to other parties, has a right to amend its claims or defenses when doing so does not unreasonably delay the proceeding or otherwise result in injustice. In particular, amendments may be justified to take account of events occurring after those alleged in earlier pleadings, newly discovered facts or evidence that could not previously have been obtained through reasonable diligence, or evidence obtained through exchange of evidence.

14.2 Leave to amend must be granted on such terms as are just, including, when necessary, adjournment or continuance, or compensation by an award of costs to another party.

14.3 The amendment must be served on the opposing party, who has [30] consecutive days in which to respond, or such other time as the court may order.

14.4 If the complaint has been amended, default judgment may be obtained on the basis of an amended pleading only if the

amended pleading has been served on the party against whom default judgment is to be entered and the party has not timely responded.

14.5 **Any party may request that the court order another party to provide by amendment a more specific statement of that party's pleading on the ground that the challenged statement does not comply with the requirements of these Rules. This request temporarily suspends the duty to answer.**

Comment:

R-14A The scope of permissible amendment differs among various legal systems, the rule in the United States, for example, being very liberal and that in many civil-law systems being less so. In many civil-law systems amendment of the legal basis of a claim is permitted, as distinct from the factual basis, but amendment of factual allegations is permitted only upon a showing that there is newly discovered probative evidence and that the amendment is within the scope of the dispute. See Comment *R-2C* for reference to the civil-law concept of "dispute."

R-14B The appropriateness of permitting amendment also depends on the basis of the request. For example, an amendment to address material evidence newly discovered should be more readily granted than an amendment to add a new party whose participation could have been anticipated. An amendment sometimes could have some adverse effect on an opposing party. On the other hand, compensation for costs reasonably incurred by the party, or rescheduling of the final hearing, could eliminate some unfair prejudicial effects. Accordingly, exercise of judicial judgment may be required in considering an amendment. The court may postpone the award of costs until the final disposition of the case. See Rule 14.2.

R-14C In accordance with the right of contradiction stated in Principle 5, Rule 14.4 requires that if the complaint has been amended, default judgment may be obtained on the basis of an amended pleading only if the amended pleading has been served on the party against whom default judgment is to be entered. See Rules 14.3 and 15.4.

R-14D Rule 14.5 permits a party to request that another party be required to state facts with greater specificity. Failure to comply with such an order may be considered a withdrawal of those allegations. Such a request for more specific allegations temporarily suspends the duty to answer. However, a frivolous request may be the basis for sanctions.

15. Dismissal and Default Judgment

15.1 Dismissal of the proceeding must be entered against a plaintiff who without justification fails to prosecute the proceeding with reasonable efficiency. Before entering such a dismissal, the court must give plaintiff a reasonable warning thereof.

15.2 Default judgment must be entered against a defendant or other party who, without justification, fails to appear or respond within the prescribed time.

15.3 In entering a default judgment for failure to appear or respond within the prescribed time, the court must determine that:

15.3.1 There is jurisdiction over the party against whom judgment is to be entered;

15.3.2 There has been compliance with notice provisions and that the party has had sufficient time to respond; and

15.3.3 The claim is reasonably supported by evidence and is legally sufficient, including the amount of damages and any claim for costs.

15.4 A default judgment may be no greater in monetary amount or in severity of other remedy than was demanded in the complaint.

15.5 A party who appears or responds after the time prescribed, but before judgment, may be permitted to enter a defense upon offering reasonable excuse, but the court may order compensation for costs resulting to the opposing party.

15.6 The court may enter default judgment as a sanction against a party who without justification fails to offer a substantial answer or otherwise fails to continue participation after responding.

15.7 Dismissal or default judgment is subject to appeal or request to set aside the judgment according to the law of the forum.

Comment:

R-15A Default judgment permits termination of a dispute. It is a mechanism for compelling a defendant to acknowledge the court's authority. If the court lacked authority to enter a default judgment, a defendant could avoid liability simply by ignoring the proceeding and later dispute the validity of the judgment.

It is important to consider the reason why the party did not answer or did not proceed after having answered. For example, a party may have failed to answer because that party was obliged by his or her national law not to appear by reason of hostility between the countries.

Reasonable care should be exercised before entering a default judgment because notice may not have been given to a defendant, or the defendant may have been confused about the need to respond. Forum procedure in many systems requires that, after a defendant has failed to respond, an additional notice be given to the defendant of intention to enter default judgment.

R-15B A plaintiff's abandonment of prosecution of the proceeding is usually referred to as "failure to prosecute" and results in "involuntary dismissal." It is the equivalent of a default.

R-15C The absence of a substantial answer may be treated as no answer at all.

R-15D A decision that the claim is reasonably supported by evidence and legally justified under Rule 15.3.3 does not require a full inquiry on the merits of the case. The judge need only determine whether the default judgment is consistent with the available evidence and is legally justified. For that decision, the judge must analyze critically the evidence supporting the statement of claims. See Rule 21.1. The judge may request production of more evidence or schedule an evidentiary hearing.

R-15E Rule 15.4 limits a default judgment to the amount and kind demanded in the statement of claim. See Rule 12.6. This Rule is important in common-law systems in which judgment is normally not limited to the original claims made by the parties on the pleadings. In civil-law systems and some common-law systems, however, there is a traditional prohibition against a judgment that goes beyond the pleadings (*ultra petita* or *extra petita* prohibition) even if the claim is contested.

R-15F Rule 15.4 must be interpreted together with Rule 14.4, which requires an amendment to be served on the party before a default judgment may be rendered.

R-15G A party who has defaulted should not be permitted to produce evidence in an appeal, except to prove that the notice was not proper.

R-15H Every system has a procedure for invalidating a default judgment obtained without compliance with the rules governing default. In some systems, including most common-law systems, the procedure is pursued in the first-instance court, and in other systems, including many civil-law systems, it is through an appeal. This Rule defers to forum law.

16. Settlement Offer

16.1 After commencement of a proceeding under these Rules, a party may deliver to another party a written offer to settle one or more

claims and the related costs and expenses. The offer must be designated "Settlement Offer" and must refer to the penalties imposed under this Rule. The offer must remain open for [60] days, unless rejected or withdrawn by a writing delivered to the offeree before delivery of an acceptance.

16.2 The offeree may counter with its own offer, which must remain open for at least [30] days. If the counteroffer is not accepted, the offeree may accept the original offer, if still open.

16.3 An offer neither withdrawn nor accepted before its expiration is rejected.

16.4 Except by consent of both parties, an offer must not be made public or revealed to the court before acceptance or entry of judgment, under penalty of sanctions, including adverse determination of the merits.

16.5 Not later than [30] days after notice of entry of judgment, a party who made an offer may file with the court a declaration that an offer was made but rejected. If the offeree has failed to obtain a judgment that is more advantageous than the offer, the court may impose an appropriate sanction, considering all the relevant circumstances of the case.

16.6 Unless the court finds that special circumstances justify a different sanction, the sanction must be the loss of the right to be reimbursed for the costs as provided in Rule 32, plus reimbursement of a reasonable amount of the offeror's costs taking into account the date of delivery of the offer. This sanction must be in addition to the costs determined in accordance with Rule 32.

16.7 If an accepted offer is not complied with in the time specified in the offer, or in a reasonable time, the offeree may either enforce it or continue with the proceeding.

16.8 This procedure is not exclusive of the court's authority and duty to conduct informal discussion of settlement and does not preclude parties from conducting settlement negotiations outside this Rule and that are not subject to sanctions.

Comment:

R-16A This Rule aims at encouraging compromises and settlements and also deters parties from pursuing or defending a case that does not deserve a full and complete proceeding.

This Rule departs from traditions in some countries in which the parties generally do not have an obligation to negotiate or otherwise consider settlement proposals from the opposing party. It allocates risk of unfavorable outcome and is not based on bad faith or misconduct. It protects a party from the expense of litigation in a dispute that the party has reasonably sought to settle. However, it imposes severe cost consequences on a party who fails to achieve a judgment more favorable than a formal offer that has been rejected. For this reason, the procedure may be regarded as impairing access to justice.

R-16B Rule 16 is based on a similar provision under the Ontario (Canada) civil-procedure rules and Part 36 of the new English Procedural Rules. The detailed protocol is designed to permit submission and consideration of serious offers of settlement, from either a plaintiff or a defendant. At the same time, the protocol prohibits use of such offers or responses to influence the court and thereby to prejudice the parties. Experience indicates that a precisely defined procedure, to which conformity is strictly required, can facilitate settlement. The law of the forum may permit or require the deposit of the offer into court.

This procedure is a mechanism whereby a party can demand from an opposing party serious consideration of a settlement offer at any time during the litigation. It is not exclusive of the court's authority and duty to conduct informal discussions and does not preclude parties from conducting settlement negotiations by procedures that are not subject to the Rule 16.5 sanction. See Rule 16.8.

R-16C The offer must remain open for a determinate amount of time, but it can be withdrawn prior to acceptance. According to general principles of contract law, in general the withdrawal of an offer can be accomplished only before the offer reaches the offeree. See, for example, UNIDROIT's Principles of International Commercial Contracts, article 2.3. However, the context of litigation requires a different protocol designed to facilitate settlement: facts or evidence may develop, or expenses may be incurred, that justify the withdrawal, reduction, or increase of the offer. When the offer is withdrawn, there will be no cost sanctions.

The offeree may deliver a counteroffer. According to the principle of equality of the parties, a counteroffer is regulated by the same rules as the offer. See Principle 3. For example, it can be withdrawn under the same conditions as an offer can be withdrawn. In addition, the counteroffer may lead to the same sanctions as an offer.

According to general principles of private contract law, the delivery of a counteroffer means rejection of the offer. See, for example, UNIDROIT's Principles of International Commercial Contracts, article 2.11. However, the rule specified here is more effective in the context of settlement offers in litigation, in which a rejection of an offer may lead to serious consequences.

R-16D Rule 16.4 prohibits public disclosure of the offer or disclosure to the court before acceptance or entry of judgment. Parties might be reluctant to make a settlement offer if doing so could be interpreted as an admission of liability or of weakness of one's position.

R-16E Rule 16.5, permitting notice to the court of an offer that was not accepted, is linked to Rule 31.3, which provides that the court must promptly give the parties notice of judgment. When such notice has been received, the party whose offer was not accepted may inform the court, in order to obtain the cost sanctions prescribed in this Rule.

R-16F If the offeree fails to obtain a judgment that is more advantageous than the offer of settlement under this Rule, that party loses the right to be reimbursed for the costs and expenses incurred after the offer, including attorneys' fees. Instead, the offeree (even if it is the winning party) must pay the costs and expenses thereafter incurred by the offeror (even if it is the loser). The court will award an appropriate proportion of the costs and expenses taking into account the date of delivery of the offer.

According to Rule 16.6, the cost sanction in this Rule is independent from and in addition to the costs awarded according to Rule 32. If the person who has to pay the cost sanction was also the loser of the action, that person may have to pay both the opponent's fees and the cost sanction.

When the offer is partial, or the offeree fails only in part to obtain a more advantageous judgment, the sanction should be proportional. The rejection of the offer may have been reasonable under the specific circumstances of the case, and under Rule 16.6 the judge may determine the sanction accordingly.

E. General Authority of the Court

17. Provisional and Protective Measures

17.1 The court may grant provisional relief to restrain or require conduct of a party or other person when necessary to preserve the ability to grant effective relief by final judgment or to maintain or otherwise regulate the status quo. The grant or extent of the remedy is governed by the principle of proportionality. Disclosure of assets wherever located may be ordered.

17.2 The provisional relief may be issued before the opposing party has an opportunity to respond only upon proof of urgent necessity and

preponderance of considerations of fairness. The applicant must fully disclose facts and legal issues of which the court properly should be aware.

17.3 A person against whom an *ex parte* order is directed must have an opportunity at the earliest practicable time to respond concerning the appropriateness of the order.

17.4 The court may, after hearing those interested, issue, dissolve, renew, or modify an order.

17.5 An applicant for provisional relief is liable for compensation of a person against whom an order is issued if the court thereafter determines that the relief should not have been granted.

17.5.1 The court may require the applicant for provisional relief to post a bond or formally to assume a duty of compensation.

17.6 The granting or denial of provisional relief is subject to immediate appellate review.

Comment:

R-17A Provisional relief may consist of an order requiring or prohibiting the performance of a specified act, for example, preserving property in its present condition. Rule 17.1 authorizes the court to issue an order that is either affirmative, in that it requires performance of an act, or negative, in that it prohibits a specific act or course of action. The term is used here in a generic sense to include attachment, sequestration, and other directives. The concept of regulation of the status quo may include measures to ameliorate the underlying dispute, for example, supervision of management of a partnership during litigation among the partners. Availability of provisional remedies or interim measures, such as attachment or sequestration, should be determined by forum law, including applicable principles of international law. A court may also order disclosure of assets wherever located, or grant provisional relief to facilitate arbitration or to enforce arbitration provisional measures.

R-17B If allowed by forum law, the court may, upon reasonable notice to the person to whom an order is directed, require persons who are not parties to the proceeding to comply with an order issued in accordance with Rule 17.1 or to retain a fund or other property the right to which is in dispute in the proceeding, and to deal with it only in accordance with an order of the court. See Comment *R-20A*.

R-17C Rule 17.2 authorizes the court to issue an order without notice to the person against whom it is directed where doing so is justified by urgent necessity. "Urgent necessity," required as a basis for an *ex parte* order, is a practical concept, as is the concept of preponderance of considerations of fairness. The latter term corresponds to the common-law concept of "balance of equities." Considerations of fairness include the strength of the merits of the applicant's claim, the urgency of the need for a provisional remedy, and the practical burdens that may result from granting the remedy. Such an order is usually known as an *ex parte* order. In common-law procedure such an order is usually referred to as a "temporary restraining order." See Rule 10.4.

The question for the court, in considering an application for an *ex parte* order, is whether the applicant has made a reasonable and specific demonstration that such an order is required to prevent an irreparable deterioration in the situation to be addressed in the litigation and that it would be imprudent to postpone the order until the opposing party has opportunity to be heard. The burden is on the party requesting an *ex parte* order to justify its issuance. However, opportunity for the opposing party or person to whom the order is addressed to be heard should be afforded at the earliest practicable time. The party or person must have the opportunity of a de novo consideration of the decision, including opportunity to present new evidence. See Rule 17.3.

R-17D Rules of procedure generally require that a party requesting an *ex parte* order make full disclosure to the court of all aspects of the situation, including those favorable to the opposing party. Failure to make such disclosure is grounds to vacate an order and may be a basis of liability for damages against the requesting party.

R-17E As indicated in Rule 17.4, if the court has declined to issue an order *ex parte*, it may nevertheless issue an order upon a hearing. If the court previously issued an order *ex parte*, it may revoke, renew, or modify its order in light of the matters developed at the hearing. The burden is on the party seeking the order to show that the order is justified.

R-17F Rule 17.5.1 authorizes the court to require a bond or other compensation as protection against the disturbance and injury that may result from an order. The particulars should be determined by reference to the law of the forum.

R-17G Review of an order granting or denying provisional relief is provided under Rule 33.2 and should be afforded according to the procedure of the forum.

18. Case Management

18.1 The court should assume active management of the proceeding in all stages of the litigation. Consideration should be given to the transnational character of the dispute.

18.2 The court should order a planning conference early in the proceeding and may schedule other conferences thereafter. A lawyer for each of the parties and an unrepresented party must attend such conferences and other persons may be ordered to do so.

18.3 In giving direction to the proceeding, the court, after discussion with the parties, may:

18.3.1 Suggest amendment of the pleadings for the addition, elimination, or revision of claims, defenses, and issues in light of the parties' contentions at that stage;

18.3.2 Order the separation for a preliminary or separate hearing and decision of one or more issues in the case and enter an interlocutory judgment addressing such issues and their relation to the remainder of the case;

18.3.3 Order the separation or consolidation of cases pending before itself, whether those cases proceed under these Rules or those of the forum, when doing so may facilitate the proceeding and decision;

18.3.4 Make decisions concerning admissibility and exclusion of evidence; the sequence, dates, and times of hearing evidence; and other matters to simplify or expedite the proceeding; and

18.3.5 Order any person subject to the court's authority to produce documents or other evidence, or to submit to deposition as provided in Rule 23.

18.4 To facilitate efficient determination of a dispute, the first-instance court may take evidence at another location or delegate taking of evidence to another court of the forum state or of another state or to a judicial officer specially appointed for the purpose.

18.5 The court may at any time suggest that the parties consider settlement, mediation, or arbitration or any other form of alternative dispute resolution. If requested by all parties, the court must stay the proceeding while the parties explore those alternatives.

18.6 In conducting the proceeding the court may use any means of communication, including telecommunication devices such as video or audio transmission.

18.7 Time limits for complying with procedural obligations should begin to run from the date of notice to the party having the obligation.

Comment:

R-18A This Rule determines the role of the court in organizing the case and preparing for the final hearing. The court has wide discretion in deciding how to conclude the interim phase, and in determining how to provide for the following final phase of the proceedings.

R-18B The court should order a planning conference early in the proceeding and may decide that, in order to clarify the issues and to specify the terms of the dispute at the final hearing, one or more further conferences may be useful. The court may conduct a conference by any means of communication available such as telephone, videoconference, or the like.

R-18C The court fixes the date or dates for such conferences. The parties' lawyers are required to attend. Participation of lawyers for the parties is essential to facilitate orderly progression to resolution of the dispute. Lawyers in many systems have some authority to make agreements concerning conduct of the litigation. Parties may have additional authority in some systems. If matters to be discussed are outside of the scope of the lawyers' authority, the court has authority to require the parties themselves to attend in order to discuss and resolve matters concerning progression to resolution, including discussion of settlement. The rule does not exclude the possibility of *pro se* litigants.

R-18D In conferences after the initial planning conference, the court should discuss the issues of the case; which facts, claims, or defenses are not disputed; whether new disputed facts have emerged from disclosure or exchange of evidence; whether new claims or defenses have been presented; and what evidence will be admitted at the final hearing. The principal aim of the conference is to exclude issues that are no longer disputed and to identify precisely the facts, claims, defenses, and evidence concerning those issues that will be addressed at the final hearing. However, exceptionally, the court may decide that a conference is unnecessary, and that the final hearing may proceed simply on the basis of the parties' pleadings and stipulations if any.

R-18E After consultation with the parties, the court may give directives for the final hearing as provided in Rule 18.3. The court may summarize the terms of claims and defenses, rule on issues concerning admissibility of evidence, specify the items of admissible evidence, and determine the order of their examination. The court may also resolve disputed claims of privilege. The court should fix the date for final hearing and enter other orders to ensure that it will be carried on in a fair and expedited manner.

Rule 18 authorizes various measures by the court to facilitate an efficient hearing. It is often useful to isolate one or more issues for hearing upon one occasion, with other issues reserved for consideration later if necessary. So also, it is often useful that a hearing be consolidated with another case when the same or substantially similar issues are to be considered. As recognized in Rule 18.3.4, it is often convenient for the court to rule on admissibility of evidence before its presentation, especially evidence that is complicated, such as voluminous documents.

R-18F The court may consider the possibility that the parties may settle the dispute or refer it to a mediator. In such a case the court, before entering the rulings described in Rule 18.3, may fix a hearing to explore the possibility of a settlement, if necessary with the mediation of the court itself, or a referral of the dispute to mediation or any other form of alternative dispute resolution. This Rule authorizes the court to encourage discussion between the parties, but not to exercise coercion.

If a settlement is reached, the proceedings ordinarily are terminated and judgment entered or the case dismissed with prejudice. If the parties agree about a deferral to mediation or arbitration, that agreement should be put into the record of the case and the proceeding suspended.

R-18G A judicial officer especially appointed for the purpose of taking evidence at another location might be a single judge, a special master, a magistrate, an auditor, a referee, or a law-trained person specifically appointed by the court.

19. Early Court Determinations

19.1 On its own motion or motion of a party, the court at any stage before the final hearing may:

19.1.1 Determine that the dispute is not governed by these Rules or that the court lacks competence to adjudicate the dispute;

19.1.2 Upon a party's motion, determine that the court lacks jurisdiction over that party;

19.1.3 Render a complete or partial judgment by deciding only questions of law;

19.1.4 Render a complete or partial judgment on the basis of evidence immediately available, in which case the court must have regard for the opportunity under these Rules for offering contradictory evidence or obtaining evidence before making such a determination.

19.2 Before rendering a decision under this Rule, the court must allow the party against whom the determination is made reasonable opportunity to amend its statement of claims or defense when it appears that the deficiency can be remedied by amendment and that affording such opportunity will not unreasonably postpone the proceeding or otherwise result in injustice.

Comment:

R-19A It is a universal procedural principle that the court may make determinations of the sufficiency of the pleadings and other contentions, concerning either substantive law or procedure, that materially affect the rights of a party or the ability of the court to render substantial justice. In civil-law systems, the court has an obligation to scrutinize the procedural regularity of the proceeding. In common-law systems, authority to make such determinations ordinarily is exercised only upon initiative of a party made through a motion. However, the court in common-law systems may exercise that authority on its own initiative and in civil-law systems the court may do so in response to a suggestion or motion of a party.

According to Rule 13.5, the objections referred to in Rules 19.1.1 and 19.1.2 can be made by defendant either by a motion or by answer to the complaint.

R-19B Rules 19.1.1 and 19.1.2 express a universal principle that the court's competence over the dispute and its jurisdiction over the parties may be questioned. A valid objection of this kind usually requires termination of the proceeding. A similar objection may be made that the dispute is not within the scope prescribed in Rule 2 and hence is not governed by these Rules. Among factors that may be considered under Rule 19.1.1 is dismissal for *forum non conveniens*. See Rule 4.6.2. Procedural law varies as to whether there are time limitations or other restrictions on delay in making any of these objections, and whether participation in the proceeding without making such an objection results in its waiver or forfeiture.

R-19C Rules 19.1.3 and 19.1.4 empower the court to adjudicate the merits of a claim or defense at the preliminary stage. Such an adjudication may be based on matters of law or matters of fact, or both. Judgment is appropriate when the claim or defense in question is legally insufficient as stated. Evidence may be in the form of written testimony as provided in Rule 23.4. Judgment is also appropriate when it is demonstrated that evidence to support or refute the claim or defense is incontrovertible. When it is contended that the evidence is incontrovertible, the court should consider whether exchange of evidence might disclose sufficient proof to support the claim or defense at issue.

Rules 19.1.3 and 19.1.4 authorize the court, prior to the final hearing, to make a partial award of some proportion of the debt or damages, when part of the dispute is not controverted or when it can be decided with the evidence available in the record.

In civil-law systems, the foregoing powers are exercised by the court as a matter of course. In common-law systems, the power to determine that a claim or defense is substantively insufficient derives from the old common-law demurrer and the modern motions for dismissal for failure to state a claim and for summary judgment and is usually exercised on the basis of a motion by a party. Examples of claims that typically may be so adjudicated are claims based on a written contract calling for payment of money, or to ownership of specific property, when no valid defense or denial is offered. Examples of defenses that typically may be so adjudicated are the defense of elapse of time (statute of limitations or prescription), release, and res judicata.

20. Orders Directed to a Third Person

20.1 The court may order persons who are not parties to the proceeding:

20.1.1 To give testimony as provided in Rules 23 and 29; and

20.1.2 To produce information, documents, electronically stored information, or other things as evidence or for inspection by the court or a party.

20.2 The court shall require a party seeking an order directed to a third person to provide compensation for the costs of compliance.

20.3 An order directed to a third person may be enforced by means authorized against such person by forum law, including imposition of cost sanctions, a monetary penalty, *astreintes*, contempt of court, or seizure of documents or other things. If the third party is not subject to the court's jurisdiction, any party may seek assistance of a court that has such jurisdiction to enforce the order.

Comment:

R-20A In some common-law countries, the court has broad authority to order nonparties to act or refrain from acting during pendency of the litigation, to preserve the status quo, and to prevent irreparable injury. In various situations a person may be involved in a suit without being a party, but should be subject to orders in the interest of justice in the proceeding. The right of contradiction stated in Principle 5 should be respected at all times. Therefore, interested persons should be notified and afforded a reasonable opportunity to respond. In civil-law countries, such in personam authority is not recognized: a court's authority is generally limited to relief in rem through attachment of property. The Anglo-American solution may be very effective, especially in international litigation, but also may be subject to abuse. See Comment *R-17B*.

R-20B When a nonparty's testimony is required, on a party's motion or on the court's own motion, the court may direct the witness to give testimony in the hearing or through deposition.

R-20C When a document or any other relevant thing is in possession of a nonparty, the court may order its production at the preliminary stage or at the final hearing.

R-20D An order directed to a third party is enforced by sanctions for noncompliance authorized by forum law. These sanctions include a monetary penalty or other legal compulsion, including contempt of court. When it is necessary to obtain evidentiary materials or other things, the court may order a direct seizure of such materials or things, and define the manner of doing it.

F. Evidence

21. Disclosure

21.1 In accordance with the court's scheduling order, a party must identify to the court and other parties the evidence on which the party intends to rely, in addition to that provided in the pleading, including:

21.1.1 Copies of documents or other records, such as contracts and correspondence; and

21.1.2 Summaries of expected testimony of witnesses, including parties, other witnesses, and experts, then known to the party. Witnesses must be identified, so far as practicable, by name, address, and telephone number.

21.1.3 In lieu of a summary of expected testimony, a party may present a written statement of testimony.

21.2 A party must amend the specification required in Rule 21.1 to include documents or witnesses not known when the list was originally prepared. Any change in the list of documents or witnesses must be immediately communicated in writing to the court and to all other parties, together with a justification for the amendment.

21.3 To facilitate compliance with this Rule, a lawyer for a party may have a voluntary interview with a potential nonparty witness. The interview may be on reasonable notice to other parties, who may be permitted to attend the interview.

Comment:

R-21A Rule 21.1 requires that a party disclose documents on which that party relies in support of the party's position. A party must also list the witnesses upon whom it intends to rely and include a summary of expected testimony. The summary of expected testimony should address all propositions to which the witness will give testimony and should be reasonably specific in detail. See Rule 23.4.

If a party later ascertains that there are additional documents or witnesses, it must submit an amended list, as provided in Rule 21.2. See also Rule 22.5. In accordance with Rules 12.1 and 13.4, the parties must state with reasonable detail the facts and the legal grounds supporting their position.

R-21B Under the concept of professional ethics in some civil-law systems, a lawyer should not discuss the matters in dispute with prospective witnesses (other than the lawyer's own client). That norm is designed to protect testimony from improper manipulation, but it also has the effect of limiting the effectiveness of a lawyer in investigating and organizing evidence for consideration by the court. In discussion with a prospective witness, the lawyer should not suggest what the testimony should be nor offer improper inducement. Although there is some risk of abuse in allowing lawyers to confer with prospective witnesses, that risk is less injurious to fair adjudication than is the risk that relevant and important evidence may remain undisclosed.

R-21C Rule 21.3 permits a voluntary *ex parte* interview by a lawyer with a witness. Such an interview is not a deposition, which is a formal interrogation, conducted before a court official. See Rule 23.

R-21D Rule 21.3 provides the alternative that the lawyer initiating the interview may give notice to other parties, inviting them to attend voluntarily. This procedure can foreclose or ameliorate subsequent objection that the interview was improperly suggestive and therefore that the witness's testimony is suspect. In some circumstances a lawyer would prefer to risk such subsequent recrimination and therefore interview the witness in private.

22. Exchange of Evidence

22.1 A party who has complied with disclosure duties prescribed in Rule 21, on notice to the other parties, may request the court to order production by any person of any evidentiary matter, not protected by confidentiality or privilege, that is relevant to the case and that may be admissible, including:

22.1.1 Documents and other records of information that are specifically identified or identified within specifically defined categories;

22.1.2 Identifying information, such as name and address, about specified persons having knowledge of a matter in issue; and

22.1.3 A copy of the report of any expert that another party intends to present.

22.2 The court must determine the request and order production accordingly. The court may order production of other evidence as necessary in the interest of justice. Such evidence must be produced within a reasonable time prior to the final hearing.

22.3 The court may direct that another judge or a specially appointed officer supervise compliance with an order for exchange of evidence. In fulfilling that function, the special officer has the same power and duties as the judge. Decisions made by the special officer are subject to review by the court.

22.4 The requesting party may present the request directly to the opposing party. That party may acquiesce in the request, in whole or in part, and provide the evidence accordingly. If the party refuses in whole or in part, the requesting party, on notice to the opposing party, may request the court to order production of specified evidence. The court, after opportunity for hearing, must determine the request and may make an order for production accordingly.

22.5 A party who did not have possession of requested evidence when the court's order was made, but who thereafter comes into possession of it, must thereupon comply with the order.

22.6 The fact that the requested information is adverse to the interest of the party to whom the demand is directed is not a valid objection to its production.

22.7 The court should recognize evidentiary privileges when exercising authority to compel disclosure of evidence or other information. The court should consider whether a privilege may justify a party's failure to disclose evidence or other information when deciding whether to draw adverse inferences or to impose other indirect sanctions.

Comment:

R-22A These Rules adopt, as a model of litigation, a system consisting of preliminary hearings followed by a concentrated form of final hearing. The essential core of the first stage is preliminary disclosure and clarification of the evidence. The principal consideration in favor of a unitary final hearing is that of expeditious justice. To achieve this objective, a concentrated final hearing should be used, so that arguments and the taking of evidence are completed in a single hearing or in a few hearings on consecutive judicial days. A concentrated final hearing requires a preliminary phase (called pretrial in common-law systems) in which evidence is exchanged and the case is prepared for concentrated presentation.

R-22B Rules 21 and 22 define the roles and the rights of the parties, the duty of voluntary disclosure, the procedure for exchange of evidence, the role of the court, and the devices to ensure that the parties comply with demands for evidence. Proper compliance with these obligations is not only a matter of law for the parties, but also a matter of professional honor and obligation on the part of the lawyers involved in the litigation.

R-22C The philosophy expressed in Rules 21 and 22 is essentially that of the common-law countries other than the United States. In those countries, the scope of discovery or disclosure is specified and limited, as in Rules 21 and 22. However, within those specifications disclosure is generally a matter of right.

R-22D Discovery under prevailing U.S. procedure, exemplified in the Federal Rules of Civil Procedure, is much broader, including the broad right to seek information that "appears reasonably calculated to lead to the discovery of admissible evidence." This broad discovery is often criticized as responsible for the increasing costs of the administration of justice. However, reasonable disclosure and exchange of evidence facilitates discovery of truth.

R-22E Disclosure and exchange of evidence under the civil-law systems are generally more restricted, or nonexistent. In particular, a broader immunity is conferred against disclosure of trade and business secrets. This Rule should be interpreted as striking a balance between the restrictive civil-law systems and the broader systems in common-law jurisdictions.

R-22F Rule 22.1 requires the parties to make the disclosures required by Rule 21 prior to demanding production of evidence from an opposing party.

R-22G Rule 22.1 provides that every party is entitled to obtain from any person the disclosure of any unprivileged relevant evidence in possession of that person. Formal requests for evidence should be made to the court, and the court should direct the opposing party to comply with an order to produce evidence or information. This procedure can be unnecessarily burdensome on the parties and on the courts, especially in straightforward requests. Ideally, full disclosure of relevant evidence should result through dialogue among the parties, whereby the parties voluntarily satisfy each other's demands without intervention of the court. A party therefore may present the request directly to the opposing party, who should comply with an adequate request within a reasonable time. If the opposing party refuses, the party may request the court to order the production of the evidence. The court will then hear both parties and decide the issue. See Rule 22.4.

R-22H According to Rule 22.1, compulsory exchange of evidence is limited to matters directly relevant to the issues in the case as they have been stated in the pleadings. See Rule 25.2. A party is not entitled to disclosure of information merely that "appears reasonably calculated to lead to the discovery of admissible evidence," which is permitted under Rule 26 of the Federal Rules of Civil Procedure in the United States. "Relevant" evidence is that which supports or contravenes the allegations of one of the parties. This Rule is aimed at preventing overdiscovery or unjustified "fishing expeditions." See Principle 11.3.

R-22I Exchange of evidence may concern documents and any other things (films, pictures, videotapes, recorded tapes, or objects of any kind), including any records of information, such as computerized information. The demanding party must show the relevance of the information, document, or thing to prove or disprove the facts supporting a claim or a defense, and identify the document or thing to be disclosed, specifically identified, or defined by specific categories. Thus, a document may be identified by date and title or by specific description such as "correspondence concerning the transaction between A and B in the period February 1 through March 31." A party is not obliged to comply with a demand that does not fulfill these conditions. Disputes concerning whether the conditions of the demand have been satisfied, and whether the demand should be complied with, are resolved by the court on motion by any party. The court may declare the demand invalid or order production of the document or thing, and if necessary specify the time and mode of production.

R-22J Exchange of evidence may concern the identity of a potential witness. As used in these Rules, the term "witness" includes a person who can give statements to the court even if the statements are not strictly speaking "evidence," as is the rule in some civil-law systems concerning statements by parties. Under Rule 21.1.2 a summary of the expected testimony of a witness whom a party intends to call must be provided to other parties. A party is not allowed to examine a witness through deposition except when authorized by the court. See Rules 18.3.5, 21.3, and 23.

R-22K In general, parties bear the burden of obtaining evidence they need in preparation for final hearing. However, disclosure obtained by the parties on their own motion may be insufficient or could surprise the court or other parties. To deal with such inconvenience, the court may order additional disclosure on its own initiative or on motion of a party. For example, the court may order that a party or a prospective witness submit a written deposition concerning the facts of the case. The court may also subpoena a hostile witness to be orally deposed. See Rule 23.

R-22L In cases involving voluminous documents or remotely situated witnesses, or in similar circumstances of practical necessity, the court may appoint someone as a special officer to supervise exchange of evidence. A person so appointed should be impartial and independent, and have the same powers and duties as the judge, but decisions by such an officer are reviewable by the appointing court. See Rule 22.3.

R-22M If a party fails to comply with a demand for exchange of evidence, the court may impose sanctions to make disclosure effective. The determination of sanctions is within the discretion of the court, taking into account relevant features of the parties' behavior in accordance with Principle 17.

The sanctions are:

1) Adverse inferences against the noncomplying party including conclusive determination of the facts.
2) A monetary penalty, fixed by the court in its discretion, or other means of legal compulsion permitted by forum law, including contempt of court. The court should graduate the penalty or contempt sanction according to the circumstances of the case.
3) The most severe sanction against noncompliance with disclosure demands or orders is entry of adverse judgment with respect to one or

more of the claims. The court may enter a judgment of dismissal with prejudice against the plaintiff or a judgment by default against the defendant or dismiss claims, defenses, or allegations to which the evidence is relevant. This sanction is more severe than the drawing of an adverse inference. The adverse inference does not necessarily imply that the party loses the case on that basis, but dismissal of claims or defenses ordinarily has that result. Unless the court finds that special circumstances justify a different sanction, the preferred sanction is to draw adverse inferences. Dismissal and entry of adverse judgment is a sanction of last resort.

23. Deposition and Testimony by Affidavit

23.1 A deposition of a party or other person may be taken by order of the court. Unless the court orders otherwise, a deposition may be presented as evidence in the record.

23.2 A deposition must be taken upon oath or affirmation to tell the truth and transcribed verbatim or recorded by audio or video, as the parties may agree or as the court orders. The cost of transcription or recording must be paid by the party who requested the deposition, unless the court orders otherwise.

23.3 The deposition must be taken at a specified time and place upon notice to all parties, at least [30] days in advance. The examination must be conducted before a judge or other official authorized under forum law and in accordance with forum-law procedure. All the parties have the right to attend and to submit supplemental questions to be answered by the deponent.

23.4 With permission of the court, a party may present a written statement of sworn testimony of any person, containing statements in their own words about relevant facts. The court, in its discretion, may consider such statements as if they were made by oral testimony before the court. Whenever appropriate, a party may move for an order of the court requiring the personal appearance or deposition of the author of such a statement. Examination of that witness may begin with supplemental questioning by the court or opposing party.

Comment:

R-23A A deposition is a form of taking testimony employed in common-law and in some civil-law systems. It consists of sworn testimony of a potential witness, including a party, taken outside of court prior to the final hearing. A deposition may be given orally in response to questions by lawyers for the parties or by questions from a judicial officer appointed by the court. A deposition may be conducted by electronic communication, for example, by telephone conference. It may also be given through written responses to written questions. Ordinarily, a deposition is given after commencement of litigation but also, in accordance with the law of the forum, may be given *de bene esse*, that is, prior to litigation to preserve testimony when the witness is expected to be unavailable after litigation has commenced. Questioning may seek to gather information and to test the witness's recollection and credibility. The testimony of a witness in a deposition may be presented as evidence, either in lieu of the witness or as direct testimony, but the court may require the presence of a witness who can attend in order to permit supplemental questioning. Under these Rules a deposition may be used in limited circumstances for exchange of evidence before trial.

R-23B A party is not allowed to examine a witness through deposition except when authorized by the court. See Rule 18.3.5. Rule 23.2 provides that deposition testimony be taken on oath or affirmation, as at a hearing before the court. It is to be transcribed verbatim or recorded on audio or video. The parties may agree about the form of transcription or recording, but the court may nevertheless determine what form is to be used. The party who requests the deposition must pay the cost of transcription or recording, unless the court orders otherwise.

R-23C Rule 23.3 specifies the procedure for a deposition. In general, the procedure should be similar to a presentation of the witness before the court. Time and place of the deposition may be prescribed by the court.

R-23D The general principle governing presentation of evidence is that evidence will be presented orally at the final hearing. See Principle 19 and Rule 29. However, oral examination of a witness at the final hearing may be impossible, burdensome, or impractical. Rule 23.1 permits the transcript of a deposition taken in accordance with this Rule to be presented to the court as a substitute for reception of testimony of a witness who cannot conveniently be present in court, for example, by reason of illness or because the witness is in a remote location or cannot be compelled to attend to give testimony. A deposition may also be convenient for presenting testimony in a language other than that of the court. A deposition in any event may be used as a statement against interest.

R-23E Rule 23.4 permits the presentation of testimony by means of written affidavits containing statements about relevant facts of the case. Such a statement, although upon oath or affirmation, is *ex parte* in that neither the court nor opposing parties has been permitted to question the witness. According to Principle 19.3, "Ordinarily, testimony of parties and witnesses should be received orally." Therefore, a written statement may be regarded with corresponding skepticism by the court, especially if another party denies the truth of the statements made by affidavit. However, facts not in serious dispute often may be conveniently proved by this procedure. See Rule 21.1.3. Testimony by affidavit may facilitate reception of evidence for early determination of the dispute. See Rule 19.1.4.

The practice of producing testimony through written affidavits instead of personal presence for an oral examination is becoming common in several systems. Reasons of efficiency explain this trend: quicker availability of testimony, less trouble and expense for the nonparty, and less time required for the court. These factors may be especially important in transnational litigation, for instance when a witness would be required to travel from a distant country to be examined in court. However, the court may, in its own discretion or on motion by a party, order that the author of an affidavit be examined orally. There are means of taking evidence abroad provided by international law and conventions on judicial assistance, requests by diplomatic channels, letters rogatory, etc. See, for example, The Hague Convention on the Taking of Evidence Abroad.

24. Public Proceedings

24.1 Ordinarily, oral hearings, including hearings in which evidence is presented and in which judgment is pronounced, should be open to the public. Following consultation with the parties, the court may order that hearings or portions thereof be conducted in private in the interest of justice, public safety, or privacy.

24.2 Court files and records should be public or otherwise accessible to persons with a legal interest or making a responsible inquiry, according to forum law.

24.3 In the interest of justice, public safety, or privacy, if the proceedings are public, the judge may order part of them to be conducted in private.

24.4 Judgments, and ordinarily other orders, are accessible to the public.

24.5 Information obtained under these Rules but not presented in an open hearing must be maintained in confidence in accordance with forum law.

24.6 **In appropriate cases, the court may enter suitable protective orders to safeguard legitimate interests, such as trade or business or national-security secrets or information whose disclosure might cause undue injury or embarrassment.**

24.7 **To facilitate administration of this Rule, the court may examine evidence in camera.**

Comment:

R-24A A hearing in camera is one closed to the public and, in various circumstances, closed to others. As the court may direct according to the circumstances, such a hearing may be confined to the lawyers without the parties or it may be *ex parte* (e.g., confined to a party and that party's lawyer, for example, when trade secrets are involved). In general, court files and records should be public and accessible to the public and news media. Countries that have a tradition of keeping court files confidential should at least make them accessible to persons with a legal interest or making a responsible inquiry.

25. Relevance and Admissibility of Evidence

25.1 **All relevant evidence generally is admissible. Forum law may determine that illegally obtained evidence is inadmissible and impose exclusions.**

25.2 **The facts and legal claims and defenses in the pleadings determine relevance.**

25.3 **A party, even if not allowed by forum law to give evidence, may nevertheless make statements that will be accorded probative weight. A party making such a statement is subject to questioning by the court and other parties.**

25.4 **A party has a right to proof through testimony or evidentiary statement, not privileged under applicable law, of any person, including another party, whose evidence is available, relevant, and admissible. The court may call any witness meeting these qualifications.**

25.5 **The parties may offer in evidence any relevant information, document, or thing. The court may order any party or nonparty to present any relevant information, document, or thing in that person's possession or control.**

Comment:

R-25A This Rule states principles concerning evidence, defining generally the conditions and limits of what may be properly considered as proof.

The basic principle is that any factual information that is rationally useful in reaching judgment on the relevant facts of the case should be admissible as evidence. The court may refuse to accept evidence that is redundant. The common-law concept of hearsay evidence as an exclusionary rule is generally inappropriate in a nonjury case but it does affect the credibility and weight of evidence.

R-25B In applying the principle of relevance, the primary consideration is the usefulness of the evidence. In deciding upon admissibility of the evidence, the court makes a hypothetical evaluation connecting the proposed evidence with the issues in the case. If a probative inference may be drawn from the evidence to the facts, then the evidence is logically relevant. See Rule 12.1 and Comment *R-12A*.

R-25C In some legal systems there are rules limiting in various ways the use of circumstantial evidence. However, these rules seem unjustified and are very difficult to apply in practice. More generally, there is no valid reason to restrict the use of circumstantial evidence when it is useful to establish a fact in issue. Therefore, generally, the court may consider any circumstantial evidence provided it is relevant to the decision on the facts of the case.

R-25D Rule 25 defers to forum law the decision of who can properly give evidence or present statements. In some national systems the rules limit the extent to which parties or "interested" nonparties can be witnesses. However, even in such systems the modern trend favors admitting all testimony. A general rule of competency also avoids the complex distinctions that exclusionary rules require. The proper standard for the submission of evidence by a witness is the principle of relevancy. This does not mean, however, that subjective or objective connections of the witness with the case must be disregarded, but only that they are not a basis for excluding the testimony. These connections, for example, kinship between the witness and a party, may be meaningful in evaluating credibility.

Any person having information about a relevant fact is competent to give evidence. This includes the parties and any other person having mental capacity. Witnesses are obligated to tell the truth, as required in every procedural system. In many systems such an obligation is reinforced by an oath taken by the witness. When a problem arises because of the religious character of the oath, the court has discretion to determine the terms of the oath or to permit the witness merely to affirm the obligation to tell the truth.

R-25E Rules 25.4 and 25.5 govern the parties' right to proof in the form of testimony, documentary evidence, and real or demonstrative evidence. A party may testify in person, whether called by the party, another party, or the court. That procedure is not always permitted in civil-law systems, where the party is regarded as too interested to be a regular witness on its own behalf.

R-25F The court may exercise an active role in the taking of testimony or documentary, real, or demonstrative evidence. For example, when the court knows that a relevant document is in possession of a party or of a nonparty, and it was not spontaneously produced, the court may on its own motion order the party or the nonparty to produce it. The procedural device is substantially an order of subpoena. The court in issuing the order may establish the sanctions to be applied in case of noncompliance.

26. Expert Evidence

26.1 The court must appoint a neutral expert or panel of experts when required by law and may do so when it considers that expert evidence may be helpful. If the parties agree upon an expert the court ordinarily should appoint that expert.

26.2 The court must specify the issues to be addressed by the expert and may give directions concerning tests, evaluations, or other procedures to be employed by the expert, and the form in which the report is to be rendered. The court may issue orders necessary to facilitate the inquiry and report by the expert. The parties have the right to comment upon statements by an expert, whether appointed by the court or designated by a party.

26.3 A party may designate an expert or panel of experts on any issue. An expert so designated is governed by the same standards of objectivity and neutrality as a court-appointed expert. A party pays initially for an expert it has designated.

26.4 A party, itself or through its expert, is entitled to observe tests, evaluations, or other investigative procedures conducted by the court's expert. The court may order experts to confer with each other. Experts designated by the parties may submit their own opinions to the court in the same form as the report made by the court's expert.

Comment:

R-26A These Rules adopt the civil-law rule and provisions of the modern English procedure according to which the court appoints a neutral expert or panel of experts. The court decides on its own motion whether an expert is needed in order to evaluate or to establish facts that because of their scientific, legal, or technical nature, the court is unable to evaluate or establish by itself. The court appoints the expert or the experts (if possible using the special lists that exist in many countries) on the basis of the expert's competence in the relevant field. If the expert's neutrality is disputed, that issue is for the court to resolve. The court, informed by the parties' recommendations, should specify the technical or scientific issues on which the expert's advice is needed and formulate the questions the expert should answer. The court also should determine which techniques and procedures the expert will apply; regulate any other aspect of the tests, inquiries, and research the expert will make; and determine whether the expert will respond orally or by submitting a written report. The court should consult with the experts as well as the parties in determining the tests, evaluations, and other procedures to be used by the experts.

R-26B The court's expert is neutral and independent from the parties and from other influence and ordinarily is expected to be sound and credible. If the advice does not appear reasonable, the court may reject it or appoint another expert. However, the court is not obliged to follow the expert's advice. In such a case, the court ordinarily should explain specifically the reasons why the expert's advice is rejected and the reasons supporting the court's different conclusion.

R-26C Rule 26 recognizes that the status of an expert is somewhat different from that of a percipient witness and that experts have somewhat different status in various legal systems.

R-26D In common-law systems an expert is presented by the parties on the same basis as other witnesses, recognizing that the role usually is one of interpretation rather than recounting firsthand observations. In civil-law systems the parties may present experts but ordinarily do so only to supplement or dispute testimony of a court-appointed expert.

This Rule adopts an intermediate position. The court may appoint experts but the parties may also present experts whether or not the court has done so. In addition, if the parties agree upon an expert, the court ordinarily should appoint that expert. Such an expert is obliged to perform this task in good faith and according to the standards of the expert's profession. Both a court-appointed expert and a party-appointed expert are subject to supplemental examination by the court and by the parties.

R-26E Under Rule 26.2 the court may examine the expert orally in court or require a written report and afford oral examination of the expert after the report has been submitted. When the court receives oral testimony from the court's expert, the parties' experts should be similarly heard. When the court's expert submits a written report, the parties' experts should also be allowed to do so. The court may order all the experts to confer with each other in order to clarify the issues and to focus their opinions. The advice of the parties' experts may be taken into account by the court and the court may adopt a party's expert advice instead of that of the court's expert.

27. Evidentiary Privileges

27.1 Evidence may not be elicited in violation of:

27.1.1 The legal-profession privilege of confidentiality under forum law, including choice of law;

27.1.2 Confidentiality of communications in settlement negotiations;

27.1.3 [Other specified limitations].

27.2 A privilege may be forfeited by, for example, omitting to make a timely objection to a question or demand for information protected by a privilege. The court in the interest of justice may relieve a party of such forfeiture.

27.3 A claim of privilege made with respect to a document shall describe the document in detail sufficient to enable another party to challenge the claim of privilege.

Comment:

R-27A Privileges exclude relevant evidence. They have evolved over time and reflect various social interests. Organized professions (e.g., doctors, psychiatrists, accountants, lawyers) are interested in protecting their clients and their members' professional activities by means of the privilege not to disclose information acquired during such an activity. Statutory law and case law have extended the list of professional privileges. However, the recognition of such privileges has significant cost in the quality of proof and discovery of truth.

R-27B Rule 27.1.1 gives effect to a "legal-profession privilege." The concept of this privilege is different in the common-law and civil-law systems but this Rule includes both concepts. The common law recognizes an "attorney–client privilege," which enables the client to object to inquiry into confidential communications between client and lawyer that were made in connection with the provision of legal advice or assistance. Under U.S. law and some other common-law systems a similar protection, called the "lawyer work product" immunity, additionally shields materials developed by a lawyer to assist a client in litigation. The civil law confers the same protections but under the concept of a professional right or privilege of the lawyer. See also Rule 22.7.

R-27C Rule 27.1.2 reflects the universal principle that confidentiality should be observed with regard to communications in the course of settlement negotiations in litigation. Some systems presume that only correspondence between lawyers is confidential, whereas many other systems extend this privilege to party communications concerning settlement. The precise scope of confidentiality of communications concerning settlement is determined by the law governing the communications, but the general principle stated above should be considered in determining the matter. See also Rule 24.

R-27D Rule 27.1.3 may be used to accord protection to other privileges under the law of the forum, such as those involving financial advisers or other professionals. In general, the civil-law systems accord privacy to the communications of many professionals. Many legal systems have additional privileges, usually in qualified form. Thus, the European Court of Human Rights has recognized various professional privileges under various circumstances, for example, for bankers, accountants, and journalists, and many countries also have a privilege for communications between family members. Many state jurisdictions in the United States have an accountant privilege and some have a "self-evaluation privilege" on the part of hospitals and some other jural entities. However, in some civil-law systems the court may examine otherwise protected confidences if they appear highly relevant to the matter in dispute. Such an approach is known in the common law as a conditional privilege. However, if the court permits receipt of such evidence, it should protect the confidential information from exposure except as required for consideration in the dispute itself.

R-27E The court may make a determination whether to receive conditionally privileged information through an in-camera hearing, in which the participants are limited to the court itself, the parties, and the parties' lawyers. See Rule 24.7. The same device may be used concerning nonprivileged information when the court finds that publication could impair some important private or public interests, such as a trade secret. The taking of evidence in a closed hearing should be exceptional, having regard for the fundamental principle of the public nature of hearings.

R-27F A person who is entitled to a privilege may forfeit it, in which event evidence in the privileged communication is received without limitation. The privilege may be lost by means of an explicit statement or tacitly, for example, by failing to assert a timely claim of privilege. However, in the interest of justice, the court may decline to enforce a forfeiture.

R-27G Rule 27.3 prescribes a procedure for claims of privilege with respect to documents. The claimant is required to identify the document in sufficient detail to permit an opposing party to make an intelligent disputation of the claim of privilege, for example, that the document had been distributed to third persons.

R-27H Regarding the legal consequences of claiming privileges, see Principles 18.2 and 18.3 and Rule 22.7.

28. Reception and Effect of Evidence

28.1 A party has the burden to prove all the material facts that are the basis of that party's case.

28.2 The court should make free evaluation of the evidence and attach no unjustified significance to evidence according to its type or source. Facts are considered proven when the court is reasonably convinced of their truth.

28.3 The court, on its own motion or motion of a party, may:

28.3.1 Order reception of any relevant evidence;

28.3.2 Exclude evidence that is irrelevant or redundant or that involves unfair prejudice, cost, burden, confusion, or delay; or

28.3.3 Impose sanctions on a person for unjustified failure to attend to give evidence, to answer proper questions, or to produce a document or other item of evidence, or who otherwise obstructs the proceeding.

Comment:

R-28A Rule 28 specifies various aspects of the authority of the court with reference to evidence. The court may exercise such powers on its own motion or on motion of a party.

Rule 28.3.2 gives the court the power to exclude evidence on various grounds, including irrelevancy of the evidence or its redundant or cumulative character. Redundant or cumulative evidence is theoretically relevant if considered by itself but not when considered in the context of the other evidence adduced. The court may in the course of a final hearing admit evidence that was preliminarily excluded because it had appeared irrelevant, redundant, or cumulative. The standard of exclusion by reason of "unfair prejudice, cost, burden, confusion, or delay" should be applied very cautiously. The court should use this power primarily when a party adduces evidence with the apparent aim of delaying or confusing the proceedings.

R-28B Rule 28.3.3 provides for various sanctions, including *astreintes*. The court may draw an adverse inference from the behavior of a party such as failing to give testimony, present a witness, or produce a document or other item of evidence that the party could present. Drawing an adverse inference means that the court will interpret the party's conduct as circumstantial evidence contrary to the party.

Drawing an adverse inference is a sanction appropriate only against a party. Sanctions applied to nonparties include contempt of court and imposing a fine, subject to the limitation in Rule 35.2.4. The conduct that may be sanctioned includes failing to attend as a witness or answer proper questions and failing without justification to produce documents or other items of evidence. See Principles 17, 18.2, and 18.3.

G. Final Hearing

29. Concentrated Final Hearing

29.1 So far as practicable, the final hearing should be concentrated.

29.2 The final hearing must be before the judge or judges who are to render the judgment.

29.3 Documentary or other tangible evidence may be presented only if it has previously been disclosed to all other parties. Testimonial evidence may be presented only if notice has been given to all other parties of the identity of the witness and the substance of the contemplated testimony.

29.4 A person giving testimony may be questioned first by the court or the party seeking the testimony. All parties then must have opportunity to ask supplemental questions. The court and the parties may challenge a witness's credibility or the authenticity or accuracy of documentary evidence.

29.5 The court on its own motion or on motion of a party may exclude irrelevant or redundant evidence and prevent embarrassment or harassment of a witness.

Comment:

R-29A Rule 29.1 establishes a general principle concerning the structure of the final hearing. It is consistent with the common-law "trial" model and the modern model of a prepared final hearing in civil-law systems, according to which the taking of evidence not previously received should be made in a single hearing. When one day of hearing is insufficient the final hearing should continue in consecutive days. The concentrated hearing is the better method for the presentation of evidence, although several systems still use the older method of separated hearings. Exception to the rule of the concentrated hearing can be made in the court's discretion when there is good reason, for example, when a party needs an extension of time to obtain evidence. In such a case the delay should be as limited as possible. Dilatory behavior of the parties should not be permitted.

R-29B In some civil-law systems, a party's statement is regarded as having lesser standing than testimony of a nonparty witness; and in some systems a party cannot call itself as a witness or can do so only under specified conditions. The common law treats parties as fully competent witnesses and permits parties to call themselves to the stand and obliges them to testify at the instance of an opposing party, subject to privileges such as that against self-incrimination. These Rules adopt the common-law approach, so that a party has both an obligation to give evidence if called by the opposing party and a right to do so on its own motion. See Rule 25.3. Failure without explanation or justification to present such evidence may justify the court's drawing an adverse inference concerning the facts, or, in common-law countries, if a party disobeys an order to testify, holding the party in contempt. However, a party's failure to comply may have some reasonable explanation or justification. Sanctions may be gradually increased until the party decides to comply.

R-29C Rule 29.4 governs the examination of witnesses. The traditional distinction between common-law systems, which are based upon direct and cross-examination, and civil-law systems, which are based upon examination by the court, is well known and widely discussed in the comparative legal literature. Equally well known are also the limits and defects of both methods. The chief deficiency in the common-law procedure is excessive partisanship in cross-examination, with the danger of abuses and of distorting the truth. In the civil law the chief deficiency is passivity and lack of interest of the court while conducting an examination, with the danger of not reaching relevant information. Both procedures require efficient technique, on the part of the judge in civil-law systems and the lawyers in common-law systems. The problem is to devise a method effective for a presentation of oral evidence aimed at the search for truth. The rules provided here seek such a balanced method.

R-29D For a witness called by a party, the common-law system of direct and supplemental examination by the parties is the most suitable for a thorough examination. The witness is first questioned by the lawyer of the party who called the witness, and then questioned by the lawyers for the other parties. Further questioning is permitted by the court when useful. To prevent abuses by the lawyers, the court should exclude, on the other party's objection or on its own motion, questions that are irrelevant or improper or which subject the witness to embarrassment or harassment.

R-29E The civil-law method, in which the court examines the witness, has advantages in terms of the neutral search for the truth and of eliciting facts that the court considers especially relevant. The court therefore is afforded an active role in the examination of witnesses, an authority that is also recognized in common-law systems. The court may also clarify testimony during the questioning by the parties or examine the witness after the parties' examinations.

R-29F The opinion of a witness may be admitted when it will clarify the witness's testimony. In the recollection of facts, knowledge and memory are often inextricably mixed with judgments, evaluations, and opinions, often elaborated unconsciously. Sometimes a "fact" implies an opinion of the witness, as for instance when the witness interprets the reasons for another person's behavior. Therefore, a rule excluding the opinions of witnesses is properly understood as prohibiting comments that do not aid in the reconstruction of the facts at issue.

R-29G The credibility of any witness, including experts and parties, can be disputed on any relevant basis, including questioning, prior inconsistent statements, or any other circumstance that may affect the credibility of the witness, such as interest, personal connections, employment or other relationships, incapacity to perceive and recollect facts, and inherent implausibility of the testimony. Prior inconsistent statements may have been made in earlier stages of the same proceedings (for instance, during deposition) or made out of the judicial context, for instance before the beginning of the litigation.

However, the right to challenge the credibility of an adverse witness may be abused by harassment of the witness or distortion of the testimony. The court should prevent such conduct.

R-29H The authenticity or the reliability of other items of evidence, either documents or real and demonstrative evidence, may also be disputed by any party. Special subproceedings to determine the authenticity of public or private documents exist in many national systems. They should be used when the authenticity of a document is doubtful or contested. Scientific and technical evidence may also be scrutinized if its reliability is doubtful or disputed.

30. Record of the Evidence

30.1 A summary record of the hearings must be kept under the court's direction.

30.2 Upon order of the court or motion of a party, a verbatim transcript of the hearings or an audio or video recording must be kept. A party demanding such a record must pay the expense thereof.

Comment:

R-30A With regard to the record of the evidence, two principal methods can be used. One is typical of some common-law jurisdictions and consists of the verbatim transcript of everything said in the presentation of evidence. The other is typical of civil-law systems and consists of a summary of the hearing that is written by the court's clerk under the direction of the court, including the matters that in the court's opinion will be relevant for the final decision. In some civil-law systems there is no procedure for making a verbatim transcript. A verbatim transcript is complete and provides a good basis both for the final decision and for the appeal, but in many cases it is exceedingly burdensome and expensive.

R-30B A summary record should include all relevant statements made by the parties and the witnesses, and other events that might be useful for the final evaluation concerning the credibility of witnesses and the weight of proofs. The parties may ask for and the court grant inclusion of specific statements.

R-30C If a party requests a verbatim transcript or audio or video recording of the final hearing, the court should so order. The party or parties requesting the transcript should pay the expense. The court should be provided a copy of the transcript or recording at the expense of the party or parties who requested it, and the other parties are entitled to have a copy upon paying their share of the expense. The court may, on its own initiative, order a verbatim transcript of the hearing. A verbatim transcript does not take the place of the official record that must be kept according to Rule 30.1 unless so ordered by the court.

31. Final Discussion and Judgment

31.1 After the presentation of all evidence, each party is entitled to present a closing statement. The court may allow the parties' lawyers to engage with each other and with the court in an oral discussion concerning the main issues of the case.

31.2 The judgment must be rendered within [60 days] thereafter and be accompanied by a written reasoned explanation of its legal, evidentiary, and factual basis.

31.3 Upon rendering judgment, the court must promptly give written notice thereof to the parties.

Comment:

R-31A The final hearing ends when all the evidence has been presented. The parties have a right to present oral or written closing statements, according to the direction of the court.

R-31B Rule 31.2 requires the court to issue a written opinion justifying its decision. The publication is made according to the local practice, but a written notice must be sent to the parties. See Rule 31.3. All parties should be sent a copy of the entire judgment. The date of the judgment, determined according to forum law, is the basis for determining the time for appeal and for enforcement.

The justificatory opinion must include the findings of fact supported by reference to the relevant proofs, the court's evaluations of evidence, and the principal legal propositions supporting the decision.

R-31C If the court is composed of more than one judge, in some countries a member of the tribunal may give a dissenting or concurring opinion, orally or in writing. Such opinions, if in writing, are published together with the court's opinion.

32. Costs

32.1 Each party must advance its own costs and expenses, including court fees, attorneys' fees, fees of a translator appointed by the party, and incidental expenses.

32.2 The interim costs of the fees and expenses of an assessor, expert, other judicial officer, or other person appointed by the court must be paid provisionally by the party with the burden of proof or as otherwise ordered by the court.

32.3 The winning party ordinarily should be awarded all or a substantial portion of its reasonable costs. It must present a request promptly after the judgment.

32.4 The losing party must pay promptly the amount requested except for such items as it disputes. Disputed items shall be determined

by the court or by such other procedure as the parties may agree upon.

32.5 **The court may withhold or limit costs to the winning party when there is clear justification for doing so. The court may limit the award to a proportion that reflects expenditures for matters in genuine dispute and award costs against a winning party who has raised unnecessary issues or been otherwise unreasonably disputatious. The court in making cost decisions may take account of any party's procedural misconduct in the proceeding.**

32.6 **The court may delegate the determination and award of costs to a specialized costs official.**

32.7 **Payment of costs may be stayed if appellate review is pursued.**

32.8 **This Rule also applies to costs and expenses incurred on appellate review.**

32.9 **A person may be required to provide security for costs, or for liability for provisional measures, when necessary in the interest of justice to guarantee full compensation of possible future damages. Security should not be required solely because a party is not domiciled in the forum state.**

Comment:

R-32A The rule governing allocation of costs and expenses of litigation in ordinary civil proceedings, recognized almost universally except in the United States, China, and Japan, is that the prevailing party is entitled to reimbursement of attorneys' fees from the losing party. That principle is adopted here. The prevailing party must submit a statement seeking reimbursement.

Under the "American" rule in the United States, each party bears its own costs and expenses, including its attorneys' fees, except as statutes, rules, or contracts specifically provide otherwise or in case of exceptional abuse of process. The American rule creates incentives for a party to bring litigation or to persist in defense of litigation that would not be maintained under the generally recognized rule.

However, the rules concerning costs in common-law systems and some civil-law systems confer authority on the court to modify the normal allocation of costs to the losing party. Rule 32.5 adopts such a position.

R-32B The parties are permitted, in accordance with applicable law, to contract with their lawyers concerning their fees. Costs awarded should be reasonable, not necessarily those incurred by the party or the party's lawyer. If it was reasonably appropriate that a party retain more than one firm of lawyers, those fees and expenses may be recovered. The party seeking recovery of costs has the burden of proving their amount and their reasonableness. The award belongs to the party, not the lawyer, subject to any contractual arrangement between them.

R-32C Rule 32.9 recognizes that, if it is not inconsistent with constitutional provisions, the court may require posting of security for costs. In several legal systems a requirement of security for costs is considered a violation of the due-process guarantee in connection with the principle of equal treatment under the law. Security for costs could entail discrimination against parties unable to give such a security, and, correspondingly, constitute preferential treatment for parties who can. On the other hand, in some countries it is considered as a normal means to ensure the recovery of costs.

In the context of transnational commercial litigation such concerns may be less important than in the usual domestic litigation. Moreover, there is a higher risk of being unable to recover costs from a losing party who is not a resident of the forum state. These Rules leave the imposition of security for costs to the discretion of the court. The court should not impose excessive or unreasonable security.

H. Appellate and Subsequent Proceedings

33. Appellate Review

33.1 Except as stated in Rule 33.2, an appeal may be taken only from a final judgment of the court of first instance. The judgment is enforceable pending appeal, subject to Rules 35.3 and 35.4.

33.2 An order of a court of first instance granting or denying an order sought under Rule 17 is subject to immediate review. The order remains in effect during the pendency of the review, unless the court of first instance or the reviewing court orders otherwise.

33.3 Orders of the court other than a final judgment and an order appealable under Rule 33.2 are subject to immediate review only upon permission of the appellate court. Such permission may be granted when an immediate review may resolve an issue of general legal importance or of special importance in the immediate proceeding.

33.4 Appellate review is limited to claims (including counterclaims) and defenses addressed in the first-instance proceeding, but the

appellate court may consider new facts and evidence in the interest of justice.

33.5 **Further appellate review of the decision of a second-instance court may be permitted in accordance with forum law.**

Comment:

R-33A A right of appeal is a generally recognized procedural norm. It would be impractical to provide in these Rules for the structure of the appellate courts and the procedure to be followed in giving effect to this right. It is therefore provided that appellate review should be through the procedures available in the court system of the forum. "Appeal" includes not only appeal formally designated as such but also other procedures that afford the substantial equivalent, for example, review by extraordinary order (writ) from the appellate court or certification for appeal by the court of first instance.

R-33B Rule 33.1 provides for a right of appeal from a final judgment. The only exceptions are those stated in Rules 33.2 and 33.3. Thus, interlocutory appellate review is not permitted from other orders of the first-instance court, even though such review might be available under the law of the forum. In some countries, especially those of common-law tradition, some of the decisions in a proceeding are made by adjuncts within the first-instance tribunal, such as magistrate judges. These decisions are usually appealable to or made under the supervision of the first-instance judge who delegated the issue. Rule 33.1 does not apply to this practice.

R-33C The rule of finality is recognized in most legal systems. However, procedure in many systems permits formal correction of a judgment under specified conditions. All systems impose time limits on use of such procedures and generally require that they be invoked before the time to appeal has expired.

R-33D Rule 33.2 permits interlocutory appellate review of orders granting or denying an injunction. See Rule 17.6. The injunction remains in effect during the pendency of the review, unless the reviewing court orders otherwise. That court or the court of first instance may determine that an injunction should expire or be terminated if circumstances warrant.

R-33E Rule 33.3 permits interlocutory appeal of orders other than the final judgment at the authorization of the appellate court. The judges of the appellate court must determine that the order is of the importance defined in Rule 33.3. Permission for the interlocutory appeal may be sought by motion addressed to the appellate court. The appellate court may take account of the first-instance judge's views about the value of immediate appeal if such views are offered.

R-33F The restriction upon presenting additional facts and evidence to the second-instance court reflects the practice in common-law and in some civil-law systems. However, that practice is subject to the exception that an appellate court may consider additional evidence under extraordinary circumstances, such as the uncovering of determinative evidence after the appeal was taken and the record had been completed in the first-instance court.

R-33G Most modern court systems are organized in a hierarchy of at least three levels. In many systems, after appellate review in a court of second instance has been obtained, further appellate review is available only on a discretionary basis. The discretion may be exercised by the higher appellate court, for example, on the basis of a petition for hearing. In some systems such discretion may be exercised by the second-instance court by certifying the case or an issue or issues within a case to the higher appellate court for consideration.

Rule 33.5 adopts by reference the procedure in the courts of the forum concerning the availability and procedure for further appellate review. It is impractical to specify special provisions in these Rules for this purpose.

34. Rescission of Judgment

34.1 A final judgment may be rescinded only through a new proceeding and only upon a showing that the applicant acted with due diligence and that:

34.1.1 The judgment was procured without notice to or jurisdiction over the party seeking relief;

34.1.2 The judgment was procured through fraud;

34.1.3 There is evidence available that would lead to a different outcome and that was not previously available or that could not have been known through exercise of due diligence, or by reason of fraud in disclosure, exchange, or presentation of evidence; or

34.1.4 The judgment constitutes a manifest miscarriage of justice.

34.2 An application for rescission of judgment must be made within [90] days from the date of discovery of the circumstances justifying rescission.

Comment:

R-34A As a general rule a final judgment should not be reexamined except in appellate review according to the provisions included in Rule 33. Only in exceptional circumstances may it be pursued through a new proceeding. A rescission proceeding ordinarily should be brought in the court in which the judgment was rendered. The relief may be cancellation of the original judgment or substitution of a different judgment.

R-34B Reexamination of a judgment may be requested in the court that rendered the judgment. In seeking such a reexamination a party must act with due diligence. The grounds for such an application are: (1) the court had no jurisdiction over the party asking for reexamination; (2) the judgment was procured by fraud on the court; (3) there is evidence not previously available through the exercise of due diligence that would lead to a different outcome; or (4) there has been a manifest miscarriage of justice.

R-34C The challenge under Rule 34.1.1 should be allowed only in case of default judgments. If the party contested the case on the merits without raising this question, the defense is waived and the party should not be allowed to attack the judgment on those grounds.

R-34D The court should consider such an application cautiously when Rule 34.1.3 is invoked. The applicant should show that there was no opportunity to present the item of evidence at the final hearing and that the evidence is decisive, that is, that the final decision should be changed.

R-34E In interpreting Rule 34.1.4, it should be recognized that the mere violation of a procedural or substantive legal rule, or errors in assessing the weight of the evidence, are not proper grounds for reexamining a final judgment, but are proper grounds for appeal. See Rule 33. A manifest miscarriage of justice is an extreme situation in which the minimum standards and prerequisites for fair process and a proper judgment have been violated.

35. Enforcement of Judgment

35.1 **A final judgment, as well as a judgment for a provisional remedy, is immediately enforceable, unless it has been stayed as provided in Rule 35.3.**

35.2 **If a person against whom a judgment has been entered does not comply within the time specified, or, if no time is specified, within 30 days after the judgment becomes final, enforcement measures may be imposed on the obligor. These measures may include compulsory revelation of assets wherever they are located and a**

monetary penalty on the obligor, payable to the judgment obligee, to the court, or to whomever the court may direct.

35.2.1 Application for such a sanction must be made by a person entitled to enforce the judgment.

35.2.2 An award for noncompliance may include the cost and expense incurred by the party seeking enforcement of the judgment, including attorneys' fees, and may also include a penalty for defiance of the court, generally not to exceed twice the amount of the judgment.

35.2.3 If the person against whom the judgment is rendered persists in refusal to comply, the court may impose additional penalties.

35.2.4 A penalty may not be imposed on a person who demonstrates to the court financial or other inability to comply with the judgment.

35.2.5 The court may order nonparties to reveal information relating to the assets of the judgment debtor.

35.3 The court of first instance or the appellate court, on motion of the party against whom the judgment was rendered, may grant a stay of enforcement of the judgment pending appeal when necessary in the interest of justice.

35.4 The court may require a suitable bond or other security from the appellant as a condition of granting a stay or from the respondents as a condition of denying a stay.

Comment:

R-35A Rule 35.1 provides that a final judgment is immediately enforceable. If the judgment will be enforced in the country of the court in which the judgment was entered, the enforcement will be based on the forum's law governing the enforcement of final judgments. Otherwise, the international rules such as the Brussels I Regulation and the Brussels and Lugano Conventions on Jurisdiction and Enforcement of Judgments will apply. When a monetary judgment is to be enforced, attachment of property owned by the judgment obligor, or obligations owed to the obligor, may be ordered. Monetary penalties may be imposed by the court for delay in compliance, with discretion concerning the amount of the penalty.

R-35B Rule 35.2 authorizes the court, upon request of the judgment holder, to impose monetary penalties upon the judgment obligor that take effect if the obligor does not pay the obligation within the time specified, or within 30 days after the judgment has become final if no time is specified. The monetary penalties are to be imposed according to the following standards:

1) Application for the enforcement costs and penalties may be made by any party entitled to enforce the judgment.
2) Enforcement costs include the fees required for the enforcement, including the attorneys' fees, and an additional penalty in case of defiance of the court. An additional penalty may not exceed twice the amount of the judgment. The court may require the penalty to be paid to the person obtaining the judgment or to the court or otherwise.
3) Additional penalties may be added against an obligor who persists in refusal to pay, considering the amount of the judgment and the economic situation of the parties. Here, too, the court may require the penalty to be paid to the person obtaining the judgment or to the court, or otherwise.
4) No penalty will be imposed on a person who satisfactorily demonstrates to the court an inability to comply with the judgment.
5) "Nonparties" includes any institution that holds an account of the debtor.

R-35C Rule 35.3 permits either the first-instance court or the appellate court to grant a stay of enforcement when necessary in the interest of justice. Rule 35.4 authorizes the court to require a bond or other security as a condition either to permit or to stay the immediate enforcement.

36. Recognition and Judicial Assistance

36.1 A final judgment in a proceeding conducted in another forum in substantial compliance with these Rules must be recognized and enforced unless substantive public policy requires otherwise. A provisional measure must be recognized in the same terms.

36.2 Courts of states that have adopted these Rules must provide reasonable judicial assistance in aid of proceedings conducted under these Rules in another state, including provisional remedies, assistance in the identification or production of evidence, and enforcement of a judgment.

Comment:

R-36A It is a general principle of private international law that judgments of one state will be recognized and enforced in the courts of other states. The extent of such assistance and the procedures by which it may be provided are governed in many respects by the Brussels I Regulation and the Brussels and Lugano Conventions.

R-36B Rule 36 provides that, as a matter of the domestic law of the forum, assistance to the courts of another state is to be provided to such extent as may be appropriate, including provisional measures. The general governing standard is the measure of assistance that one court within the state would provide to another court in the same state.

A BIBLIOGRAPHY OF WRITINGS ABOUT THE ALI/UNIDROIT PROJECT[1]

The following listing is limited to the writings that have been addressed to the project itself, a literature remarkably rich both in the breadth of its critique and the diversity of its approaches. These writings, representing a wide range of viewpoints and national perspectives, pragmatic as well as scholarly, have been of great value to the Reporters in enabling them to refine the scope of their work. Arranged chronologically in order to help the interested reader to discern more readily the interdependence of work and commentary as both evolved in the course of the project's successive drafts, this Bibliography provides a useful starting point for additional research and reflection.

Michele Taruffo, "Drafting Rules for Transnational Litigation." *Zeitschrift für Zivilprozess International* 449 (1997).

John Barcelo, III, "Transnational Rules of Civil Procedure: Introduction." *Cornell International Law Journal*, vol. 30, no. 2 (1997), 493.

Edición Especial (Special Issue): *Proyecto de Normas Transnacionales del Proceso Civil (Transnational Rules of Civil Procedure)*: 52 Derecho PUC (1998 & 1999). Geoffrey C. Hazard, Jr., "Civil Litigation Without Frontiers: Harmonization and Unification of Procedural Law," 575; Geoffrey C. Hazard, Jr., "Litigio Civil Sin Fronteras: Armonización y Unificación del Derecho Procesal," 583; Antonio Gidi, "Apresentação ao Projeto de Normas Transnacionais de Processo Civil," 593; Antonio Gidi, "Presentación del Proyecto de Normas Transnacionales del Proceso Civil," 607; Geoffrey C. Hazard, Jr., and Michele Taruffo, "Discussion Draft No. 01, Transnational Rules of Civil Procedure," 621; Geoffrey C. Hazard, Jr., and Michele Taruffo, "Proyecto de Normas Transnacionales del Proceso Civil," 679; Geoffrey C. Hazard, Jr., and Michele Taruffo, "Normas Transnacionais de Processo Civil," 1047.

Symposium: *Texas International Law Journal*, vol. 33 (1998). Gary Born, "Critical Observations on the Draft Transnational Rules of Civil Procedure," 387; Russell J. Weintraub, "Critique of the Hazard-Taruffo Transnational Rules of Civil Procedure," 413; Jacob Dolinger and Carmen Tiburcio, "The Forum Law

[1] Compiled by Antonio Gidi.

Rule in International Litigation – Which Procedural Law Governs Proceedings to Be Performed in Foreign Jurisdictions: Lex Fori or Lex Diligentiae?" 425; Gerhard Walter and Samuel P. Baumgartner, "Utility and Feasibility of Transnational Rules of Civil Procedure: Some German and Swiss Reactions to the Hazard-Taruffo Project," 463; Catherine Kessedjian, "First Impressions of the Transnational Rules of Civil Procedure," 477; Geoffrey C. Hazard, Jr., "Transnational Rules of Civil Procedure: Preliminary Draft No. 1," 499.

Joaquim-J. Forner Delaygua, "El Proyecto del American Law Institute 'Transnational Rules of Civil Procedure': La Cooperación Judicial." *Annuario Español de Derecho Internacional Privado* (2000), 275.

Rolf Stürner, "Règles Transnationales de Procédure Civile? Quelques Remarques d'un Européen sur un Nouveau Projet Commun de l'American Law Institute et d'UNIDROIT." *Revue Internationale de Droit Comparè* 845 (2000).

Rolf Stürner, "Some European Remarks on a New Joint Project of The American Law Institute and UNIDROIT (Foreign Law Year in Review: 1999)." *International Lawyer*, vol. 34, no. 3 (2000), 1071.

Antonio Gidi, "Normas Transnacionais de Processo Civil." *8 Revista dos Mestrandos em Direito Econômico da UFBA* 54 (2000).

José Lebre de Freitas, "O Anteprojecto Hazard-Taruffo para o Processo dos Litígios Comerciais Internacionais." 2 *Themis. Revista da Faculdade de Direito da Universidade Nova de Lisboa* 19 (2000).

Eduard Kunštek, "Transnacionalna Pravila Gradanskog Postupka." *21 Zbornik Pravnog Fakulteta Sveučilišta U Rijeci* 351 (2000).

Antonio Gidi, "Apresentação às Normas Transnacionais de Processo Civil." 8 *Revista dos Mestrandos em Direito Econômico da UFBA* 40 (2000) [Brazil], also published in 52 *Derecho PUC* 593 (1999) [Peru], in *Roma e America* 335 (2000) [Italy], and in 102 *RePro* 185 (2001) [Brazil].

Antonio Gidi, "Iniciativas para la formulación de normas uniformes en el ámbito del derecho procesal civil internacional." 54 *Derecho PUC* 245 (2001) [Peru], also published in 11 *Tribunales de Justicia* 21 (2002) [Spain], and in 26 *Revista de Direito Processual Civil* 749. (2002) [Brazil]; Geoffrey C. Hazard, Jr., Rolf Stürner, Michele Taruffo, and Antonio Gidi, "Principios fundamentales del proceso civil transnacional," 54 *Derecho PUC* 253 (2001), also published in 11 *Tribunales de Justicia* 27 (2002) [Spain], and in 26 *Revista de Direito Processual Civil* 754. (2002) [Brazil]; Geoffrey C. Hazard, Jr., Michele Taruffo, Rolf Stürner, and Antonio Gidi, "Normas del proceso civil transnacional" 54 *Derecho PUC* 263 (2001), also published in 11 *Tribunales de Justicia* 31 (2002) [Spain], and in 26 *Revista de Direito Processual Civil* 761 (2002) [Brazil].

Vers un Procès Civil Universel? Les Règles Transnationales de Procédure Civile de l'American Law Institute, edited by Philippe Fouchard, (Paris: Editions Panthéon-Assas, 2001). Lance Liebman, "Allocution," 11; Philippe Fouchard, "Introduction," 13; Michele Taruffo, "La Genèse et la finalité des Règles Proposées par l'American Law Institute," 19; Pierre Mayer, "L'Utilité des Règles

Transnationales de Procédure Civile: Une vue Critique," 23; Horatia Muir Watt, "Quelle Méthode?" 39; Marie-Laure Niboyet, "Quels Litiges?" 51; Hélène Gaudemet-Tallon, "Quel Juge?" 67; Geoffrey C. Hazard, Jr., "Le Déroulement du Procès," 81; Jacques Normand, "La Confrontation des Principes Directeurs," 89; Catherine Kessedjian, "Quelques Réflexions en Matière de Preuves," 109; Loïc Cadiet, "Quelles Preuves? Discovery, Témoins, Experts, Rôle Respectif des Parties et du Juge," 115; Antonio Gidi, "'Vers un Procès Civil Transnational': Une Première Réponse aux Critiques," 139; Philippe Fouchard, "Clôture," 151; Gabriele Mecarelli, "Les Principes Fondamentaux de Procédure Civile Transnationale et les 'nouvelles' Règles Transnationales: Premières Observations, 157; "Annexes," 171.

Special Issue, *Harmonising Transnational Civil Procedure: The ALI/UNIDROIT Principles and Rules [Vers Une Procédure Civile Transnationale Harmonisée: Les Principes et Règles ALI/UNIDROIT], Uniform Law Review [Revue de Droit Uniforme]*, NS – vol. 6, no. 4 (2001). Herbert Kronke, "Efficiency, Fairness, Macro-Economic Functions: Challenges for the Harmonisation of Transnational Civil Procedure," 740; Herbert Kronke, "Efficacité, impartialité, fonctions macro-économiques: les objectifs de l'harmonisation de la procédure civile transnationale," 741; Geoffrey C. Hazard, Jr., "Fundamentals of Civil Procedure," 753; Marcel Storme, "Procedural Law and the Reform of Justice: from Regional to Universal Harmonisation," 763; Philippe Fouchard, "Une procédure civile transnationale: Quelle fin et quels moyens?," 779; Stephen Goldstein, "The Proposed ALI/UNIDROIT Principles and Rules of Transnational Civil Procedure: The Utility of Such a Harmonization Project," 789; Janet Walker, "The Utility of the ALI/UNIDROIT Project on Principles and Rules of Transnational Civil Procedure," 803; Antonio Gidi, "Notes on Criticizing the Proposed ALI/UNIDROIT Principles and Rules of Transnational Civil Procedure," 819; Haimo Schack, "Transnational Service of Process: A Call for Uniform and Mandatory Rules," 827; L. J. Priestley, "Transnational Civil Procedure – Fact Pleading v. Notice Pleading: Its Significance in the Development of Evidence," 841; Edward H. Cooper, "Transnational Civil Procedure: Fact Pleading or Notice Pleading? A Viewpoint from the USA," 857; Rolf Stürner, "Transnational Civil Procedure: Discovery and Sanctions Against Non-compliance," 871; Pierre Lalive, "Principe d'inquisition et principe accusatoire dans l'arbitrage commercial international," 887; Gabriele Mecarelli, "Quelques réflexions en matière de discovery," 901; Aída Kemelmajer de Carlucci, "La charge de la preuve dans les Principes et Règles ALI/UNIDROIT relatifs à la procédure civile transnationale," 915; Jean-Paul Béraudo, "Réflexions sur les Principes ALI/UNIDROIT à propos de la preuve," 925; Neil Andrews, "Provisional and Protective Measures: Towards a Uniform Protective Order in Civil Matters," 931; Bryan Beaumont, "The Proposed ALI/UNIDROIT Principles of Transnational Civil Procedure and their Relationship to Australian Jurisdictions," 951; Sheldon H. Elsen, "An American Lawyer Looks at Litigation under the Proposed ALI/UNIDROIT Principles and Rules of Transnational Civil

Procedure," 971; Valentinas Mikelėnas, "The Proposed ALI/UNIDROIT Principles and Rules of Transnational Civil Procedure and the New Code of Civil Procedure in Lithuania," 981; "Frédérique Ferrand, Les 'Principes' relatifs à la procédure civile transnationale sont-ils autosuffisants? – De la nécessité ou non de les assortir de 'Règles' dans le projet ALI/UNIDROIT," 995; Thomas Pfeiffer, "The ALI/UNIDROIT Project: Are Principles Sufficient, Without the Rules?" 1015; ANNEX I: "ALI/UNIDROIT Draft Principles and Rules of Transnational Civil Procedure," 1035; ANNEXE II: "Projet ALI/UNIDROIT de Principes et Règles relatifs à la procédure civile transnationale," 1105.

New York University Journal of International Law and Politics, vol. 33 (2001). Geoffrey C. Hazard, Jr., Michele Taruffo, Rolf Stürner, and Antonio Gidi, "Introduction to the Principles and Rules of Transnational Civil Procedure," 769; Geoffrey C. Hazard, Jr., Rolf Stürner, Michele Taruffo, and Antonio Gidi, "Fundamental Principles of Transnational Civil Procedure," 785; Geoffrey C. Hazard, Jr., Michele Taruffo, Rolf Stürner, and Antonio Gidi, "Rules of Transnational Civil Procedure," 793.

Essays on Transnational and Comparative Civil Procedure, edited by Federico Carpi and Michele Lupoi (Torino: Giappichelli, 2001).

Gerhard Walter and Samuel P. Baumgartner, *Improving the Prospects of the Transnational Rules of Civil Procedure Project: Some Thoughts on Purpose and Means of Implementation*, 6 Zeitschrift für Zivilprozeß International (2000), also published in 18 Ritsumeikan L. Rev. 169 (2001).

El Proyecto de las "Normas de Proceso Civil Transnacional," 11 Tribunales de Justicia 19 (2002) [Spain]. Lorena Bachmaier Winter, "El Proyecto de las 'Normas de Proceso Civil Transnacional,'" 19; Antonio Gidi, "Iniciativas para la formulación de normas uniformes en el ámbito del derecho procesal civil internacional," 21; Geoffrey C. Hazard, Jr., "Litigio civil sin fronteras: armonización y unificación del derecho procesal," 24; Geoffrey C. Hazard, Jr., Rolf Stürner, Michele Taruffo, and Antonio Gidi, "Principios fundamentales del proceso civil transnacional," 27; Geoffrey C. Hazard, Jr., Michele Taruffo, Rolf Stürner, and Antonio Gidi, "Normas del proceso civil transnacional," 31.

Samuel P. Baumgartner, *Gaining a Worldly Perspective for the World in Our Courts*, unpublished manuscript (on file with ALI).

Jorge Sánchez Cordero and Antonio Gidi, *Las reglas y procedimientos del derecho procesal civil transnacional*. El Proyecto American Law Institute-UNIDROIT (2003).

Frédérique Ferrand, *La Procédure Civile Mondiale Modélisée: Le projet de l'American Law Institute et d'Unidroit de Principes et Règles de procédure civile transnationale: Actes du colloque de Lyon du 12 juin 2003, Collection Droit et Procédures* (2004). Guy Lavorel, "Allocution d'ouverture," 9; Olivier Moréteau, "Allocution," 11; Herbert Kronke, "Le cadre du projet ALI-Unidroit," 17; Geoffrey C. Hazard, Jr., "Les objectifs du projet ALI-Unidroit," 23; Frédérique Ferrand, "Rapports entre Principes et Règles dans le projet ALI-Unidroit," 27; Jacques Junillon, "Le projet ALI-Unidroit, vue critique d'un praticien du droit," 35; Tony Moussa, "Le Projet ALI-Unidroit, vue critique d'un magistrat," 47; Hélène Gaudemet-Tallon, "Les aspects de droit international privé du Projet ALI-Unidroit," 71; Hervé Croze, "L'introduction de l'instance," 93; Jacques Normand, "Le rôle respectif des parties et du juge dans les Principes de procédure civile transnationale," 103; Loïc Cadiet, "La preuve," 119; Gabriele Mecarelli, "Sanctions, frais et dépens. Les aspects financiers de la procédure," 139; Serge Guinchard, "Rapport de synthèse," 155; Geoffrey C. Hazard, Jr., "Postface," 345.

The Future of Transnational Civil Litigation: English Responses to the ALI/UNIDROIT Draft Principles and Rules of Transnational Civil Procedure (London: The British Institute of International and Comparative Law, Mads Andenas, Neil Andrews, and Renato Nazzini eds., 2004). Geoffrey Hazard, Jr., "The ALI/UNIDROIT Project," 3; Rolf Stürner, "Anglo-American and Continental Civil Procedure: The English Reform as a Model for Further Harmonization?" 9; Cyril Glasser, "Do We Need a Transnational Civil Procedure Code? A Critical Comment," 13; Jeremy Lever, "Comparative Reflections," 17; Neil Andrews, "Embracing the Noble Quest for Transnational Procedural Principles," 21; Anthony May, "The ALI/UNIDROIT Rules of Transnational Civil Procedure in the Perspective of the New English and Welsh Rules," 43; Henry Brooke, "The 'Overriding Objective,' Procedural Sanctions, and Appeals," 51; Bernard Rix, "First Instance and Appellate Proceedings in Commercial Matters," 65; Robert Turner, "The Proactive Judge and the Provision of a Single Transnational Case Management System and Its Associate Procedures," 73; Renato Nazzini, "Transnational Litigation and ADR: The Philosophy of the CPR," 91; Adam Johnson, "Interim Measures under the Draft Principles and Rules of Transnational Civil Procedure: Some Reflections from the English Perspective," 109; Adrian Zuckerman, "Compliance with Process Obligations and Fair Trial," 127; Charles Hollander, "Documentary Disclosure: Lessons from the English Experience," 151; Michele Taruffo, "Admissions and Presentation of Evidence," 161.

ALI Project Drafts[2]

Preliminary Draft No. 1 (1998)
Preliminary Draft No. 1A (1998)
Interim Revision (1998)
Discussion Draft No. 1 (1999)
Preliminary Draft No. 2 (2000)
Discussion Draft No. 2 (2001)
Council Draft No. 1 (2001)
Discussion Draft No. 3 (2002)

[2] From 2000 on, the ALI and UNIDROIT documents have practically the same substantive content.

Preliminary Draft No. 3 (2002)
Discussion Draft No. 4 (2003)
Council Draft No. 2 (2003)
Proposed Final Draft (2004)

UNIDROIT Studies, Reports, Drafts, and Proposed Final Draft[3]

1999 – Study LXXVI – Doc. 1 (Feasibility Study)
2000 – Study LXXVI – Doc. 2 (Preliminary Draft)
2001 – Study LXXVI – Doc. 3 (Secretary's Report)
2001 – Study LXXVI – Doc. 4 (Draft)
2001 – Study LXXVI – Doc. 5 (Remarks and Comments)
2002 – Study LXXVI – Doc. 6 (Secretary's Report)
2002 – Study LXXVI – Doc. 7 (Draft)
2002 – Study LXXVI – Doc. 8 (Secretary's Report)
2002 – Study LXXVI – Doc. 9 (Draft)
2003 – Study LXXVI – Doc. 10 (Draft)
2004 – Study LXXVI – Doc. 11 (Draft)
2004 – Study LXXVI – Doc. 12 (Draft)

[3] From 2000 on, the ALI and UNIDROIT documents have practically the same substantive content.

INDEX

References are to Principles, Rules, and Comments

Access to Information and Evidence, Prin. 16. *See also* Burden and Standard of Proof; Burden of proof; Commencement of Proceeding and Notice; Disclosure; Discovery; Due Notice/Right to Be Heard; Evidence; Evidentiary Privileges; Evidentiary Privileges and Immunity; Exchange of Evidence; Expert Evidence; "Facts and evidence"; Model Code of Evidence project of ALI; Oral and Written Presentations; Reception and Effect of Evidence; Record of Evidence; Relevance and Admissibility of Evidence; Taking of Evidence Abroad
- compensating nonparty's costs in, Prin. 16.2, Com. *P-16C*
- confidentiality protection, Prin. 16.5
- disclosure, Prin. 16.2, Com. *P-16C*
- facilitation with, Prin. 16.3
- fishing expedition, Com. *P-16A*
- free evaluation of evidence in, Prin. 16.6, Com. *P-16G*
- International Judicial Cooperation and, Prin. 31, Com. *P-31C*
- jury trials, Com. *P-16I*
- nonadmissibility of statements in, Com. *P-16B*
- no special legal value in, Prin. 16.6, Com. *P-16G*
- physical/mental examinations as part of, Com. *P-16E*
- sanctions, Com. *P-16H*
- tainting of witness in, Com. *P-16D*
- testimony elicitation, Prin. 16.4, Com. *P-16F*
- types of information/evidence, Prin. 16.1

Adversary system, 7

Advocates, common-law, 6, 10

ALI. *See* The American Law Institute

ALI/UNIDROIT Working Group, 4

Amendments, Rule 14. *See also* Pleading Stage
- appropriateness of permitting, Com. *R-14B*
- court-ordered providing of, Rule 14.5
- default judgment based on, Rule 14.4, Com. *R-14C*
- opposing party serving of, Rule 14.3
- parties right for claim/defense with, Rule 14.1
- right of, Rule 14.2
- scope of permissible, Com. *R-14A*
- stating facts with greater specificity for, Com. *R-14D*

American continent, legal approximation openness of, xxxix

The American Law Institute (ALI), xxiii, xlii
- Advisers, xlv, 4
- agenda of, xxiii–xxiv, xlii
- International Consultants, xlv
- Members Consultative Group, xlv, 4
- Model Code of Evidence project of, xlii
- Model Penal Code project of, xlii
- proceedings, xlv
- project beginnings of, xxxi
- Reporters, xlv
- Restatements of the Law project of, xlii

Amicus Curiae Submission, Prin. 13, Rule 6
civil-law countries, Com. *P-13C*, Com. *R-6B*
court's relationship with, Com. *P-13B*
nonauthorization of third persons, Com. *P-13D*
purpose of, Com. *P-13A*, Com. *R-6A*
written comment submission, Com. *P-13E*
Appeal, Prin. 27. *See also* Appellate and Subsequent Proceedings; Appellate Review; Finality, second-instance review and
expeditiousness of review in, Prin. 27.1
new fact/evidence consideration with, Prin. 27.3, Com. *P-27B*
objections, Com. *P-27C*
procedural variance for, Com. *P-27A*
scope of, Prin. 27.2
Appellate and Subsequent Proceedings (Rules), 150–156. *See also* Appeal; Appellate Review; Finality, second-instance review and
Appellate Review, Rule 33. *See also* Appeal; Appellate and Subsequent Proceedings; Finality, second-instance review and
appeal taken from final judgment of court of first instance in, Rule 33.1
appellate court's permission for, Rule 33.3
exception considered by, Com. *R-33F*
interlocutory, Com. *R-33D*
interlocutory appeal, Com. *R-33E*
limitation of, Rule 33.4
order of court of first instance subject to immediate review in, Rule 33.2
right of appeal, Com. *R-33A*, Com. *R-33B*
rule of finality, Com. *R-33C*
second-instance court involvement in, Rule 33.5
three-level hierarchy, Com. *R-33G*
Approximation, xxxvii–xxxviii
American continent's, xxxix
substantive law and, 1
Approximation project (Storme), 3
Arbitration
international, 3
multinational, xxxiv, 3
Attorney-client privilege. *See* Evidentiary Privileges
Bonell, M. J., xliv
Burden and Standard of Proof, Prin. 21. *See also* Access to Information and Evidence; Burden of proof; Evidence; Reception and Effect of Evidence; Relevance and Admissibility of Evidence
determining, Com. *P-21A*
facts, courts, and, Prin. 21.2
failure to produce evidence for, Prin. 21.3
individual responsibility for, Prin. 21.1
parties' good faith for, Com. *P-21C*
"reasonably convinced" standard of, Com. *P-21B*
Burden of proof, xli. *See also* Burden and Standard of Proof

Canada, xxxvii, xlii
Case Management, Rule 18. *See also* Structure of Proceedings
communication in, Rule 18.6
conference aims in, Com. *R-18D*
court's directives for final hearings in, Com. *R-18E*
court's role in, Rule 18.1, Com. *R-18A*
dispute resolution in, Rule 18.5, Com. *R-18F*
first-instance court decisions in, Rule 18.4
judicial officer (defined) for, Com. *R-18G*
mediation in, Com. *R-18F*
party participation, Rule 18.2, Rule 18.5, Com. *R-18C*, Com. *R-18E*, Com. *R-18F*
planning conference for, Rule 18.2, Com. *R-18B*
setting conference dates in, Com. *R-18C*
suggestions, orders, and decisions by court in, Rule 18.3, Rule 18.3.1, Rule 18.3.2, Rule 18.3.3, Rule 18.3.4, Rule 18.3.5
time limits with, Rule 18.7
Civil disputes, xlviii
Civil-law systems, xxvii, xlix
common-law versus, xxxvi, 5, 6, 9–10
documents, 9
judge in, 6
judgment in, 6
juries in, li, 6
litigation in, xlvii, li, 6
origination of, 5–6

Index

Civil Procedural Law, xxxi
Civil procedure
  principles of, xxxvi
  rules of, xxvii
Civil Procedure Model (Latin America), xxxiv
Claims, rules for formulation of, 7
Code Pleading, 7
Columbia Law School, xlv
Commencement of Proceeding and Notice, Rule 11. *See also* Due Notice/Right to Be Heard
  plaintiff's submission of statement of claim during, Rule 11.1
  rule for commencement of suit for, Com. *R-11A*
  "service of process" of, Com. *R-11B*
  time of lodging of complaint in, Rule 11.2
Commerce
  international, xxix
  transnational, xxix
Commercial disputes, xlix
Commercial transactions, xlix
Common-law systems, xxvii, xlix
  advocates of, 6, 10
  American version of, 6–7
  civil law versus, xxxvi, 5, 6, 9–10
  jurisdictions, 8
Community
  global, xxix
  human, 1
  international legal, xxxii, xxxv
Composition and Impartiality of Court (Rules), 108–110. *See also* Composition of the Court; Impartiality of Court; Independence, Impartiality, and Qualifications of Court and Its Judges; Judges, civil-law system
Composition of the Court, Rule 9. *See also* Composition and Impartiality of Court
  adjudicating disputes governed by Rules, Com. *R-9A*
  jury trial as constitutional right, Com. *R-9C*
  number of judges in, Com. *R-9B*
Concentrated Final Hearing, Rule 29, Rule 29.1
  allowable evidence at, Rule 29.3
  appearance before judge rendering judgment at, Rule 29.2
  civil-law method advantages for, Com. *R-29E*
  common-law system structure for, Com. *R-29D*
  evidentiary reliability, Com. *R-29H*
  examining witnesses at, Com. *R-29C*
  excluding irrelevant/redundant evidence at, Rule 29.5
  opinion of witness at, Com. *R-29F*
  party's statement versus nonparty witness at, Com. *R-29B*
  person giving testimony questioned first at, Rule 29.4
  structure of, Com. *R-29A*
  witness credibility for, Com. *R-29G*
Contractualization, xxxiv
Convention on International Interests in Mobile Equipment (Capetown, 2001), xxiii
Conventions. *See* Human-rights conventions
Cooper, Edward H., xlv
Cooperation, international, xxx
Cornell International Law Journal, vol. 30, no. 2 (1997), 12
Costs, Prin. 25, Rule 32
  "American" rule, Com. *P-25A*, Com. *R-32A*
  appellate review, Rule 32.8
  attorney's fees, Com. *P-25A*
  court's delegation for determining, Rule 32.6
  court's limitation of, Rule 32.5
  each party bearing own, Rule 32.1
  "English" rule, Com. *P-25A*, Rule 25.1, Rule 32.3, Rule 32.4, Com. *R-32A*
  losing party's obligation to pay, Rule 32.4, Com. *R-32A*
  parties' contract with lawyers regarding, Com. *R-32B*
  payment of interim, Rule 32.2
  rule of, 7
  security provision for, Rule 32.9, Com. *R-32C*
  staying of, Rule 32.7
  types of, Prin. 25.1

Costs, Prin. 25, Rule 32 (*cont.*)
winning party's awarding of, Rule 32.3, Com. *R-32A*
withholding/limiting/declining of, Prin. 25.2, Com. *P-25B*
Court Responsibility for Direction of Proceeding
consultation with parties, Prin. 14.2
court's active management, Prin. 14.1
order determination, Prin. 14.3
standing orders, Prin. 7.2, Com. *P-9A*, Com. *P-14A*
Cultural dissonance, xlix
Cultural diversity, xxxv

Decision and Reasoned Explanation, Prin. 23
award specific, Prin. 23.1
further proceedings for, Com. *P-23B*
judgments, Prin. 23.2
prompt judgments, Prin. 23.1
subsequent specification, Com. *P-23C*
written decisions, Com. *P-23A*
Defendants. *See* Jurisdiction Over Parties; Multiple Claims and Parties; Intervention; Obligations of Parties/Lawyers; Party Initiative/Scope of Proceeding
Deposition and Testimony by Affidavit, Rule 23. *See also* Depositions; Evidence
authorization to examine witness by, Com. *R-23B*
court order of, Rule 23.1
deposition defined, Com. *R-23A*
oath of truth/payment of, Rule 23.2
procedure for, Com. *R-23C*
specified time/place of, Rule 23.3
transcript substituted as, Com. *R-23D*
written statement of sworn testimony as, Rule 23.4, Com. *R-23E*
Depositions, li. *See also* Deposition and Testimony by Affidavit; Evidence
Disclosure, Rule 21. *See also* Evidence; Exchange of Evidence
amendments of specifications in, Rule 21.2
facilitating compliance with, Rule 21.3
identification of evidence in, Rule 21.1, Rule 21.1.1, Rule 21.1.2, Rule 21.1.3
lawyer's *ex parte* interview as, Com. *R-21C*
listing of witnesses/documents as, Com. *R-21A*
nonsuggesting of testimony as, Com. *R-21B*
notification/invitation to other parties during, Com. *R-21D*
Discovery, xli, xlix
American rules of, 6
comprehensive, li
Dismissal and Default Judgment, Prin. 15, Com. *P-17B*, Rule 15
absence of substantial answer in, Com. *R-15C*
amendment served on party before, Com. *P-15F*
amount of, Prin. 15.4
appeal/rescission of, Prin. 15.5, Rule 15.7
claim's reasonable support in, Prin. 15.3.3, Com. *P-15D*
consistency of, Com. *R-15D*
court's determinations regarding, Prin. 15.3, Prin. 15.3.1, Prin. 15.3.2, Prin. 15.3.3, Com. *P-15D*, Rule 15.3, Rule 15.3.1, Rule 15.3.2, Rule 15.3.3
defendant's failure to appear/respond leading to, Rule 15.2, Rule 15.6
dismissal of proceeding against plaintiff leading to, Rule 15.1
dispute termination permitted by, Com. *R-15A*
excuse offering, Com. *P-15G*
"failure to prosecute" resulting in, Com. *R-15B*
limitations on, Com. *P-15E*, Com. *R-15E*
monetary amount of, Prin. 15.4, Rule 15.4
nonpermission to produce evidence, Com. *P-15G*
notification, Com. *P-15F*
parties' lateness of appearance leads to, Com. *P-15B*
procedure for invalidating, Com. *P-15H*
purpose of, Com. *P-15A*
reasonable care with, Com. *P-15C*
timeframe for entering, Prin. 15.2, Rule 15.5
warning of plaintiff in, Prin. 15.1

Index

Disputes
civil legal, xlviii, li
commercial, xlix
dealing with, xxix
resolving, xxix
transnational, xxix
Disputes to Which These Rules Apply (Rules), Rule 2
application of Rules, Com. *R-2A*
changing Rule status in, Com. *R-2H*
contractual option in case of arbitration in, Com. *R-2F*
"dispute" connotations in, Com. *R-2C*
dispute types, Rule 2.1, Rule 2.1.1, Rule 2.1.2, Rule 2.1.3
enlarging/restricting scope of application in, Com. *R-2J*
excluded categories from application in, Rule 2.3
habitual residence determination, Com. *R-2D*
multiple claims/multiple parties, Rule 2.2, Rule 2.2.1, Rule 2.2.2
multiple substantive legal bases, Com. *R-2G*
"Party"/"Person"/"Witness" in, Com. *R-2I*
property claims, Com. *R-2E*
scope of application of Rules in, Com. *R-2B*
Documents, civil-law systems and, 9
Due Notice/Right to Be Heard, Prin. 5, Rule 7. *See also* Commencement of Proceeding and Notice
civil-law/common-law giving of notice in, Com. *R-7A*
communication among parties, Com. *R-7C*
court's consideration of contentions, Prin. 5.6
default judgments for international litigation, Com. *P-5B*
ex parte orders, Prin. 5.8
ex parte proceedings propriety, Com. *P-5G*
expediting communication in, Prin. 5.7, Com. *P-5F*
formal notice for, Rule 7.1, Rule 7.2, Rule 7.2.1, Rule 7.2.2, Rule 7.2.3, Rule 7.2.4
language of documents of, Prin. 5.2, Com. *R-7B*
making facts/rules of law known in, Com. *P-5D*
nonconsideration of contentions for, Com. *P-5E*
notice of motions/applications/determinations for, Prin. 5.3
notice procedures, Com. *P-5A*
notice to parties, Prin. 5.1, Com. *P-17B*
notification of claims, Rule 7.3
parties' response to contentions in, Prin. 5.5
right to be informed in, Com. *P-5C*
submission of contentions of fact/law/supporting evidence with, Prin. 5.4
summons, Com. *R-7A*, Com. *R-11B*

Early Court Determinations, Rule 19, Rule 19.1, Rule 19.1.1, Rule 19.1.2, Rule 19.1.3, Rule 19.1.4
adjudication of claim in, Com. *R-19C*
amendment opportunities in, Rule 19.2
right to question court in, Com. *R-19B*
scrutiny by courts in, Com. *R-19A*
Effective Enforcement, Prin. 29
archaic/inefficient procedures of, Com. *P-29A*
Enforcement of Judgment, Rule 35
court-imposed monetary penalties in, Com. *R-35B*
final judgment immediately enforceable in, Rule 35.1, Com. *R-35A*
measure taken for noncompliance in, Rule 35.2, Rule 35.2.1, Rule 35.2.2, Rule 35.2.3, Rule 35.2.4, Rule 35.2.5
security/bond requirements, Rule 35.4
stay granted by court of first instance in, Rule 35.3, Com. *R-35C*
English Judicature Acts (1873, 1875), 9
European Civil Procedure Codes, xxxiv
European Court of Human Rights, Com. *R-27D*
European Union, xxxvii

Evidence (Rules), 128–144. *See also* Access to Information and Evidence; Disclosure; Exchange of Evidence
  burden of proof. *See* Burden and Standard of Proof; Burden of proof; Reception and Effect of Evidence; Relevance and Admissibility of Evidence
  exchange of, 8–9
  presentation of, 9–10
Evidentiary Privileges, Rule 27. *See also* Evidentiary Privileges and Immunity
  attorney-client privilege, Com. *R*-27A, Com. *R*-27B
  challenge to claim of, Rule 27.3
  common-law/civil-law recognition of, Com. *R-27B*
  confidentiality of communications regarding, Com. *R-27C*
  forfeit of, Rule 27.2, Com. *R-27F*
  in camera hearing, Com. *R-27E*
  legal consequences of, Com. *R-27H*
  legal-profession privilege, Rule 27.1.1, Com. *R*-27A, Com. *R*-27B
  procedure for claims of, Com. *R-27G*
  professional privilege, Com. *R*-27A, Com. *R-27D*
  protection to other privileges, Com. *R-27D*
  recognition of during exchange of evidence, Rule 22.7
  relevant evidence exclusions, Com. *R-27A*
  violations regarding, Rule 27.1, Rule 27.1.1, Rule 27.1.2, Rule 27.1.3
Evidentiary Privileges and Immunity, Prin. 18. *See also* Evidentiary Privileges
  court's recognition of protection for, Prin. 18.3
  direct versus indirect sanctions in, Prin. 18.2, Prin. 18.3, Com. *P-18C*
  drawing adverse influences with, Prin. 18.2
  evidence disclosure/other information, Prin. 18.1
  imposing indirect sanctions with, Prin. 18.2
  nonrecognition of privilege *sua sponte*, Com. *P-18D*
  types of, Com. *P-18A*
  weighting of, Com. *P-18B*
Exchange of Evidence, Rule 22. *See also* Disclosure; Evidence
  broad discovery for, Com. *R-22D*
  civil-law restrictedness with, Com. *R-22E*
  compliance with order for, Rule 22.5, Com. *R-22B*
  court-ordered additional disclosure during, Com. *R-22K*
  disclosure prior to demanding production in, Com. *R-22F*
  evidence relevance in, Com. *R-22H*, Com. *R-22I*
  non-U.S. common-law countries and, Com. *R-22C*
  nonvalid production objection in, Rule 22.6
  parties' right of disclosure in, Com. *R-22G*
  reasonable time frame for, Rule 22.2
  recognizing evidentiary privileges during, Rule 22.7
  requesting court order production in, Rule 22.1, Rule 22.1.1, Rule 22.1.2, Rule 22.1.3
  requesting party interacting with opposing party during, Rule 22.4
  revealing identities of witnesses during, Com. *R-22J*
  sanctions imposed during, Com. *R-22M*
  special officer appointment for, Com. *R-22L*
  stages in, Com. *R-22A*
  supervised compliance for, Rule 22.3
Expert Evidence, Rule 26
  civil-law rule and provisions, Com. *R-26A*, Com. *R-26D*
  common-law systems on, Com. *R-26D*
  court-appointed neutral expert(s), Rule 26.1
  designation of experts for, Rule 26.3
  nonobligation to follow advice of, Com. *R-26B*
  specifying issues for, Rule 26.2
  status of expert, Com. *R-26C*
  written/oral examination of expert, Com. *R-26E*

Index

"Facts and evidence," xlviii
Federal Rules of Civil Procedure (U.S.), xlv, xlviii, 3–4
  adoption of, 7
  ambiguity avoided by, l
  amendments to, 8
Final Discussion and Judgment, Rule 31
  60-day rendering of judgment, Rule 31.2
  court's prompt written notice for, Rule 31.3, Com. *R-31B*
  entitlement to closing statement in, Rule 31.1
  final hearing's end, Com. *R-31A*
  tribunal involvement in, Com. *R-31C*
Final Hearing (Rules), 144–150
Finality, second-instance review and, 10. *See also* Appeal; Appellate and Subsequent Proceedings; Appellate Review
"Fishing expedition," l
Forum and Territorial Competence, Rule 3
  establishing specialized courts with, Com. *R-3B*
  first-instance court jurisdiction with, Rule 3.2
  specialized jurisdiction for commercial disputes with, Rule 3.1
  territorial competence establishment, Rule 3.3
  "venue," Com. *R-3A*
Free-trade zones, xxxvii

General Authority of Court (Rules), 120–128
German Civil Justice (Murray), xliii
Gidi, Antonio, xxiv, xliv
Global community, xxix
Globalization, xxvii
Goldstein, Stephen, xxxiii
Guidelines Applicable to Court-to-Court Communications in Cross-Border Cases, xxx

Hague Conventions on the Service Abroad, 2
Harmonization, xxxiii
  defined, 1, 11
  impediments to, 2
  procedural law's international, 1–4
  substantive law and, 1
Harvard Law School, xliii
Hazard, Jr., Geoffrey C., xxiv, xxxi
Human community, 1
Human-rights conventions, xxxv

"il principio del finalismo," xxxviii
Immediate Enforceability of Judgments, Prin. 26
  appeal of, Prin. 26.2
  civil-law, 6
  immediate enforceability of, Prin. 26.1
  losing party's time compliance, Com. *P-26B*
  partial, Com. *P-26C*
  principle of finality, Com. *P-26A*
  security required from appellant in, Prin. 26.3
Impartiality of Court, Rule 10. *See also* Composition and Impartiality of Court; Composition of the Court; Independence, Impartiality, and Qualifications of Court and Its Judges; Judges, civil-law system
  court's nonacceptance of communications, Rule 10.4
  ex parte communications prohibition, Com. *R-10D*
  judge required to be impartial in, Com. *R-10A*
  nonparticipation by judge in, Rule 10.1
  persons having "decisional authority" in, Com. *R-10B*
  right to challenge impartiality of judge in, Rule 10.2, Rule 10.3, Com. *R-10C*
Independence, Impartiality, and Qualifications of Court and Its Judges. *See also* Composition and Impartiality of Court; Composition of the Court; Impartiality of Court; Judges, civil-law system
  addressing judicial bias by, Com. *P-1D*
  communication with, Prin. 1.4
  contentions considered by, Prin. 5.6
  ex parte proceedings of, Com. *P-1E*
  impartiality of, Prin. 1.3

Independence, Impartiality, and Qualifications of Court and Its Judges (*cont.*)
  independence of, Prin. 1.1
  independence versus impartiality of, Com. *P-1A*
  internal/external influence by, Com. *P-1B*
  judge's familiarity with law in, Com. *P-1F*
  judicial independence of, Prin. 1.2
  knowledge/experience of, Prin. 1.5
  language chosen by, Com. *P-6A*
  term of judges serving, Com. *P-1C*
Insolvency systems, xxx
International Commercial Arbitration, xxxviii
International Institute for the Unification of Private Law (UNIDROIT), xxiii. *See also* Working Group of ALI/UNIDROIT
  evaluation by, xliii–xliv
  Governing Council, xxxvi
  partnership, 4
International Judicial Cooperation, Prin. 31
  international recognition and, Com. *P-31A*
  judge's communication with judges, Com. *P-31B*
  significance of "evidence" with, Prin. 16, Com. *P-31C*
International trade, xxix, 1
Interpretation and Scope (Rules), 100–102
Investments, international, xxix
Isolationism, xxvii

Japan, xxxvii
Joinder. *See* Multiple Claims and Parties; Intervention
Judges, civil-law system, 6. *See also* Composition and Impartiality of Court; Composition of the Court; Impartiality of Court; Independence, Impartiality, and Qualifications of Court and Its Judges
  decisions. *See* Case Management, first-instance court decisions in; Case Management, suggestions, orders, and decisions by court in; Decision and Reasoned Explanation; Relevance and Admissibility of Evidence, decisions of who gives evidence in
Judicial Cooperation. *See* International Judicial Cooperation
Judicial organization, xxxiii
Juries
  civil litigation and, li, 6
  trials and, li, lii
Jurisdiction, Prin. 2. *See also* Jurisdiction, Joinder, and Venue; Jurisdiction Over Parties
  common-law, 8
  countries' variance in rules of, Com. *P-12B*
  court's exercise of, Com. *P-2A*
  court's granting provisional measures for, Prin. 2.3
  decline of, Prin. 2.4, Prin. 2.5, Prin. 2.6
  exclusive agreement for, Com. *P-2E*
  exercising, Prin. 2.1, Prin. 2.2
  "forum necessitatis," Com. *P-2C*
  forum non conveniens, Com. *P-2F*
  "long-arm," 5
  personal, 2
  state's exercise of, Com. *P-2D*
  stay of proceedings for, Com. *P-2G*
  "substantial connection" standard for, Com. *P-2B*
  suspension of, Prin. 2.5, Prin. 2.6
  "tag," 5
  U.S. aberrance towards, 5
Jurisdiction, Joinder, and Venue (Rules), 103–108. *See also* Jurisdiction; Jurisdiction Over Parties
Jurisdiction Over Parties, Prin. 2, Rule 4. *See also* Jurisdiction; Jurisdiction, Joinder, and Venue
  in absence of forum, Prin. 2.2, Prin. 2.2.1, Prin. 2.2.2
  common-law rule of *forum non conveniens* in, Com. *P-2F*, Com. *R-4D*
  consent/absence of consent in, Com. *P-2A*
  corporations, Prin. 2.1.2, Com. *P-C*, Rule 4.2, Rule 4.2.3, Com. *R-2I*, Com. *R-4B*
  court granting provisional measures for, Prin. 2.3, Rule 4.5
  declining, Prin. 2.4, Prin. 2.5, Prin. 2.6, Rule 4.6, Rule 4.6.1, Rule 4.6.2, Rule 4.6.3

establishment of, Rule 4.2, Rule 4.2.1, Rule 4.2.2, Rule 4.2.3
exclusivity in, Com. *P-2E*
"forum necessitatis," Com. *P-2C*
jural entities, Prin. 2.1.2, Com. *P-C*, Rule 4.2, Rule 4.2.3, Com. *R-2I*, Com. *R-4B*
"jural entity" concept, Com. *R-4B*
means of exercising, Prin. 2.1, Prin. 2.1.1, Prin. 2.1.2
nationals, Prin. 2.2.1, Com. *P-B*, Com. *P-C*, Com. *P-2B*, Com. *P-2F*
person claiming interest in property in, Rule 4.3
plaintiffs, Rule 4.1
reinstatement of proceeding, Rule 4.7
residents, Prin. 2.12, Com. *P-C*, Com. *P-2F*
sequestration or attachment of property in, Com. *P-2D*, Com. *R-4C*
"substantial connection" standard, Com. *P-2B*, Com. *R-4A*
when no other forum is available, Rule 4.4, Rule 4.4.1, Rule 4.4.2
Jury trials, 6
Justinian tradition, xlvi

Kane, Mary Kay, xlv
Kemelmajer de Carlucci, Aída R., lii
Kerameus, Konstantinos D., xxxii–xxxiii
Kronke, Herbert, xxxiii

Languages, Prin. 6, Rule 8
court's choice of, Com. *P-6A*
examining by deposition option in, Com. *R-8C*
language of document, Prin. 5.2
proceeding in court's language, Prin. 6.1, Rule 8.1, Com. *R-8A*
providing translation option in, Prin. 6.3, Com. *P-6B*, Rule 8.3, Com *R-8B*
use of other languages, Prin. 6.2, Rule 8.2
Las Leñas, xxxiv
Latin America
legal subsystem of, xxxvi–xxxvii
Law
harmonization of, 11
procedural, xxxii, xxxiii, 1
secured-transactions, xxiii
substantive, xxiii
Lawyers. *See* Obligations of Parties/Lawyers; Right to Engage Lawyers
League of Nations, xxiii
Legal community, international, xxxii, xxxv
Legal systems
approximation of, xxxvii–xxxviii
Mexican, xxxviii
reconciling needs of, xxxv
reducing differences between, xxxv
Ley de Enjuiciamiento Civil (Spain), xxxiv
Libonati, Berardino, xxxii
Liebman, Lance, xlv
Lis Pendens and *Res Judicata*, Prin. 28. *See also* Jurisdiction Over Parties; Party Initiative/Scope of Proceeding; *Res judicata*
issue preclusion, Prin. 28.3
repetitive litigation avoidance, Com. *P-28A*
scope of claim(s), Prin. 28.2
scope of proceedings, Prin. 28.1
strict versus flexible rules of, Prin. 2.6, Prin. 10.3, Com. *P-28B*
Litigants, fair procedures for, 11
Litigation
civil-law, xlvii, 6
international, 3
personal-injury, xlvii
U.S. and, xlix

Mercosur region protocols, xxxiv
Mexican Code of Commerce (Co. Com.), xxxviii
Mexican Supreme Court, xxxvii
Mexico, xxxvi, xxxvii, xlii
jurisdiction of, xxxix
legal system of, xxxviii
Meza, Silva, xxxviii
Model Code of Civil Procedure Project of the Conference of Chief Justices of Mexico, xxxvii
Model Code of Evidence project of ALI, xlii
Model Penal Code project of ALI, xlii
Multinational arbitration, xxxiv
Multiple Claims and Parties; Intervention, Prin. 12, Rule 5. *See also* Orders Directed to a Third Person
applying to intervene, Prin. 12.2, Rule 5.3

Multiple Claims and Parties; Intervention, Prin. 12, Rule 5 (*cont.*)
assertion of claim, Prin. 12.1, Com. *P-12A*, Rule 5.1, Com. *R-5A*
countries' variance in jurisdiction rules with, Com. *P-12B*
court authority for claim separation for, Com. *P-12F*
court-ordered separation of claims, issues, parties with, Prin. 12.5, Rule 5.6
joinder of interpleading parties with, Com. *P-12C*
party added to proceeding in, Rule 5.4
person substituted for party in, Prin. 12.3, Rule 5.5
replacement/addition of parties in, Com. *P-12E*
rights/obligations of participation/cooperation in, Prin. 12.4
summoning of third person made party in, Rule 5.2
third-person intervention in, Com. *P-12D*, Com. *R-5B*
Murray, Peter L., xliii

NAFTA. *See* North American Free Trade Agreement
National borders, abolishment of, xxxix
National sovereignty, xxxiii
New York University Journal of International Law and Politics, vol. 33, no. 3 (2001), 12
Nhlapo, Ronald T., xliv
North American Free Trade Agreement (NAFTA), xxiv
Notice. *See* Commencement of Proceeding and Notice; Due Notice/Right to Be Heard
Notice Pleading, 7
Nouveau Code de procédure civile (France), xxxiv

Obligations of Parties/Lawyers, Prin. 11. *See also* Defendants; Plaintiffs; Procedural Equality of Parties; Right to Engage Lawyers
assistance observing procedural obligations as, Prin. 11.5
failure to support substantial contention in, Prin. 21.3, Com. *P-11C*, Com. *P-17B*
fair dealings with all parties as, Com. *P-11D*
good-faith conduct as, Prin. 11.1
good-faith obligations as, Com. *P-11A*
speedy resolution of proceeding as, Prin. 11.2
"sufficient specification" requirement, Prin. 11.3, Com. *P-11B*
support of allegations as, Prin. 11.3, Com. *P-11B*
timely response failure as, Prin. 11.4
Oral and Written Presentations, Prin. 19. *See also* Access to Information and Evidence; Due Notice/Right to Be Heard
electronic communication used with, Com. *P-19B*
final hearings of, Prin. 19.2
interrogation during, Com. *P-19C*
limitations of, Prin. 19.4
pleadings, motions, legal arguments of, Prin. 19.1
testimony procedures during, Prin. 19.3
written statement replacement during, Com. *P-19A*
Orders Directed to a Third Person, Rule 20, Rule 20.1, Rule 20.1.1, Rule 20.1.2, Rule 20.3, Com. *R-20A*. *See also* Multiple Claims and Parties; Intervention
compensation for compliance as, Rule 20.2
direct seizure of materials as, Com. *R-20D*
enforcement of, Rule 20.3
producing document at preliminary stage as, Com. *R-20C*
witnesses giving testimony/deposition as, Com. *R-20B*
Organization, judicial, xxiii
Ouro Preto, xxxiv

Parties. *See* Defendants; Plaintiffs
Party Initiative/Scope of Proceeding, Prin. 10. *See also* Defendants; Plaintiffs
amending claims for, Prin. 10.4
determining, Prin. 10.3, Com. *P-22C*
initiation of proceeding, Prin. 10.1
just adjudication by courts, Com. *P-10A*
litigation commencement, time limits for, Com. *P-10B*

lodging complaint timing in, Prin. 10.2
new claim introduction, Com. *P-10D*
nondiscontinuance of action, Com. *P-10E*
pleading amendment rights with, Com. *P-10C*
voluntary termination/modification, Prin. 10.5
Personal-injury litigation, xlvii
Peruvian Guano case, l, 9
Plaintiffs. *See also* Jurisdiction Over Parties; Multiple Claims and Parties; Intervention; Obligations of Parties/Lawyers; Party Initiative/Scope of Proceeding
allegations of, xlix
lawyers of, xlviii
"notice pleading" of, xlviii
Pleading Stage (Introduction; Rules), 7, 8, 110–120. *See also* Amendments; Notice Pleading; Plaintiffs, "notice pleading" of; Statement of Claim (Complaint); Statement of Defense and Counterclaims
Plenary hearing, 9–10
Principles and Rules
administration of, xlvii
finality conditions defined by, 10
international translations of, 13
prior drafts of, 12
procedural system of, xlvii
purpose of, 11–12
recognition of, 10–11
scope limitations of, xlvii
Principles of International Commercial Contracts, xxiii
Principles of Transnational Civil Procedure
exclusions from, xlvii
preparation of, 4
Privacy, l
Privileges. *See* Evidentiary Privileges; Evidentiary Privileges and Immunity
Procedural Equality of Parties. *See also* Obligations of Parties/Lawyers
avoiding illegitimate discrimination as, Prin. 3.2
illegitimate discrimination defined, Com. *P-3B*
litigant's equal treatment as, Prin. 3.1
litigant's special protection as, Com. *P-3C*
nonimposition of burden of access, Prin. 3.4
nonrequirement of security with, Prin. 3.3
"reasonable" defined, Com. *P-3A*
security requirements with, Com. *P-3D*
venue rules, Com. *P-3E*
Procedural law, xxxii
conventions for dealing with, 2
international harmonization of, xxxii, xxxiii, 1–4
substantive, xxxiii
Procedural systems
differences among, 5–7
similarities in, 4–5
Procedures, dispute-resolution, xxix
Prompt Rendition of Justice
accessibility to, Com. *P-7B*
dispute resolution for, Prin. 7.1
moving adjudication forward for, Com. *P-7A*
parties' duty to cooperate for, Prin. 7.2
prompt rendition of, Prin. 7
Provisional and Protective Measures, Prin. 8, Rule 17
appellate review, Com. *P-8G*, Rule 17.6
applicant's disclosure of facts, Prin. 8.2
balance of equities, Com. *P-8B*
bond/other compensation requirements with, Prin. 8.3, Com. *P-8F*, Com. *R-17F*
compensation liability with, Rule 17.5, Rule 17.5.1
concept of injunction, Com. *P-8A*
court-ordered compliance for, Com. *R-17B*
court's ordering provisional relief as, Prin. 8.2
ex parte order for, Com. *P-8C*, Rule 17.3, Com. *R-17E*
full disclosure to court with, Com. *P-8D*, Com. *R-17D*
granting provisional relief, Prin. 8.1, Rule 17.1
order modification by court for, Com. *P-8E*, Rule 17.4
posting of bond/assuming duty of compensation, Prin. 8.3, Com. *P-8F*
"provisional relief" defined, Com. *P-8A*, Com. *R-17A*
review of relief order for, Com. *R-17G*

Provisional and Protective Measures, Prin. 8, Rule 17 (*cont.*)
temporary restraining order as, Com. *R-17C*
urgent necessity with, Rule 17.2, Com. *P-8B*, Com. *R-17C*
Provvedimenti urgenti per il processo civile (Italy), xxxiv
Public Proceedings, Prin. 20, Rule 24
court-ordered protective orders during, Rule 24.6
evidence in camera examined during, Rule 24.7
files/records, Prin. 20.2
hearing in camera during, Com. *R-24A*
information confidentiality during, Rule 24.5
judge accessibility during, Rule 24.4
judgments, Prin. 20.4
open court files/records for, Rule 24.2
privacy of, Com. *P-20B*
private versus, Rule 24.1, Rule 24.3
public versus private, Prin. 20.1, Prin. 20.3, Com. *P-20A*

Reception and Effect of Evidence, Rule 28. *See also* Access to Information and Evidence; Burden and Standard of Proof; Burden of proof; Evidence; Relevance and Admissibility of Evidence
burden to prove all material facts, Rule 28.1
court's free evaluation of evidence in, Rule 28.2
court's motions in, Rule 28.3, Rule 28.3.1, Rule 28.3.2, Rule 28.3.3
evidentiary authority for court in, Com. *R-28A*
sanctions/*astreintes* in, Com. *R-28B*
Recognition and Judicial Assistance, Rule 36
final judgments from other forums, Rule 36.1
interstate, Rule 36.2, Com. *R-36A*
interstate assistance for, Com. *R-36B*
Recognition of judgments, Prin. 30
firm rules of, Com. *P-30A*
standards set by, Com. *P-30B*
Record of Evidence, Rule 30
court's keeping summary record of hearing as, Rule 30.1
methodology regarding, Com. *R-30A*
parties' request for verbatim transcript, audio/video recording as, Com. *R-30C*
summary record inclusions, Com. *R-30B*
verbatim transcript, audio/video recording required as, Rule 30.2
Regimes, civil law/common law, xlii
Relevance and Admissibility of Evidence, Rule 25, Rule 25.1. *See also* Access to Information and Evidence; Burden and standard of proof; Evidence; Reception and Effect of Evidence
circumstantial evidence limitations with, Com. *R-25C*
court's active role in taking testimony in, Com. *R-25F*
decisions of who gives evidence in, Com. *R-25D*
determination of, Rule 25.2
information regarding, Rule 25.5
parties right to proof in, Com. *R-25E*
principles concerning evidence of, Com. *R-25A*
probative weight, statements regarding, Rule 25.3
proof through testimony, Rule 25.4
usefulness of evidence, Com. *R-25B*
Rescission of Judgment, Rule 34
appellate review of, Com. *R-34A*
application for, Rule 34.2, Com. *R-34D*
default judgments challenge in, Com. *R-34C*
grounds for, Com. *R-34E*
reasons for, Rule 34.1, Rule 34.1.1, Rule 34.1.2, Rule 34.1.3, Rule 34.1.4
request for reexamination of judgment, Com. *R-34B*
Res judicata, xli. *See also* Jurisdiction Over Parties; *Lis Pendens* and *Res Judicata*; Party Initiative/Scope of Proceeding
Responsibility for Determination of Fact and Law, Prin. 22
amendments by parties, Prin. 10.3, Com. *P-22C*
court-appointed experts, Prin. 22.4, Prin. 22.4.1, Prin. 22.4.2, Prin. 22.4.3

Index

court-assigned delegates, Prin. 22.3
courts and, Prin. 22.1
determination of issues, Com. *P-22A*
expert's testimony, Com. *P-22D*
foreign law, Com. *P-22B*
response of parties, Prin. 22.2, Prin. 22.2.1, Prin. 22.2.2, Prin. 22.2.3
Restatements of the Law projects of ALI, xlii
Restraining order, temporary. *See* Provisional and Protective Measures
Right to be heard. *See* Due Notice/Right to Be Heard
Right to Engage Lawyers. *See also* Obligations of Parties/Lawyers
attendance of foreign, Com. *P-4B*
client relationship with, Com. *P-4C*
common-law, 4
forum's admittance of, Com. *P-4A*
legal ethics variance of, Com. *P-4D*
professional independence of, Prin. 4.2
rights for engagement of, Prin. 4.1
Rome, Italy, xxiii
Rules
Anglo-Saxon preference for, xxxv
pleading, 8
transnational-civil-procedure, xxxi
uniform civil-procedure, xxvii
universal procedural, xxvii, xxxi
universal process, xxxvi

Sanctions, Prin. 17
additional, Prin. 17.4
direct versus indirect, Prin. 18.2, Prin. 18.3, Com. *P-18C*
dismissal/entering of judgment, Prin. 5.1, Prin. 15, Prin. 21.3, Com. *P-17B*
noncompliance, Prin. 17.1
reasonable/proportionate, Prin. 17.2
types of, Prin. 17.3
variance, Com. *P-17A*
Scope and Implementation, 16–50
applicability to international arbitration, Com. *P-E*
citizenship determination, Com. *P-C*
commercial/transnational, Com. *P-B*
multiple parties/multiple claims in, Com. *P-D*
national system of, Com. *P-A*
Second-instance review, finality and. *See* Finality, second-instance review and
Secured-transactions law, xxiii
Settlement, Prin. 24. *See also* Settlement Offer
alternative dispute resolution, Prin. 24.2
award of costs, Prin. 24.3
court's encouragement of, Prin. 24.1
court's noncoercion of parties in, Com. *P-24A*
nonobligation to negotiate, Com. *P-24B*
Settlement Offer, Rule 16. *See also* Settlement
compromise/settlements encouraged with, Com. *R-16A*
condition leading to rejected, Rule 16.3
court giving parties notice of judgment in, Com. *R-16E*
court-imposed sanction of, Rule 16.5, Rule 16.6
court without knowledge of, Com. *16-D*, Rule 16.4
determinate time for, Com. *R-16C*
loss or reimbursement rights in, Com. *R-16F*
noncompliance with, Rule 16.7
nonexclusiveness of court's authority with, Rule 16.8
offer and counteroffer in, Rule 16.2, Com. *R-16C*
party's delivery of, Rule 16.1
permit submission and consideration of, Com. *R-16B*
South African Law Commission, xliv
Standards of interpretation, Rule 1
matters not addressed in Rules, Rule 1.2
nonauthorization of local concepts, Com. *R-1A*
noncomprehensive "code," Com. *R-1B*
Principles of Transnational Civil Procedure interpretation, Rule 1.1
Statement of Claim (Complaint), Rule 12. *See also* Amendments; Pleading Stage; Statement of Defense and Counterclaims
alternative statement of facts as, Rule 12.4
challenge to application, Com. *R-12C*
claims prior to litigation, Com. *R-12D*
determining legal validity of, Rule 12.2

legal grounds for claim, Com. *R-12B*
plaintiff responsibilities with, Rule 12.1, Rule 12.5
plaintiff statement of facts with, Com. *R-12A*
remedy requested statement as, Rule 12.6
statement of money demanded as, Com. *R-12E*
time, place, participants, events of, Rule 12.3
Statement of Defense and Counterclaims, Rule 13. *See also* Amendments; Pleading Stage; *Statement of Claim (Complaint)*
60 days' response time, Com. *R-13C*
affirmative defense, Com. *R-13B*
allegations addressed by defendant, Com. *R-13B*
alternate statement of facts, Com. *R-13B*
counterclaim by defendant, Rule 13.3, Com. *R-13E*
defendant's answer of complaint, Rule 13.1, Rule 13.2
details of defendant's statement, Com. *R-13D*
negative defense, Com. *R-13B*
objection motion, Rule 13.5, Com. *R-13F*
statement of claim's details, Rule 13.4
time frame for defendant's response, Com. *R-13A*
State sovereignty prerogative, xxxiii
Storme, Marcel, 3
Structure of Proceedings, Prin. 9, Com. *P-9A*, Com. *P-14A*. *See also* Case Management
addressing jurisdiction with, Com. *P-9E*
final hearings, Com. *P-9C*
final phase, Prin. 9.4
interim phase, Prin. 9.3
orderliness of schedule, Com. *P-9B*
phases, Prin. 9.1
pleading phase, Prin. 9.2
preliminary hearings, Com. *P-9C*
summary judgments, Com. *P-9D*
Stürner, Rolf, xxiv, xxxii, xliii, 4
Substantive law, xxiii
Supreme Court of the Justice of Mexico (SC), xxxviii, xxxix
Systems
civil law, xxvii, xxxvi
civil-law systems, xxvii
common law, xxvii, xxxvi
common-law systems, xxvii
insolvency, xxx

Taking of Evidence Abroad, 2. *See also* Deposition and Testimony by Affidavit; Depositions; Evidence
Taruffo, Michele, xxiv, xxxi
credentials of, xli–xlii
Temporary restraining order. *See* Provisional and Protective Measures
Texas International Law Journal, vol. 33, no. 3 (1998), 12
Trade, international, xxix, 1
Transnational civil procedure
need for, xxviii, xxxi
Principles of, xxxi
Rules of, xxxi
Transnational commerce, xxix, xxxv
Transnational disputes, xxix
Traynor, Michael, xlv
Trials, li, 6

UNCITRAL. *See* United Nations Commission on International Trade Law
UNIDROIT. *See* International Institute for the Unification of Private Law
United Kingdom, xxxvi
United Nations Commission on International Trade Law (UNCITRAL) xxxiv, xxxviii
United States, xxxvii
adversary system of, 7
common-law system of, xxvii, 6–7
constitutional jury trials in, li–lii
discovery rules of, 6
Federal Rules of Civil Procedure, xlv, xlviii, l
jurisdiction aberrance of, 5
litigation in, xlix
peculiarities of, xxvii
Uniform Commercial Code of, xlii
University of Freiburg, xliii
University of Pennsylvania Law School, xxxi

Index

Witnesses, interrogation of, Prin. 16.4, Com. *P-16E*
Woolf reforms, xxxvi
Working Group of ALI/UNIDROIT, xxiv, xxxv, xxxvi, xliii–xliv. *See also* International Institute for the Unification of Private Law (UNIDROIT)
  common aim of, xliv
  first meeting of, xlv–xlvi
  mandate of, xliv
  members of, xliii–xliv
World, direction of, xxvii
World Trade Organization (WTO), xxiv
Wright, Charles Alan, xlv
WTO. *See* World Trade Organization